T0328459

THE RISE OF THE

PROJECT WORKFORCE

THE RISE OF THE
PROJECT WORKFORCE

Managing People and Projects in a Flat World

RUDOLF MELIK

John Wiley & Sons, Inc.

Published by John Wiley & Sons, Inc., Hoboken, New Jersey
Published simultaneously in Canada.

Wiley Bicentennial Logo: Richard J. Pacifico

For general information on our other products and services or for technical support, please contact our Customer Care Department within the United States at (800) 762-2974, outside the United States at (317) 572-3993 or fax (317) 572-4002.

Wiley also publishes its books in a variety of electronic formats. Some content that appears in print may not be available in electronic books. For more information about Wiley products, visit our web site at www.wiley.com.

Library of Congress Cataloging-in-Publication Data:

Melik, Rudolf.
  The rise of project workforce : managing people and projects in a flat world / Rudolf Melik.
    p. cm.
    Includes index.
    ISBN 978-0-470-12430-7 (cloth)   ISBN 978-1-119-11393-5 (paperback)
  1. Project management.   I. Title.
  HD69.P75M453 2007
  658.4'04—dc22

                                               2007008874

10 9 8 7 6 5 4 3 2 1

Contents

PART III
Implementation

Foreword

"Don't mess with my powder, dude." Such was the rather flippant response by an engineering graduate to a job offer from a leading architectural/engineering company. "You spoke about your regular Tuesday project meetings, the weekly afternoon Thursday update sessions, and your 9-to-5 culture. And I'm sitting there thinking all the time that there's fresh powder on the hills, and you're messing with my boarding time."

The CEO of the organization was explaining this story to me while we discussed the global trends that I should address during my upcoming presentation to staff of the organization.

"What's with these kids?" he asked.

The answer to that question is not that difficult to understand. And it is by thinking about the context of such things as today's prevailing attitudes toward work and life that you will realize the importance of everything you will learn from reading this book.

We are in an era of massive transformation of the modern organization. We are buffeted by rapid market change, regular, constant product and service innovation, increased globalization, heightened competition, and the ever-increasing specialization of skills as a result of accelerated knowledge growth.

Organizations have learned that the way forward is not by relying on solid, unyielding, slow-to-respond corporate structures of the last century. They have realized that to deal with the high-velocity future, they must be able to swiftly assemble and disassemble teams that will focus on specific projects. They know that they will staff these projects with individuals who will work on these projects for very short periods of time. They will then quickly disassemble the project and the team that goes with it, in order to move on to next project. They will be juggling dozens and dozens, and hundreds and hundreds of such projects.

They know that their ability to manage a workforce that is sometimes temporary, always transient, part-time in nature and multiskilled in background will become a key leadership skill. They know, however, that project and skills management probably isn't a core skill that they possess.

Which is why they—you—are reading this book.

What does this have to do with the snowboarder? There are dozens of complexities that come with the project-oriented economy. For example:

- Finding the right skills, at the right time, for the right purpose, at the right price
- Managing complex, real time projects that span the globe in terms of partners and skills
- Learning how to veer a project toward a new, unforeseen goal as a result of rapid market change
- And yes, attracting to a project team a generation that has a completely different concept toward the idea of work

Seven years ago, as the parents of two very busy young sons, my wife and I decided that we should take up skiing as a family activity. The first year, we could barely get down the hill. Today, as I write this, we are about to head off for a week at a mountain ski resort, where we will be able to navigate some of the most difficult hills. Not with ease, but at least with enthusiasm!

Going downhill is the fast part of skiing. The social part of the sport is, of course, après-ski, but also takes place during the ride up the hill. You get to meet a fascinating array of people from different backgrounds while on a chair lift: different age groups, locales, and career types. Everyone talks to their gondola partner; it's part of the culture of the sport.

Through the years, I have come to a quirky but fascinating conclusion about these conversations: Different generations have very different attitudes toward their life and their careers. For example, baby boomers inevitably ask me the question, "What do you do for a living?" Being in my late 40s, I can understand that much of how we define ourselves is based on how well we've done with our career.

Snowboarders, on the other hand, who almost always inevitably seem to be younger than 25 (though yes, I know, there are millions of 30, 40, and 50 year-olds who snowboard) always tend to ask me a different question: "What do you like to do?"

And that comes to the heart of the question asked by the CEO: What's with these kids? If they can't find a career that provides an adequate fit between what they do for fun (boarding) and what they do for a living (designing), they'll turn down the opportunity.

I worked into my presentation to that company two fascinating statistics: More than 50 percent of American kids now believe that self-employment is more secure than a full-time job. And a survey of engineering students indicated that the majority believed that a full-time career was about two to five years long.

What's going on here? Massive transformation in attitudes toward the world of work, organizational structure, and careers. This is but one of dozens of trends that are coming together leading us toward the project-based economy. Quite simply, there is an entire generation who would prefer a career of dozens of short-term, project-oriented assignments, rather than long-term, thoroughly dull, career paths.

Boomers are the last generation of a world in which people defined themselves in terms of their career. They went to school, obtained a set of skills, and began to apply those skills to a career with the expectation that this is what they would do with their lives. With this expectation, however, came the rude awakening of the end of the job for life, the end of the concept of a career-for-life, and perhaps even the concept of a "job."

Boomers are the vanguard of the last-century organizational structure and career concepts: one that is focused on the concept of employment and on the concept of a career.

Generation-connect (as I have begun to call them) on the other hand, have a mindset that is perfectly in tune with the project-oriented economic and career structure of this new century: one that is based upon an ongoing stream of short-term, project-oriented work assignments.

These statistics clearly indicate that the younger generation is very different when it comes to careers. It's easy to understand why: they've seen their parents right-sized, out-sourced, reengineered, and transformed. They've come to understand that there are no guarantees, nothing is long term, and that much of their success will come from their ability to constantly reinvent themselves.

And they get very bored, very quickly. They are the first generation to grow up in the global data-cloud; they've been weaned on Xbox and MSN and YouTube. They are immersed from birth in a world in which they can be doing multiple things at once, and which their minds are always very active.

They are coming to expect the same degree of heightened stimulation in the workplace. They expect to have multiple different careers; they want to be provided with a regular stream of new projects and varied assignments and responsibilities. They fully expect a career path that will allow for multiple different jobs and careers throughout their lifetime, simply to avoid the boredom and tedium that comes with routine.

And they define themselves not by what they do for a living, but by what they like to do. The latter includes sports, socializing, hanging out, chatting online, and, well, a few careers and jobs and projects and things to do along the way.

They are a generation that is fiercely collaborative and extremely team oriented. While their older baby boomer parents talk of change management workshops and the need for "team collaboration" within existing corporate structures, this next generation just "does" stuff. They can instantly take on the most complex of projects and work in a manner that draws together the talents of many, many people.

Their uniqueness is such that they are the vanguard of the next phrase of the massive restructuring of the modern business organization. Quite simply, they don't subscribe to the concept of a corporate work philosophy that says you have to come to a certain location every day to do things. They find the concept to be entirely laughable, with the result that those organizations that have yet to adopt a workplace culture that supports irrelevancy-of-location as a cornerstone will be unable to attract their talent and skills.

In other words, if you mess with their powder time, you likely won't be able to interest them. And in an economy in which the war for talent will be the defining factor for future success, that could be a pretty big problem.

A huge amount of my time is spent, as a futurist, trends, and innovation expert, on providing insight to some of the largest organizations in the world.

I'm helping them with what they must do in order to adapt to an ever more rapidly changing economy, collapsing product life cycles, fiercer market competition, the rapid emergence of new competitors, challenging new workforce attitudes, not to mention the necessity of gaining access to ever more specialized skill sets. In doing so, I've come to learn that many leading thinkers of our age truly don't appreciate just how quickly the world is changing.

For example, I often tell the story on stage of a hypothetical "GoogleCar." I suggest to the audience that we live in an era in which Google could choose to become a car company—and could jump into the business pretty quickly if it wanted to. All it would have to do is line up the proper partners for the project: today's economic winners excel by putting together rapid, global, sophisticated, knowledge-deep partners.

In the global economy of today, the capabilities needed to design, build, and deliver a sophisticated new automobile can become accessible at the drop of a hat. Well, perhaps not that easily, but learning how to manage a project of such scope and scale will become one of the critical success factors for any organization in the future.

You might need to learn to assemble rapid, global, sophisticated project partners—the insight provided by this book—faster than you might think!

After I tell my story of the GoogleCar, I explain that Google's founders are now significant equity participants in a new California car company, Tesla Motors—an organization that has brought to market, rather quickly, a fascinating new electric vehicle. It did so by bringing together a wide number of partners to the project, each bearing their own unique expertise and skills.

We live in a time in which things are happening so fast that predictions go from fantasy to reality in a matter of months.

Today, we can see an ever-increasing reliance on project-based "workforce for hire." Companies are aggressively focused on becoming leaner than ever before. They continue to reorganize themselves around a small, core group of staff responsible for keeping the business running, and they focus on obtaining the rest of their needed expertise through an ongoing and ever-growing reliance on short-term, contract workers. The increasing specialization of knowledge, rapid career evolution, relentless market and business change, and globalization have led to a world in which skills access is critical: it's all about getting the right skills, at the right time, for the right purpose.

In the future, we will continue to see companies relentlessly focused on obtaining the best talent they can, regardless of where they might be. In the hyper-innovative global economy, the only thing that counts is knowledge. If the knowledge is accessible from anywhere in the world, then companies will find themselves in the position of being able to choose the best talent and expertise they need to do a particular job from a group of global, skilled experts.

That's why *The Rise of the Project Workforce* is such an important book. It provides you with the insight, knowledge, and best practices to access, manage, and deploy the critical skills that you need to compete and thrive in the global economy—which is one of the defining characteristics of the successful organizations of tomorrow.

And it might help you understand that the simple issue of "What do you do for a living?" being replaced by the question, "What do you like to do?" is one of the fundamental changes occurring around us today. That this issue has tectonic consequences in the project and workforce management landscape.

JIM CARROLL

Jim Carroll is a strategic thinker and thought leader with deep insight into trends, the future, creativity, and innovation. He was named by BusinessWeek as one of four leading sources for insight on innovation and creativity. An author, columnist, media commentator, and consultant, he has a client base that includes the Walt Disney Organization, Nestle, Monster.com, Motorola, DaimlerChrysler, the BBC, and the Swiss Innovation Forum. He has researched key innovation success factors for dozens of industries, associations, professions, companies, and individuals. He is a frequent keynote speaker with highly customized presentations. He learned to ski at the age of 40 and now organizes his professional career activities during the winter around his skiing time. He welcomes your comments at jcarroll@jimcarroll.com.

Preface

This book is ideal for managers, directors, and executives who are looking for a project-based approach to apply to their business, to standardize work processes, and to improve collaboration across the workforce.

The Rise of the Project Workforce is a practical guide to Project Workforce Management for project managers, human resources directors, finance and payroll professionals, compliance officers, executives, system implementers, and consultants. It also serves as an excellent introduction to the topic for students and beginners.

This book introduces the concepts, tools, and technologies that, combined with accounting, payroll, human resources, and customer relationship management applications, result in improved productivity and greatly reduce compliance and overhead costs, resulting in substantial profit and revenue increases for an organization.

Part I provides an introduction to the market realities, competitive pressures, project execution, and service delivery challenges that have led to the emergence of the Project Workforce.

Part II serves as an in-depth discussion of concepts, technologies, and tools facilitating project management, workforce management, and workflow that are of interest to project managers and operational executives.

Part III provides consultants, administrators, system integrators, and implementers with a phased implementation roadmap, a primer on integration points between various enterprise systems, predeployment planning checklists, and an administration handbook. It also shows how you can build a thorough business case and prepare for the user adoption challenges a Project Workforce Management initiative is likely to face.

Acknowledgments

As we express our gratitude, we must never forget that the highest appreciation is not to utter words, but to live by them.

—John Fitzgerald Kennedy

This book, as with everything else I have created in my life, is the result of great teamwork. My thanks and deepest gratitude to:

- Nouchig, my wife, for helping me edit this book and for supporting me during the long road and late nights it took to complete this project
- My business partners for taking care of business while I was busy writing, and for giving me the time and the opportunity to work on this extremely demanding yet very exciting project
- Anna Chang, Ara Israilian, Fady Risk, Kevin Charbonneau, Ludwig Melik, Sammy Wahab, Rafat Hilal, Randy Urquhart, and Michael McRae for their reviews, feedback, and contributions to various chapters
- Edna Badalian, Carol Beaulieu, and Roberto Bonaduce for their work on the book's cover, graphics and Web content
- Jan Sisko, Paul McKeon, Terrie O'Hanan, and Veronica Brown from the Content Factor for their reviews and contributions to various chapters
- Special thanks to Matt Holt for his editorial insight and to the Wiley publishing team, including Shannon Vargo, Christine Kim, and all the others at Wiley who helped us put this book together
- Last but certainly not least, to Jim Carroll for writing the Foreword to this book and for helping me introduce this new topic to the business and academic community

Thank you all.

PART I

Working in a Flat World

The Rise of the Project Workforce

I think it's going to be one of the biggest middle-class jobs—
collaborators. Collaborators are people who are good at working as
part of global knowledge, manufacturing or supply chains.

—Thomas Friedman

The World Is Flat—Again

In his seminal work: *The World Is Flat* (New York: Farrar, Straus and Giroux, 2006) author and "presentist" Thomas Friedman describes a highly integrated world where business is done instantaneously with billions of people across the planet. As a result of the lowering of trade and political barriers and the technical advances of the digital revolution, a new flat world has emerged in which a call center in the Philippines answers support questions from a distributor in England for software that was designed in California, coded in India, and tested in Ireland.

For some of us on the leading edge of global commerce, these developments may not come as a big surprise. But Friedman convinces us that the new flat world is no longer the stuff of futurists or presentations at the World Economic Forum. Outsourcing and collaboration are facts of life, and much more the norm than the insulated small manufacturer based in the heartland of the United States.

As organizations and executives find themselves with two feet planted firmly in a fully interconnected, truly global economy, one truth is evident for all enterprises; and particularly for project- or service-driven businesses that rely heavily on project teams and information workers:

> Our established ways of getting work done, of accounting for this work, of monitoring compliance, and of analyzing work in progress for intelligence that will help us

do future work faster, better, cheaper, and smarter are through. They are no longer enough.

In his seminal work *Only the Paranoid Survive* (New York: Random House, 1999) then Intel Corporation CEO Andy Grove coined what would become the de facto phrase for points in time such as *strategic inflection points.* Strategic inflection points mark full-scale changes in the way business is conducted. The ways we work, the ways we compete, and the ways we win require a new approach, a new outlook beyond simply making our existing systems bigger, better, faster. During strategic inflection points, businesses that "get it" and change, achieve unprecedented gains—those that do not, stumble and fade.

Driving our current strategic inflection point is the underlying social, economic, and world infrastructure transformation of what globalization guru, author, and Pulitzer Prize winning *New York Times* columnist Thomas Friedman calls a "flat world." In a flat world, Friedman explained to *Wired* magazine, organizations compete on a "level, global, Web-enabled playing field that allows for multiple forms of collaboration without regard to geography or distance—or soon, even language."

Friedman goes on to tell us that while Fortune 500 firms are willing participants in this global business revolution, they are not driving it. Rather they are being pulled along by groups of highly innovative, widely dispersed project teams. Most of the individuals that comprise these teams are working from basements and boiler rooms, not skyscrapers. In essence, the new flat world is being driven by a corresponding flat hierarchy of small, co-equal teams interconnected by a series of co-dependent projects. And these teams are working fast!

Futurist, trends, and innovation expert Jim Carroll concurs with Friedman and notes the increased pace at which change occurs in this new flat world. In his book, *What I Learned from Frogs in Texas* (Toronto, Canada: Oblio Press, 2004), he writes:

> As globalization and technological advances converge, competition is changing overnight, and product lifecycles often last for just a few months. Permanence has been torn asunder. We are in a time that demands a new agility and flexibility: leaders must have the skill and insight to prepare for a future that is rushing at them faster than ever before.

While star journalists like Thomas Friedman and Jim Carroll are free to chronicle the emergence of the flat world, it is left to the rest of us to figure out how to better manage and work in it, without falling off the edge. That's where this book comes in. It's a practical guide to organizing and getting work done in an environment that Friedman further describes as:

> More people than ever collaborating and competing in real time with more other people on more different kinds of work from more different corners of the planet and on a more equal footing than at any previous time in the history of the world. (p. 8)

Today's business systems are simply not designed to plan, schedule, manage, audit, and optimize work that gets done in a flat world. In fact, the origin of double-entry accounting actually dates back to the last time the world was flat: the days of Columbus. More modern versions of business automation tools such as enterprise resource planning (ERP), customer relationship management (CRM), and project management software want to impose a certain rigidity within business processes, and fail to address the dynamic interplay and constantly shifting relationship between projects and people, which occurs naturally in the flat world and characterizes today's business.

To help you navigate the flat world, this book is organized into three main sections:

Part I: Working in a Flat World is an executive's guide to the trends and implications of this new business world order.

Part II: Project Workforce Management describes how a new class of software and associated best practices can help businesses better manage and produce work in the flat world.

Part III: Implementation details how best to implement Project Workforce Management in your company.

Market Dynamics That Challenge Traditional Project Management

The following major market dynamics not only contribute to the flattening of the world, but also challenge the management capabilities of the processes and systems we use:

- *Globalization:* At the start of this shift, organizations moved simple tasks like assembly and manufacturing to developing countries where this work could be completed more economically. In globalization's current wave, organizations are outsourcing knowledge work as well. At first, only large multinational corporations outsourced operations. In the current wave, all organizations—even ones with just a few employees—are outsourcing and conducting business globally. The Internet, fast networks, and a globally connected workforce are the driving forces behind this trend.

- *Increased regulatory scrutiny:* As organizations have become more fragmented, they also have become subject to greater regulatory scrutiny. They must achieve and maintain compliance with regulations such as Sarbanes-Oxley, which directly impact project and workforce management and execution. To comply, companies need more thorough and expansive systems for assigning, tracking, and managing accountability for the work being done. These controls protect everyone—workers, customers, suppliers—effectively, all of the organization's stakeholders.

- *Flattened hierarchy:* In a flat world, top-down decision making is replaced by bottom-up empowerment. Widely distributed companies cannot use an authoritative command-and-control structure. Instead, market leaders will find ways to remove the red tape shackles from their project teams and empower them to get work done and make local decisions.
- *Fragmented enterprises:* Today's work is defined by atomized segments that are delivered by specialized workers both inside and outside the company. Organizations assign work to internal or outsourced teams based on costs, available talent, the nature of work, and customer expectations.

A Flat World Demands Collaboration and Cooperation

The net result of a flat world is an overriding need for collaboration and cooperation. The problem is that companies are not really all that adept at collaborating; too many enterprises struggle with thinking innovatively about how they work. They fail to create processes and systems that support cooperative collaboration.

In *What I Learned from Frogs in Texas*, Jim Carroll reports the results of a survey by Collaborative Strategies LLC. It revealed that 32 percent of the time in a typical working week is spent on helping others resolve questions. Of these questions, 54 percent have been answered before, yet the answers are not recorded in any type of accessible knowledge base so that they can be institutionalized. Instead, organizations continue to waste time answering the same questions—despite the fact that 81 percent of the workers surveyed believed it was important to share such knowledge.

Often, the desire to collaborate is not supported by processes and systems that make collaboration easy, or better yet, a natural part of the way work flows. Instead, entrenched roadblocks and business challenges such as those that follow get in the way:

- Employees and contractors are working very long hours to deliver projects, but management cannot report on the reasons why resources are so overloaded. As a result, management also lacks the insight to create innovative long-term solutions for balancing resource demand and availability.
- Businesses lack tangible measures of the value versus the effort of different internal departments.
- Manual data collection processes cause management to receive reports on billable utilization and capacity planning after month end—too late to make corrections on work in process or to take corrective action before initiating new projects.
- Information Technology (IT) or engineering is unable to produce a report that shows the cost breakdown of effort across different types of projects—

such as research and development or client and maintenance assignments—so that work allocations can be optimized to meet the organization's goals.

- Business reporting comes after the fact. Organizations do not have standardized processes and systems for capturing the details of work. They often use "pillars of disconnected data" that sometimes conflict. For example, they track time using spreadsheets, multiple information systems, or a variety of timesheet and expense reporting systems (one for payroll, another for project tracking, and yet another for billable work). The information in these systems does not always agree. Managers use manual entry (such as merging spreadsheets) to integrate the data for reporting and decision making—this consumes time and resources, often resulting in inaccuracies.

- Decentralized shared resource pools spread across business units, cities, countries, and time zones. They often lack systems to enable the real-time collaboration and data access that their work requires.

- Compliance costs are escalating as regulations become more stringent, while the way work gets done becomes more fluid. The lack of process automation results in high additional costs for internal and external compliance audits and any process reimprovement initiative.

- Various departments and geographically dispersed resource groups use completely different or disconnected systems to manage the same processes, thus hindering collaboration and knowledge sharing.

New Nature of Work

The new nature of work lies at the crossroads of a flat world and the heightened demand for collaborative organizations. Today, work is increasingly *differentiated*, meaning it is compartmentalized into units of subject matter expertise, delivered by collaborating specialized workers both inside and outside the company. While only a short while ago, just a small percentage of an enterprise's work was formed around collaborative projects and differentiated time, today, about more than half is, and the trend toward compartmentalization of work is expected to accelerate.

This shift in the way work gets done requires organizations to track differentiated time and expenses, to allocate costs (whether or not they are billable) to the right projects, and to examine as well as justify spending and labor costs across both internal and external business units.

The empowered collaborative workforce in today's flat world has a substantial impact on how we track and measure work:

- *Work is delivered or centered on an initiative or a project.* Since the mid-1990s, renowned author and speaker Tom Peters has been telling anyone who would listen that business professionals should consider work and career as a succession of discrete projects to be strung together in consecutive stages of advancement and accomplishment. Modern companies embody this principle in reverse, as they quickly assemble teams of geographically dispersed, highly specialized professionals (referred to as the *Project Workforce*) to execute specific projects. These teams are formed for varying durations depending on the nature of each project and are dismantled just as quickly as initiatives are completed. Some have called this the "Hollywood Model" of work: bringing together the best resources to make a movie, then disbanding and forming other teams to make other movies.

- *It is no longer sufficient to analyze customers, projects, employees, and financial data as separate entities.* These elements are too interdependent to be tracked by different executives, each using their own tools and policies for monitoring and reporting. A new global system of record is required that combines the customer, the talent, and the project.

Traditional Systems Prevent Progress in a Flat World

Inadequate and *disconnected* describe most of the systems in use today. Traditional ERP systems fail to provide a single system of record that unifies customer, project, and workforce management. Whether they use an ERP system, most organizations (and all Global 2000 companies) have deployed multiple enterprise applications and heavy customizations, including but not limited to:

- *Customer relationship management* (CRM) *systems,* such as salesforce .com, Microsoft CRM, and Sugar CRM
- *Project scheduling and project collaboration software,* such as Microsoft Project, Primavera
- *Portfolio management solutions,* such as Primavera or Computer Associate's Clarity (used by internal IT departments to prioritize projects, conduct what-if-analysis, and align projects with company objectives)
- *Portal development and document management software,* such as Microsoft's SharePoint or Captaris' Alchemy
- *Time and attendance tracking software,* whether ERP customizations or separate systems from companies, such as Kronos or Workbrain
- *Travel and entertainment expense tracking software,* whether ERP customizations or systems from companies such as Concur

- *Billable time tracking software,* whether ERP customizations or separate systems, such as Sage Carpe Diem
- *Business process management software,* such as Ultimus or Lombardi to automate business processes that are not addressed in other enterprise applications

Often, these applications have their own databases, rules, and policies. Sometimes they are completely disconnected from the company's ERP, accounting, or payroll systems. Disconnected systems result in dozens and, in large corporations, easily hundreds of spreadsheets to track work; to import and export data; and to report on customers, projects, and workers. To further complicate matters, some of these applications are used on-demand (like salesforce.com) while others remain on-premise systems.

In addition, spreadsheet-based tracking and reporting is used as a "cure-all-remaining-gaps" approach that creates a blizzard of assorted and often conflicting data. Disconnected or manually integrated systems, a mish-mash of unapproved data, and a wild e-mail exchange of spreadsheets leads to an environment that is ripe for revenue leakage, errors, fraud, and systemic control weakness.

Project Workforce Management: A New System for a Flat World

To operate effectively, businesses must combine:

- Human capital management,
- Project management,
- Business process management, and
- Cost/revenue accounting

into a synthesized solution called *Project Workforce Management.*

The underlying business process management workflow in this approach adapts to each process, project, business unit, and organization. It automates accounting for time and expenses of a project workforce—both within the company and without, to include its service providers. The software can be configured to work the way the company does, and fundamentally empower individuals and decentralized organizations.

Project Workforce Management enables companies to meet the cooperative collaboration challenges of a flat world. It establishes a new system of record that links the customer, the project, and the workforce (talent) to identify interdependencies and to simplify priority setting, as well as talent sourcing, while balancing project profitability with customer satisfaction (Figure 1.1). Customer Relationship Management systems (where the "customer" is the system of record), Project Management systems (where the "project" is the system of record), and Human Capital Management systems (where the "employee" is the system of record), cannot alone accommodate these interdependencies.

The fundamental building blocks of Project Workforce Management are:

- Global system of record that combines the customer, the project, and the talent
- Hierarchical organization and work breakdown structures
- Workflow platform

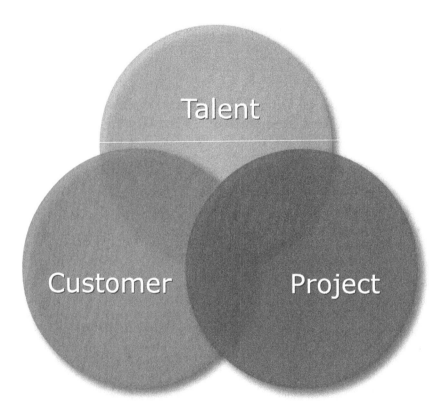

Figure 1.1   Project Workforce Management Links the Customer, the Project, and the Talent to Create a Global System of Record.

Project Workforce Management
Identifies Interdependencies

The global "projectization" and fragmentation of work in the flat world has resulted in these business requirements, which a Project Workforce Management solution fulfills:

- Project Workforce Management helps design and oversee the process itself, providing real-time visibility into the financial implications of project and service delivery. It provides a set of workflow driven services that link into a single solution—a control hub—for total visibility and management. Examples include:
  —Cost accounting and billing for differentiated time and expenses
  —Productivity analysis
  —Budget-versus-actual comparisons
  —Resource utilization trends
  —Segmented reporting to fully understand the effectiveness and profitability of each separate project, resource group, and customer.
- Change is a constant. Project Workforce Management solutions make it easy for managers to change processes as they learn more about a project, resource group, or customer. Process workflows are depicted graphically and can be changed using simple modeling tools. Organizations also can standardize these changes locally or worldwide, if necessary.
- Work has been broken down into smaller pieces that sometimes overlap: business units, countries, outsourced teams, cost centers, and individual resources must collaborate, cooperate, and handle more than one project at a time. A Project Workforce Management solution mirrors this reality by breaking down work and organizational breakdown structures into microcomponents that can be tracked and summarized in any combination.
- A Project Workforce Management system provides an interactive environment for the real-time tracking and analyzing of project workforce data that complies with established policies and best practices, yet enables immediate decision making.

Workflow: Connects Projects and People
to Business Processes

Every project workforce activity is driven by an underlying business process. The workflow platform allows managers to model project, workforce, and financial processes; and subsequently to embed them into the software (Figure 1.2).

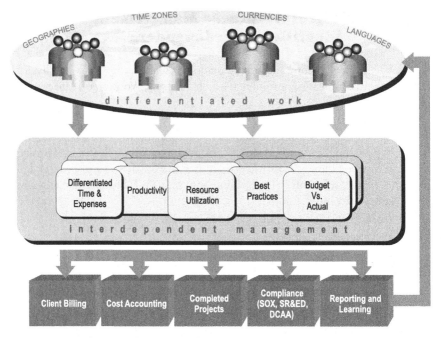

Figure 1.2   Software Is Designed to Plan, Manage, Track, and Report. Work Differentiated in an Interdependent and Holistic Way Helps Companies Remain Competitive and Meet the Significant Challenges of Today's Flat World Business Environment.

This platform graphically represents work processes so that they can be designed, configured, and changed by authorized business process owners without requiring programming resources. The workflow interface enables users to visually define, control, track, and audit approvals, routing, role-based assignments and notifications. All business processes use the same workflow concepts and management interface. By leveraging the same visual framework and concepts, users experience a consistent interface that is easy to learn and use to manage any work process.

Functions of a Project Workforce Management System

Project Workforce Management centrally manages project workforce related data, eliminating many of the spreadsheets used to track projects, time, and labor, expenses, interdepartmental chargebacks, and billable work (Figure 1.3). Project Workforce Management encompasses and integrates:

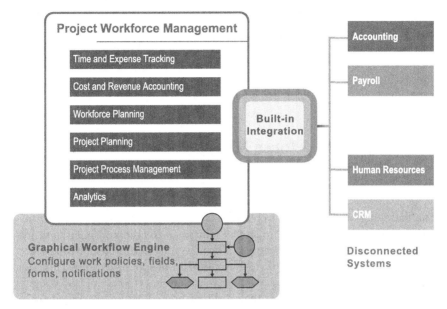

Figure 1.3   The Components of a Project Workforce Management System

- *Time and expense tracking:* Tracks all differentiated time and expenses, billable or not.
- *Cost and revenue accounting:* Attributes all revenue (and chargebacks), spending, and labor costs to specific projects, and establishes a formal chargeback system for shared service departments such as IT and engineering. Formalize and enforce a revenue accounting and recognition policy that is in compliance with regulations. Produce customer invoices, or chargeback to other business units, on a project basis for all billable work, spending, and labor costs, or based on predefined billing schedules.
- *Workforce planning:* Handle competency and capacity planning. Optimally schedule a distributed global workforce by locating the most optimal available resources to accomplish specific roles in a project.
- *Project planning:* Build a detailed project plan including the project's work breakdown structure and the project team. Assign resources to work on the tasks. Perform real-time earned value reporting and analysis.
- *Project process management:* Manage project processes, including project initiation, risk and issue reporting, and scope control using policy-based and enforced best practices.
- *Analytics:* Analyze consolidated, real-time and dynamic views of the company's projects, processes, and workforce, with a special emphasis on reporting the financial perspective.

Project Workforce Management modules tightly integrate with CRM, human resources, accounting, and payroll systems. The same reviewed and approved costs, expenses, and differentiated time that are utilized to update and report on project status can also be used to process payroll, reimburse expenses, invoice for any billable work and spending, and update the accounting system with summary or detailed cost-revenue transactions.

Project Workforce Management: A Common Launching Point for All Explorers of the Flat World

The flattening of the world has created a strategic inflection point that organizations must address in order to survive: the need to accomplish, account for, monitor, analyze, and improve work in this new era of the Project Workforce.

Project Workforces encompass different teams of specialized subject matter experts both inside and outside of an organization that collaborate and cooperate. These teams achieve work that is differentiated, or compartmentalized, based on customer requirements, talent availability, and project scope, as well as business rules and objectives.

Traditional business management systems, which often exist in disconnected silos that provide narrow departmental or functional views, do not provide project workforces or business managers with the collaborative capabilities and integrated data they need to excel in this new business reality.

To address this need, Project Workforce Management systems have emerged. These systems bring together talent, work, and finances into one process-managed system with the following benefits:

- A common vantage point for all decision makers
- Real-time views of projects, resource groups, actual progress, and issues
- More accurate decision making, since data is generated from approved, compliant, and automated processes

In short, decisions that impact financial, team, and project performance are made faster with better information and in collaboration with stakeholders. In a flat world, an empowered project workforce can make faster localized decisions while gaining a global perspective.

While guides such as the *Project Management Body of Knowledge* (PMBOK)[1] do a very good job of explaining the ideal project management concepts and techniques, they do not provide a roadmap to achieving differentiation or market advantage.

Purely methodology-based initiatives start with many good intentions and often end with compromises on quality, consistency, efficiency, or, worse yet, ineffective project controls. Project Workforce Management builds on the excellent disciplines and methodologies described in PMBOK. However, unlike the purely software-based enterprise project management and workforce management or educational tools such as PMBOK, Project Workforce Management is both a set of disciplines and workflow—driven tools combined with an unambiguous phased deployment roadmap that will help you achieve operational excellence.

NOTE

1. For more information visit http://www.pmi.org or http://en.wikipedia.org/wiki/Project_Management_Body_of_Knowledge.

2

Managing the Project/Service Delivery Life Cycle

Everything should be made as simple as possible, but not simpler.

—Albert Einstein

"There is less to fear from outside competition than from inside inefficiency," writes famed business scholar Michael Porter on competitive advantage in his seminal work, *Competitive Strategy: Techniques for Analyzing Industries and Competitors* (New York: Free Press, 1998). In other words, companies should first "look within" to ensure their processes and systems work with efficient excellence *before* "looking without" to competitive moves.

Agile organizations maximize internal efficiency by investing only in high-performing and strategic initiatives. Project selection, return-on-investment (ROI) analysis, risk identification and mitigation, as well as continuous process improvements are imperative. In many organizations, management faces the challenge of having little visibility into the scope and progress of projects across the enterprise. *Silo thinking* prevents resources from being assigned effectively across departmental and geographical boundaries. And, without standardized project management procedures, schedules fall offline and budgets routinely exceed original resources.

Adding stress to the system are regulations that govern how time and talent must be tracked to accurately allocate cost and revenue to work performed, as described in the chapters related to compliance. Some of these regulations are labor-related—such as state-specific wage laws or federal labor laws—and some involve financial governance and accounting requirements. All require meticulous planning as well as accurate recording, tracking, and auditing to ensure full compliance.

Understanding the project/service delivery life cycle helps organizations build a shared long-term vision for managing people and projects in today's dynamic world. Therefore, this chapter:

17

- Examines how Project Workforce Management helps manage the life cycle of project and service delivery
- Shows how workflows, controls, and reporting create a corporate memory that can be used to learn from previous projects and results
- Describes the benefits of workflow-driven automation for the various user communities inside and outside the organization
- Demonstrates how companies can enforce policies and best practices throughout the organization without expending more resources

Understanding the project-delivery life cycle stages and using a workflow system to better manage project and resource processes allows companies to:

- Ensure that the right projects continue to get funding.
- Identify and evaluate poor performing projects and resource groups.
- Plan and execute projects more consistently and efficiently.
- Allocate costs to business units, invoice customers, and update financial systems without any manual or disconnected processes.
- Capture, learn, and share best practices for selecting and executing projects.

The benefits of a Project Workforce Management solution are far reaching within an organization and have a varied, yet profound effect on the different user groups. A Project Workforce Management system can be universally used to track projects from start to finish—from proposal and selection to completion.

Delivering Projects and Services

Quality is never an accident . . . it represents the wise choice of many alternatives.
—William A. Foster

Figure 2.1 diagrams the five stages in the project and service delivery cycle. Each of these steps involves choices managers must make as they "look within" to optimize the performance of the business. Companies failing to leverage the intelligence and controls available through automating the processes and decision systems will likely find themselves at a competitive disadvantage or facing regulatory compliance issues. Optimally, automation should encompass processes at each of these stages:

1. *Initiate.* First, managers define the objectives and scope of the work to be performed.
2. *Plan.* Next, managers plan the work as well as assign the resources required to deliver the project, along with key milestones to track the project's progress.

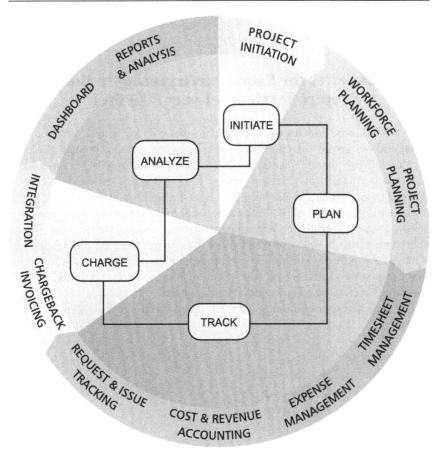

Figure 2.1 The Project Delivery Cycle Has Five Key Stages, Each with Its Own Alternative Choices, Complexities, and Challenges.

3. *Track.* Managers have now started to review time, expenses and budgets associated with each project milestone; to account for costs and revenue by resource group, project, and tasks within each project phase; and proactively handle requests, risks, and issues that affect the scope, budget, schedule, and status of the work being performed.

4. *Charge.* At this point, managers create accurate and timely chargebacks or invoices and integrate the data with the company's core information systems, including billing, finance, accounting, human resources (HR), and customer relationship management (CRM) systems.

5. *Analyze.* Finally, managers have all the information to create executive dashboards and reports to present high-level metrics that help them keep projects on track and enable them to measure revenue, utilization rates, costs, and profitability. This stage also allows them to produce

reports and analysis that assist with regulatory compliance, process improvement, and decision making.

Benefits for Users Participating in the Project/Service Delivery Life Cycle

Project Workforce Management offers benefits to the various communities inside and outside of the enterprise, including customers, sales staff, project-service delivery teams, managers, information technology (IT) specialists, finance departments, and administrative staff, as well as top-level (C-level) executives. These distinct groups have very specific needs and challenges. Each group requires certain types of information and tools to execute their tasks efficiently. Project Workforce Management systems work to reduce overhead where individuals have to enter and verify data. In addition, Project Workforce Management provides very robust, real-time reports and information that empower professionals to make quicker, yet more informed decisions based on reliable data that is captured and audited by the system.

The principal user communities of a Project Workforce Management solution are:

- Account executives
- External and internal customers
- General administrative staff
- Project and service delivery teams
- Finance team
- Project managers
- Resource managers
- IT department
- Product development teams
- C-level executives

Account Executives

- What is the status of my customers' projects and are they happy?
- Who is working on my customers' projects?
- How much was billed and what has not yet been invoiced?
- Are there any new business opportunities I can pursue?

Sales staff needs summary status and billing information on their customers' projects. They also have to be able to turn opportunities into projects by notifying the delivery teams that a new sale has closed. Project Workforce Management combined with CRM provides a 360-degree customer view available to all authorized users throughout the entire life cycle of a customer relationship—from initial discussion stages to a signed contract, hand off from sales to project and service delivery teams, through to project initiation, planning, execution, and support.

Account executives can initiate a project for formal handoff to project-service delivery teams once a deal closes. The sales team then gains access to up-to-the-minute information on customer projects, including key milestones, billing and invoicing information, service contracts near completion, and change requests that could trigger new opportunities. The sales organization has full visibility into customer engagements from the CRM interface.

Customers

Project Workforce Management supports the concept of a customer as an internal or external entity. The customer can actually be an external client being billed for services delivered or an internal business unit charged back for services rendered for cost allocation, business unit profitability assessment, and budgeting purposes. Many organizations actually track both types of "customers" using their Project Workforce Management system. By tracking all work performed for both external customers and for interdepartmental chargeback in one system, the company gains considerable insight into enterprise-wide project execution and resource utilization-related metrics that are impossible to analyze if different systems manage billable and internal projects.

EXTERNAL CUSTOMERS. Today's customers expect more instantaneous access to their own project information; principally because they want to be able to approve billable work, monitor project progress, check the status of previously reported issues or to review details of outstanding invoices. Project Workforce Management enables a service provider to present billing information online accurately and instantaneously.

The underlying workflow platform drives all issue reporting-and-resolution processes. Issues are automatically assigned to different individuals or teams internally based on the customer's specific requirements and service level agreement (SLA). Workflows use notification, automatic escalation, and conditional routing to ensure customer issues are handled in accordance with their SLA. Similarly, a workflow is used to track invoice review and approval by both internal billing managers and the customer (in the case of an online bill presentment and invoice approval process).

INTERNAL CUSTOMERS. Internal customers within a Project Workforce Management system usually include semiautonomous business units that have profit-and-loss responsibility. These internal groups are often very sophisticated and will fully utilize almost all of the reporting and analysis functionality made available to them. These business units are also among the heaviest users of business intelligence functionality. This does not come as a surprise because they juggle internal deliverables to and from various departments as well as manage other suppliers—all for the purpose of providing a product or service to a paying customer.

These business units are provided, at a minimum, with chargeback, progress, and status reports on project deliverables and milestones. In practice, however, they often demand and require much more information in the form of personalized role-based dashboards and analytics that help them monitor projects and services.

General Administrative Staff

Nonbillable resources with administrative duties reap significant benefits from a Project Workforce Management solution. Without such a solution, the general administrative staff has to deal with laborious, repetitive, manual, error-prone, and spreadsheet-intensive processes related to project management, resource management, time and expense entry, purchasing and approval tracking and follow-ups that often lead to additional overhead costs in the form of high turnover, frustrations, unmotivated employees, delays, and bottlenecks. Approval workflows, point-of-entry data validation, cost and billing engine, and reporting tools eliminate most, if not all, of these repetitive tasks.

The administrative staff's role changes from paper shuffling, e-mail processing, manual report generation, and repetitive data entry to a more sophisticated function of educating users, defining policies, identifying best practices, automating reports, and other administrative work using the Project Workforce Management solution.

Project/Service Delivery Teams

- What should I work on next week?
- What is the status of the expense report or purchase order I submitted a week ago?
- The time I was assigned is not enough; can I ask for an extension?
- Who authorizes resource allocations, purchases?

The project/service delivery staff (professional services teams in the case of a revenue-generating team) actually executes projects and delivers services. Project Workforce Management facilitates the collection of time and expense information by providing access from a variety of data-entry locations including Web browsers, phones, and personal digital assistants (PDAs), in regular use by today's mobile workforce.

Field workers report billable work while on the road or when they return to the office. And, they are automatically reminded to submit their timesheets and expense reports promptly following the customer-requested billing cycle. In addition to those in the field, other service personnel, such as support representatives, can gain access to the details of projects and engagements. Approved work items and assigned activities automatically appear on user schedules, so they know what projects or tasks to work on. Service members can quickly update the work status and enter billable charges, then immediately return to the activity at hand.

The Project Workforce Management system unravels a considerable amount of the complexity for the project/service delivery teams. A simple customer project with only a few activities that simply requires the staff to charge all their time to one budget, managed by a single project manager does not offer much of a challenge. However, it is not unusual to have staff members work on a number of different tasks for several projects, with more than one project manager, and with varying billing rates, rules, or different budgets. Regardless of the project's complexity, team members only see the work that is assigned to them and what they have been authorized to view.

Finance Team

There are three major user communities within the finance team: accounts receivable (billing), accounts payable, and payroll departments.

ACCOUNTS RECEIVABLE (BILLING)

- Which projects and expenses are billable?
- What project revenues can be recognized?
- What is our work in progress?

The billing department needs to know which projects, services, and expenses can be invoiced. Any customer approved milestones, billable work, and expenses are reported to the billing team for processing based on the customers' invoicing cycles.

Project details are not required for work in progress and revenue recognition reporting. Since project tasks are linked to general ledger accounts, Project Workforce Management is able to calculate this information for financial reporting purposes.

ACCOUNTS PAYABLE

- Who approved this vendor invoice?
- Which expenses should be reimbursed?

Using a purchase request workflow, accounts payable staff can match vendor invoices with internally approved purchase orders to verify and process payments. Meanwhile, the expense reporting system provides the staff with the list of employee incurred and manager approved expense reports that are to be reimbursed.

PAYROLL

- Have all timesheets been approved?
- Did employee A take five vacation days and how much time does he have left?
- Employee B has been sick for three days, did she have any paid sick leave available?

For every payroll cycle, payroll administrators need to know how many hours of work was done per employee and any paid/unpaid time off. Administrators have to apply pay rules such as exempt/non-exempt status, overtime calculations, paid time-off eligibility, and any bonuses due. Payroll administrators are able to make adjustments on current or past payrolls as well as enforce corporate pay rules and policies. For payroll processing, all time data is associated with one or more pay codes per user.

Project Managers

- What projects are coming and how do we prioritize them?
- What is the scope of work, including start dates and deadlines?
- How do I get the resources I need for this project?
- What is this project's health and earned value?

Project managers are daily users of a Project Workforce Management system. They define and manage critical parts of the organization and work breakdown structures (see Chapter 6), as well as plan and monitor the work of delivery teams. Project managers control budgets that fund activities, track and approve time, expenses, issues, change requests, and project-related purchases.

Project managers gain deeper visibility into the project pipeline. By getting visibility into upcoming projects, they can prepare tentative project start dates and plans as well as better assess the required resources and deliverables.

Resource Managers

- What is the current and forecasted resource utilization?
- What skill sets are required for the current project pipeline? Do we have the required talent?
- Which skills are we lacking or we have too many of?

Resource managers have the difficult task of fine-tuning the organization's capacity in response to demand changes. Project Workforce Management provides resource managers with the resource calendars, current and upcoming project plans, skill repository, resource request workflows, as well as the search and skill-matching functions they need to manage the company's resource pool.

Information Technology Department

- How is the IT spending forecast justified?
- Which IT projects are not performing?
- How can I quickly report the IT costs per business unit?
- How can we manage and report on scope change as well as project risks and issues?

IT is a budget-driven department that does not perform any direct revenue generating work. Therefore, it is a very large and highly visible cost center. The IT department is always under pressure to do more with less and to do it quickly. IT organizations are one of the first adopters of Project Workforce Management as they are constantly under pressure to manage and control IT project costs and justify any spending.

Product Development Teams

- How much did it cost to build this product?
- Is the product on schedule, on budget, and on track?
- Which products have the most defects and the highest risk?
- What should the engineers (researchers, etc.) work on next?

Product development teams have traditionally been opposed to tracking because they believe the details of what they do should stay under management's radar. There are, however, tremendous benefits for them and the company if products are treated like any other project. For example, any time (effort) and expenses can be charged back to the project and a cost-benefit analysis can be performed to assess whether the project (product) is meeting its intended cost, time, and strategy objectives.

C-Level Executives

- What is the business case for this for this project?
- Who approved these projects?
- What is the status of key projects throughout the enterprise?
- Which clients or product lines are generating the most revenue? The most profit?

- Where can I get a consolidated view of our forecasts and status of all engagements?
- Where is the cost-benefit analysis of this initiative?

Executives with profit-and-loss responsibility are among the heaviest users of Project Workforce Management dashboards and reports. Naturally as the span of control and financial responsibility grows, it becomes increasingly important to quickly identify and manage trends, slipping financial indicators, customer satisfaction, project pipeline, billing issues, revenue, cash flow, overhead, and margins.

In many cases, especially in large enterprises, specialized tools may already be in place to perform some of the financial modeling, executive and exception reporting, profitability and head-count analyses, as well as project status. Very often, all this input is packaged for the executive and referred to as an *executive dashboard*. Often these tools are so tailored to the business and culture of the enterprise that they are custom-built systems, using what were powerful tools back when the systems were first assembled. Surprisingly, executive reports are often based on spreadsheets. These reports are time consuming to generate, providing inconsistent, error-prone and out-of-date information. A Project Workforce Management solution can be configured to serve as the core executive dashboard for project and workforce information or to provide feeds into other enterprise systems for reporting.

3

Project Governance

Direct threats require decisive action.

—Dick Cheney

A variety of threats and challenges can impact projects. Understanding and proactively addressing these risks should be at the core of any company's operational efficiency, compliance, and governance initiatives. Management must evaluate whether there are any material weaknesses that can lead to a lack of effective internal controls, which is a fundamental requirement of the Sarbanes-Oxley (SOX) corporate governance law (see Chapter 4, "What Project Managers Need to Know about Sarbanes-Oxley"). Project threats are classified into four categories: financial, process, governance, or compliance. Financial threats are the result of poor budget forecasting and tracking, lack of interdepartmental chargebacks, and ineffective resource and cost-allocation tracking. Process threats grow from lack of a framework that encourages the use of methodologies, templates, best practices, and consistent processes for project initiation, scope control, status reporting, risk assessment, and issue tracking. Last, compliance and governance threats materialize when a company's internal controls demonstrate material weaknesses.

Unless immediate action is taken, internal or external auditors have an obligation to report when a company is not in compliance with any applicable regulations. Compliance threats can jeopardize projects, executives, and the success of the company when there are violations—whether intentional or unintentional—of government, industry, or accounting regulations, such as employment wage laws, Family and Medical Leave Act (FMLA) regulations, or generally accepted accounting principles (GAAP) for project-related matters, such as cost accounting, revenue recognition, work in progress reporting, and which projects to capitalize or expense.

Project and workforce governance roadmaps should be designed to address the potential threats that are presented in Figure 3.1. This chapter identifies the enterprise-wide threats and uses a symptom-cause-solution format

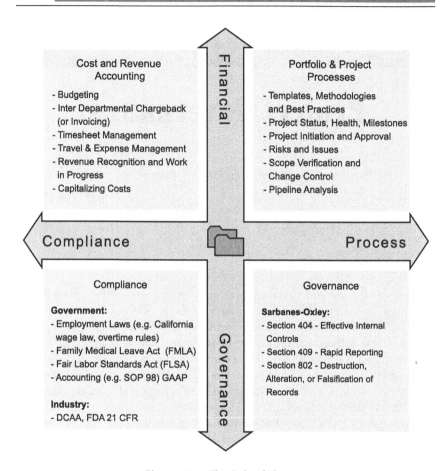

Figure 3.1   The Axis of Threats

to highlight the steps executives and project managers need to take to effectively mitigate risk and reduce the likelihood that any of these threats may damage their business. Subsequent chapters provide more detailed analyses on how to turn these threats into opportunities for improvement.

Cost Accounting

For each area, we address symptoms, causes, threats, and solutions.

Budgeting

Symptoms indicating problems in the area of budgeting include:

- Projects are over budget without clear justification.
- An internal department is forced to lay off workers due to a budget shortfall.

- Many projects are hit with unanticipated delays and scope changes.
- A company revises previous forecasts, cost estimates, profit margins, or financial reports due to forecasting errors.

Causes of these problems include:

- Company lacks a top-down budget planning process.
- There is not a systematic analysis and forecasting of spending and its impact on cash flow and profit margins.
- The company does not track budget versus estimate versus actual project results in real time or on a regular basis.

Threats to companies without disciplined budget approval processes in place include:

- They are far more likely to experience budget shortfalls, project delays, and failures.
- They may encounter poorly funded strategic projects or unjustified funding of the wrong projects, resulting in substantial damages to the company, executive careers, customer satisfaction, and investor confidence.

Tracking project time and cost budgets is one of the most important aspects of effective controls. Companies that want to neutralize the associated threats must:

- Ensure all projects have clear budget forecasts in sync with overall project schedules.
- Invest in a reporting and notification system configured to provide alerts of any budget shortfalls or over-budget activities.
- Ensure that budget-impact analysis is part of any scope change or risk assessment.
- Establish budget baselines and track budget variances.

Interdepartmental Chargebacks

Symptoms that indicate a problem include:

- Managers are unable to itemize costs of services rendered to other business units.
- A cost center's budget is consistently increasing, seemingly out of step with the growth and demand experienced by revenue and profit centers.
- The company is unable to determine every business unit's performance and profit margin.

There are many possible causes. Many internal service departments, such as information technology (IT), get a corporate budget and spend it without charging costs back to the business units that use their services or having to provide a return-on-investment report. More frequently, companies are looking to implement a zero-budget policy for internal service departments. Business units are responsible for allocating budgets to internal service departments. These budgets drive the overall funding of internal service teams; all internal spending and resource utilizations are charged back to the business unit.

Without internal chargeback and approvals of internal cost allocation:[1]

- Department managers and company executives are far more likely to allocate costs to the wrong projects.
- Profit margins may be inflated in one business unit and underreported in another.
- Executives and project managers can hide underperforming projects and budget shortfalls because they can shift costs to different projects since there is no formal chargeback process. This renders project portfolio reviews and alignment ineffective due to the lack of verifiable cost and profit information (see Chapter 18, "Project Prioritization and Selection").

The solution is to implement a top-down budget and interdepartmental chargeback process (Figure 3.2) across all business units. Business units should fund internal service departments as part of their overall budgets. An enterprise-wide, cost-tracking solution ensures spending is always aligned with corporate strategy and internal projects are initiated with clear justification, proper approval, sponsorship, and funding by the business units that ultimately benefit from such projects.

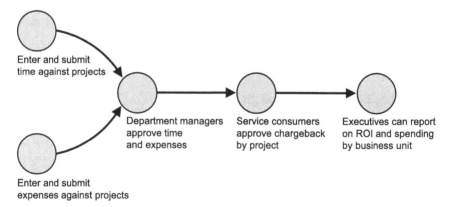

Enter and submit time against projects

Department managers approve time and expenses

Service consumers approve chargeback by project

Executives can report on ROI and spending by business unit

Enter and submit expenses against projects

Figure 3.2   Sample Chargeback Process

Timesheet Management

Symptoms of a problem are:

- There is no tangible measure of the value created versus effort of internal departments.
- Project manager notices employees are working very long hours to deliver a project, but cannot report to management regarding which resources are overloaded.
- Vice president of professional services receives a report of the billable utilization of consultants two weeks after month end because the data collection process is manual.
- COO cannot get a report showing the breakdown of effort per department across research and development (R&D), customer, and maintenance projects.

Causes include:

- Some company cultures work against using timesheets and see this as employee monitoring. Timesheet management is a fundamental requirement for earned value tracking, billing, chargeback, cost allocation, capitalization of software development costs, measurement of work in progress, and revenue recognition for partially completed projects.
- Companies track time using spreadsheets or multiple disconnected timesheet systems: one for payroll, another for project tracking, and yet another for billable work. The information in these systems is often inconsistent.
- Manual entry, processing, and reporting—such as merging of spreadsheets—is used to verify, integrate, and analyze the information collected.

Without formal time tracking a company is more likely to experience material errors, inconsistencies, and delays in its payroll, billing, as well as cost allocation and reporting. Ineffective time tracking can also result in revenue leakage, longer billing cycles, project execution problems, unhappy customers who experience the chaos, and ultimately, audit failure due to material-control weaknesses in cost accounting and billing systems.

Enterprise timesheet management helps companies track labor costs and billable time much more effectively, by providing a centralized, audited, and real-time view of the work performed. Management gains insight into how much time is spent on every project. Time reports highlight tasks that are not being performed efficiently and help pinpoint potential constraints and resource conflicts.

Travel and Entertainment Expense Management

Symptoms of problems include:

- Expenses are treated as overhead rather than being allocated to actual projects.
- An employee submitted an expense report weeks ago, but never got reimbursed. No one can quickly validate the claim or track the report's status.
- The company cannot efficiently curb rogue and discretionary travel and entertainment (T&E) expenses.

Causes of these problems include:

- Spreadsheets are used to collect and approve employee-incurred expenses. Expenses are often entered manually into accounts payable and are not properly audited or linked to any tool that reports spending by project and business unit.
- Compliance mostly depends on the integrity of the approvers. Lack of auditing, automation, and reporting are the primary sources of control weakness for T&E.

Travel and entertainment is often the second largest corporate expense after labor. Manual processes and high transaction volume can quickly lead to unnecessary expenses, errors, and outright fraud. For companies that use manual processes and spreadsheets, lack of internal controls results in the following: no accountability or traceability, inaccurate cost accounting, errors, and a control weakness that will be flagged by any capable internal or external audit committee.

Travel and entertainment expense management automates the entire expense management life cycle. Travel and entertainment software helps a company:

- Predefine expense item limits that prevent overspending or flag certain expense entries as exceptions, which require further scrutiny and approval.
- Budget for spending by project and by cost objective to detect and prevent rogue spending.
- Establish line item approvals of expenses, allocate employee spending to individual business units and projects, and update accounts payable.
- Conduct a full audit of all expense report modifications, approvals, and rejections.
- Create extensive reports on expenses by project, customer, business unit, and by expense type across the enterprise.

Revenue Recognition and Work in Progress

Symptoms of problems include:

- Project managers and the finance team are not sure when to recognize revenue for billable projects, contracts, and expenses.
- The finance team does not get an account of project overhead costs, backlog, work in progress, conditional purchases, and partially completed projects.
- Customers refuse to pay because, from their perspective, project milestones have not been reached. The finance department is unable to validate milestone approvals without constantly meeting with project managers.

Revenue recognition has not established or communicated a formal revenue recognition policy to its project and service delivery teams. The company is not able to quickly determine what project milestones have been reached. In addition, project managers perceive revenue recognition to be strictly a finance team issue.

A company without a written and strictly followed revenue-recognition policy is in danger of being forced to restate its financials. The company may have recognized revenue prematurely or underrecognized revenue that it will be forced to revise later when external or internal auditors uncover revenue-recognition errors and inconsistencies.

The first step is to write a revenue-recognition policy based on generally accepted accounting principles (GAAP). The policy should be explained to the company's revenue-generating divisions because their cooperation is needed on a regular basis to correctly report revenue. Software can be implemented to automate revenue-recognition controls. Depending on the nature of the company's business and types of customers, some billable work can be recognized as revenue while the work is being delivered. Whereas, other types of work may be recognizable only after specific milestones have been reached or customer acceptance is obtained. The company's revenue-recognition policy should account for high-risk customers and conditional purchases (see Chapter 14).

Capitalizing Costs

Symptoms of the problem include:

- Software purchases or software development projects are not capitalized.
- No distinction is made between maintenance, IT, and software development projects.

Causes of the problems might be:

- The company's management is unaware of the accounting regulation SOP 98 (capitalization of certain software costs).
- The company does not perceive software or IT projects as potential assets.
- The company does not track engineering time and is unable to measure time spent on R&D versus maintenance or other types of projects.

Threats because of these problems include:

- The company may be overstating its expenses (e.g., SOP 98 requires the capitalization of certain types of software projects).
- The company may be understating its expenses by capitalizing projects that should not be capitalized according to GAAP.
- Inaccurate cost and revenue reporting may lead to after-the-fact tax revisions, penalties, and audit failures.

The company must determine the nature of a software project as part of the project-initiation process and establish whether the project's costs are material. Whether a project is to be capitalized or expensed, must be determined in this early stage to ensure that all subsequent progress and risk reports, and interim financial reports, properly classify this project as a balance sheet (an asset class that should be depreciated according to regulations) or an income statement (an expense) item. This classification has to be done for every project phase down to the task level. A project initiation process and activity-based cost tracking accomplishes the objectives mentioned previously.

Portfolio and Project Processes

In this section, we again address the symptoms, causes, threats, and possible solutions for each area.

Templates, Methodologies, and Best Practices

Symptoms of problems include:

- New project managers do not get any training or documentation about the department's project-management processes, procedures, and methodologies.
- No standardized tracking of project artifacts, such as a charter or a closing report.
- Project managers and executives do not have immediate access to an analysis of the company's past performance on various types of projects.

Any insight comes from talking to veteran project managers and team members.

- The company does not capture and share any of its lessons learned across multiple teams and departments.
- After a status meeting, action items are e-mailed to participants without a tracking or follow-up process. Minutes with action items are hard to find after meetings.

The major cause of these problems is that project management is not recognized as a necessary and critical business function.

The threat that results is:

- Projects are more likely to experience varying degrees of success, repeat the same costly mistakes, and exhibit the same budget overruns as their predecessors.
- The ability to report on enterprise-wide projects is limited because of inconsistent tracking and reporting.

The solution involves establishing a project management office (PMO), a special group of project managers within an organization who are designated on a full-time or part-time basis to define, promote, and enforce project management standards and best practices throughout the company. The PMO:

- Implements standard project-management methodologies to reduce the training time and learning curve for new project managers.
- Trains all project-service delivery teams on project management and best practices.
- Monitors projects looking for patterns of success or failure.
- Selects and implements new project management related software that promotes and improves enterprise-wide project management.
- Defines project management best practice templates, policies, and processes.

Project Status, Health, and Milestones

Symptoms of problems include:

- Project status seems to change weekly—from everything going well one week to a seemingly unmanageable number of issues and obstacles the next.
- Project delays and budget overruns are often a complete surprise. No one anticipates any problems until it is too late.
- Project status meetings lack metrics and are based on gut feeling.

Causes of these problems include:

- The company does not track measurable project status metrics for all projects.
- Projects are managed in silos without a real-time global perspective.
- Standard key performance indicators (KPI) have not been defined to quantitatively measure project health.

The threats resulting from the problems might be:

- The company is likely to experience project delays and failures.
- The company's investors may interpret lack of timely or inconsistent reporting as a sign of an incompetent or intentionally deceitful management team.
- Projects fail or succeed without any lessons learned. The company is in a constant state of struggle and crisis control.

The solution involves the PMO defining a companywide standard project-status reporting process including measurable performance indicators to:

- Collect and review periodic status reports that show a summary of every project's performance, value, costs, issues, and risks.
- Build executive dashboards and live, dynamic portfolio-management reports that indicate project health by comparing budgeted versus estimated and actual costs as well as billable amounts.

Project Initiation and Approval

Symptoms of problems include:

- Projects are initiated differently in every department, depending on a specific manager's habits or the department's relationship with the executive committee.
- No one can quickly determine who approved particular phases of a project and what the justifications were for those approvals.

The cause is that there is no companywide project approval process that is strictly enforced, regardless of the departments and executives involved.

Threats that result from these problems include:

- Questionable projects are far more likely to get funded when there is not a centralized and audited system for project initiation.

- Without reporting on how and why projects are approved or rejected, no one can be held accountable when a project fails or is not funded in the appropriate timeframe.
- Auditors may conclude that the company is not properly auditing and archiving project-related approvals and documentation, such as proposals, status reports, scope-change requests, and milestone sign-offs (a potential violation of Section 802 of Sarbanes-Oxley).

The solution involves treating project initiation and all related documentation and approvals as high-risk business-critical processes. One of the first mandates of the company's PMO is to involve all departments and project managers in the process of defining a clear policy and procedure for proposing and approving projects. Once this is done, the company can then use software to facilitate project-initiation control, as well as audit and reporting to help institutionalize and govern these vital project-related processes.

Risk Management

Symptoms of problems include:

- The company did not report to its investors newly discovered risks likely to impact the latest product release.
- The company failed to mitigate known risks that led to the project's failure.
- Risks were managed properly until the company's CIO or COO was replaced.
- Management does not know whether different teams have encountered similar risks.
- Risks are not promptly reported to management for immediate remedial action.

Causes might be:

- No formal processes have been established for risk management.
- There has not been an audit of which risks were reported, how they were addressed, and whether they are material enough to be communicated to project stakeholders.

Companies that do not have a process to manage and mitigate risks encounter the following threats:

- Severe customer and shareholder backlash when an unreported, unexpected, or unmanaged risk results in project delays and/or failures.

- Management statements and reassurances in financial reports that are in conflict with the statements and comments made by project managers and other people in the field. This is a violation of Section 409 of the Sarbanes-Oxley law—a failure to act on and report known risks in financial reports on a rapid and current basis.

The solution is to use a risk-management workflow that ensures every risk is carefully documented, assessed, and any necessary course corrections are initiated. Project stakeholders report risks as they are encountered. Based on a predefined, risk-management workflow, the risk is reported to the assessment committee, who can then discard it or take the actions necessary to address the risk. All risk, scope change, and action item related activities are tracked, audited, and reported by the risk-management system for future analysis, enterprise-wide access, management decision making, and accountability. To learn more about project risk management refer to Chapter 16, "Risk, Scope, and Issue Tracking."

Issue Management

Symptoms of the problem include:

- Some project issues go unanswered for an unreasonable amount of time.
- Project managers do not have a global perspective of project issues or priorities and do not know how other teams have managed similar issues.

Causes of the problems might be:

- The company does not have a central repository to track, report, and manage issues across multiple teams and projects.
- The company's managers and employees are not sure of the role they play in the process and sometimes feel that ignoring certain issues will make them go away.
- Service level agreement (SLA) guidelines are not enforced. Unresolved issues are rediscovered only after someone, whether inside or outside of the company, gets frustrated.

Threats that result are:

- Projects are likely to suffer "death from a thousand wounds." Without a global perspective or the benefit of past experience, high-priority issues can accumulate and become unmanageable.
- Unresolved and unmanaged high-priority issues can quickly develop into a major risk that may derail the project.

- Issues that take too long to resolve may breach the SLA that has been formally agreed on between the customer and the project-service delivery teams resulting in customer dissatisfaction.

The solution involves implementation of an enterprise-wide issue-tracking system to manage project issues and to enforce SLAs. For more information see Chapter 16, "Risk, Scope, and Issue Tracking."

Scope Verification and Change Control

Symptoms of problems include:

- People start with the assumption that project scope cannot be defined but that it will get finalized as the project progresses and needs are better understood.
- Project stakeholders do not formally verify and approve initial scope statements.
- Scope changes are approved or rejected depending on who makes the requests and when those requests are made.
- Scope changes are not tracked in any way. Project managers and team members simply revise estimates and create new baselines to indicate scope change.
- Scope is changed only to find out later that funding was not approved, the change is not exactly what the customer wanted or could have been avoided.

Causes of the problems include:

- Institutionalized processes for scope verification and change control do not exist.
- No formal document describes the project's full scope, goals, and requirements.
- The company lets line-of-business managers or project managers decide how to manage scope, which leads to scope management based on individual styles and a lack of consistency, transparency, and accountability.
- Budget request and scope change approvals are handled in separate spreadsheets or systems with no explicit link between them.

Threats from these problems include:

- Stakeholders are not fully involved in the original scope definition, have not approved scope changes, and refuse to pay for what is being delivered.

- Projects experience *scope creep,* which can impact delivery dates and profitability.

Some companies manage project scope by maintaining a list of documents, folders, spreadsheets, and e-mails that contain scope-related content and discussion threads. This type of scope management is a control weakness because the company is not auditing scope change approvals, does not have a formal process for scope change review, and scope change is not explicitly linked to budget requests or other action items. Workflow-based scope management provides an effective solution to controlling scope. Additional information on project scope management can be found in Chapter 16, "Risk, Scope, and Issue Tracking."

Project Pipeline Analysis

Symptoms of problems include:

- The company has no more than a few weeks of visibility for upcoming projects.
- Employees, consultants, and customers exhibit stress and dissatisfaction due to shifting demands, high workloads, and delays in project starts.
- There are cash flow problems because of poor forecasting.

Causes of these problems might be:

- There is not a centralized and audited system for reviewing new initiatives.
- Projects are not classified into portfolios (see Chapter 18, "Project Prioritization and Selection"). Therefore, management is unable to prioritize and choose the right investment level for new or existing projects.
- Cash flow analysis is weak because future demand is not forecasted properly.

Threats that result from these problems include:

- Poor project and portfolio pipeline management can lead to the failure of existing projects and lack of funding for new strategic initiatives due to poor resource and logistics forecasting and planning.
- The company experiences budget and cash-flow problems since it is unable to manage current demand and meet future capacity requirements.

For visibility into future resource needs for new projects, a company needs procedures, policies, and systems that enable executives and program managers to analyze demand and collaborate on forecasting and planning for staffing levels and resource allocations. Collaborative workforce planning and project selection systems provide:

- An audited and formalized process to submit and track new initiatives. New project proposals include business-case definitions, objectives, budget and resource estimates, feasibility analysis, in addition to tracking of approvals for every stage of the initiative.
- Measures for current and past resource utilization, as well as forecasts for future skill and availability needs, helping the company plan capacity more effectively for upcoming projects.
- Visibility into the corporate customer relationship management (CRM) solution for sales-pipeline analysis to anticipate growth.

Corporate Governance

Sarbanes-Oxley will force system integration, automation, and real-time notification of events to give companies more visibility into everything that goes into their financial books.

—Aberdeen Group[2]

Sections 404 and 409: Effective Internal Controls and Rapid Reporting

Symptoms of problems include:

- A company's internal or external auditors are unable to certify that all transactions are transparent and audited.
- The company fails to report on material changes in a rapid and timely manner.
- According to auditors, the company does not have the proper processes in place to protect it against potential misallocation of funds and budget abuse.
- The company is regularly forced to spend a tremendous amount of time and resources to prepare for an audit.

Possible causes are:

- The company uses spreadsheets and manual processes to collect and consolidate project status and financial data from multiple business units.

- The management team is unable to quickly trace back the justification behind a specific event, such as a budget approval and project-related purchases.
- There is a lack of auditing and validation of project and workforce activity such as budgeting, billing, and cost accounting.

Threats that result from these problems include:

- With poor controls, the company's certifying officers are far more hesitant to sign the corporate financials and are at risk of approving financials, which are later revised and need to be restated.
- If a company fails an audit, the organization may incur substantial fines, investor backlash, and a damaged reputation.
- The cost of achieving or maintaining manual compliance is so high that it has a material effect on the company's bottom line and forces the managers to spend their time and attention on day-to-day compliance matters rather than on running the business.
- The company must be able to respond to project cost and approval-related audit inquiries for the past seven years (as required by law); lack of sufficient documentation of such transactions is an automatic audit failure.

The Sarbanes-Oxley Law does not specifically state business-process management (workflow software) as a requirement. However, companies and their management teams pay a very high price to achieve and maintain compliance using manual or disconnected processes.

Workflow systems provide automatic validation of all forms, requests, and documents at point of entry, audit all transactions, offer real-time reporting on operations, ensure that proper notifications are sent in the case of a material change in business conditions, and make certain the same consistent, predefined procedures are followed for the company's key people, project, and financial-related work processes.

Section 802: Destruction, Alteration, or Falsification of Records

Symptoms of problems include:

- Auditors cannot find certain documents, contracts, project approvals, scope changes, invoices, and chargeback approvals for completed projects or for those in progress for the past seven years.
- The company is unable to quickly locate all of the documents, scope changes, status reports, and milestone sign-offs associated with a project under audit.

- The company does not have an activity log that displays who had access to project documents and what changes were made.
- Important project documents were destroyed when an employee left the company.

Possible causes for these problems include:

- The company has not adopted consistent enterprise-wide document-retention and safeguarding policies and systems.
- Only contracts, specifications, and e-mails are treated as documents to be safeguarded. However, under Sarbanes-Oxley, all project-related content including meeting minutes of internal discussions, status reports, timesheets, expense reports, and invoices, as well as issues and risk assessments are considered documents that must be retained and safeguarded against any alteration or destruction.
- There is limited security related to accessing and altering project documents.

Threats that result are:

- Auditors identify the lack of document retention and security as control weaknesses.
- It is difficult and costly to hold project managers and executives accountable because the company cannot quickly identify what changes were made to certain documents—why, by whom, and when.
- The company may be a victim of the destruction of evidence or substantial fraud that goes undetected due to destroyed or altered documents.

For compliance with Section 802:

- Documents have to be linked to the organization and work-breakdown structures to facilitate reporting, searching, and cross-indexing.
- Secure all types of documents (described previously) so that they can only be altered by authorized users at specific stages in the document life cycle.

Compliance

Compliance involves government laws such as the California wage law, Family Medical Leave Act (FMLA), Fair Labor Standards Act (FLSA), and industry-specific regulations such as Defense Contract Audit Agency (DCAA) cost accounting guidelines. For a more detailed breakdown of these regulations see Chapter 5, "Complying with Labor Laws and Accounting Regulations."

Symptoms of problems include:

- The company is not certain whether it is in compliance with various labor laws and is concerned about the potential for employee labor law-related liability.
- Tremendous time and resources are spent preparing for government audits.
- Compliance is manual, resource intensive, and depends heavily on the individual efforts of a few managers who are in charge of the compliance process.
- Adapting to new rules or regulations requires considerable effort.

Causes of these problems include:

- The company relies instead on manual procedures to verify and enforce compliance.
- There is no automated mechanism to alert administrators of any rule violations.
- There is a lack of built-in validation, auditing and control of timesheets, time-off requests, expense reports, and purchase requests at the point of entry.

Threats that result from these problems include:

- The cost of compliance is so high that it has a material effect on the company's bottom line and occupies a great deal of management's time.
- Employee lawsuits and litigations are likely to occur and will be hard to defend because many processes were manual and, therefore, fraught with inconsistencies.

Compliance can be achieved by:

- Tracking regular work time, overtime, and shifts.
- Calculating and keeping track of paid and unpaid accrued leave time based on FLSA, FMLA, and corporate policies.
- Ensuring compliance at point of entry and displaying compliance-related information to administrators and managers.
- Asking employees to report time and expenses and approving them on a regular basis; minimizing the possibility of future lawsuits and liabilities.

Risk Management and Basel II

Basel II is a set of international standards for risk management that are specifically related to financial institutions. While compliance to these standards does not apply to most companies, the risk management principles are worth mentioning. A comparison of Sarbanes-Oxley and Basel II is helpful in the context of project governance and compliance.

Sarbanes-Oxley is focused on controls: Does the company have processes and verification systems in place to manage its business effectively, prevent fraud, and accurately report financials? And can it prove that its systems are effective?

In contrast, Basel II is focused on risks: Has the company looked at the risks in its operations? How much money needs to be set aside to cover risk exposure? What can the company do to reduce its risk exposure and therefore reduce the reserves that it has to set aside to cover the potential financial liabilities?

Controls can only be effective if a company understands and assesses its risk exposure.

NOTES

1. The WorldCom case represents a perfect example of the potential dangers of not having an audited chargeback process. More details on this case are outlined in Chapter 4, "What Project Managers Need to Know about Sarbanes-Oxley."
2. Alex Veytsel, Aberdeen Group, October 2002, "Baring the Financials: More Than the Current Financial Systems Can Bear."

4

Why Project Managers Need to Know about Sarbanes-Oxley

Integrity is doing the right thing, even if nobody is watching.
—Jim Stovall

Occupational fraud and abuse sliced 6% off corporate revenue (approximately $4,500 per employee) in 2002. Over 80% of fraud involves asset misappropriation—with cash, or its equivalents—being targeted 90% of the time. The average fraud scheme lasts about 18 months before it's detected and over half cost their victims at least $100,000; nearly one in six causes losses of $1 million or more. Those larger losses are often the work of mid- to upper-level.
—Association of Certified Fraud Examiners (CFE)[1]

As the percentage of project-centric organizations and teams as a total of the global workforce continues to increase so does the time and space in a flat world where work has become more fragmented. Many companies, recognizing this trend, are funding and promoting a new department within their organization called the Project Management Office (PMO). Now, more than ever, project managers have to gain a better understanding of the role they play in addressing compliance challenges and effective financial reporting. Today's global economy moves much faster, thus demanding that project and finance teams build stronger ties and collaborate on ensuring transparent, compliant, and responsible project selection, funding and execution.

The Sarbanes-Oxley (SOX) law has made corporate governance a mandatory element of financial reporting, operational control, and the daily management of a publicly traded company. Furthermore, institutional investors are putting significant pressure on privately held companies to comply with some of the primary concepts and guidelines established by Sarbanes-Oxley as they relate to effective governance and internal controls.

After the corporate fraud and scandals in recent years, shareholders and the government are demanding more accountability from all companies and organizations. The Sarbanes-Oxley law states that CEOs and CFOs must certify the financial reports of the organization. Noncompliant public organizations will face the swift wrath of their shareholders and creditors, as well as the Security and Exchange Commission's (SEC) investigations and severe penalties.

Forecasting cost and revenue of all project portfolios; analyzing and measuring financial risk; maintaining real-time data about where a project is against budget; having traceability of the project data; and documenting and standardizing core processes and best practices within the PMO are all examples of how project managers reinforce executive decisions and help comply with sections of Sarbanes-Oxley.

Nonformalized processes and unsystematic data capture increase the risk of inaccurate forecasts, budgets, project status, and after-the-fact untimely reporting. This irregularity provides far too much subjectivity in the financial analysis than CEOs and CFOs need to have on a monthly and quarterly basis. The penalties for noncompliance under Sarbanes-Oxley are severe and are justifiably on the minds of all executives in today's business world.

Keep in mind, compliance is possible without automation. However, companies can use Sarbanes-Oxley as a driving force to change for the better. Implementing software does not guarantee compliance, but it helps companies comply faster. Companies can also leverage this type of compliance initiative to reduce costs, improve project/service delivery, build more agile project teams, and enhance the confidence of all stakeholders including investors, employees, and customers.

How Sarbanes-Oxley Impacts Project Managers

The following sections of Sarbanes-Oxley require specific internal changes for any organization that has to comply with this law and has a direct impact on the project management community within organizations that fall under the compliance microscope:

Section 302: Expanded Representation by Certifying Officers requires CEO and CFO sign-off on the company's quarterly financial reports. The key officers must assert that the company's financial report is accurate, all material changes have been reported in a timely manner, and that the company has the appropriate internal controls to protect against any fraud or inaccuracies in its reporting.

Section 404: Effectiveness of Internal Controls relates to the ability of internal controls to intercept and detect any irregular, fraudulent, questionable, or unauthorized corporate activity. This section mandates the company to file an annual Internal Control Report (ICR), as well as quarterly reviews and reports of any material changes in internal controls. The annual ICR must communicate:

- Management's responsibility to establish and maintain internal controls over financial reporting
- The criteria used to evaluate the effectiveness of internal controls
- Management's conclusion as to the effectiveness of the established internal controls
- The fact that an auditor—a chartered public accountant—has attested to and reported on management's evaluation

According to the SEC's threshold on internal controls, management is not permitted to conclude that its internal controls are effective if there are one or more material weaknesses. If the company's management asserts that internal controls are effective, then this is also an assertion that there are no material weaknesses in such controls.

The SEC places the ultimate responsibility of financial reporting with the company's certifying officers. Consistent with the description of accounting control laws, certifying officers are responsible for ensuring all corporate transactions are properly authorized and recorded. They are responsible for the safeguarding of all company assets against unauthorized and improper use. The company must also comply with rules and regulations directly related to financial statements. However, Sarbanes-Oxley does not encompass effectiveness and efficiency of a company's operations or compliance with other regulations.

There is a significant overlap between internal controls for financial reporting and disclosure of controls as well as procedures. The former are the focus of Section 404, while the latter are addressed in Section 302. Companies need to ensure Section 404 compliance and provide assurances to certifying officers who have to sign for Section 302, that there are no internal control deficiencies. Any internal control that is a subset of disclosure control must also be evaluated on a quarterly basis and any material changes in those controls must be reported on a quarterly basis.

Section 409: Rapid Reporting requires disclosure of material changes on a "rapid and current basis" or rapid reporting. Rapid reporting implies that the company's internal control systems can report on projects and operations in real time. The company must be able to assess its current situation instantly and accurately. For example, if management is informed that a product will be released materially late due to design issues, execution challenges, or supplier delays, then it must immediately inform its investors of this change.

Section 802: Destruction, Alteration, or Falsification of Records links any knowingly falsified or altered documents to provisions of the criminal code. The company must establish strict audit records and a comprehensive document-retention policy. Company executives cannot simply say "documents were destroyed without our knowledge." This section and Section 404 mandate the company's executives to guarantee that proper systems are in place to ensure all documents are preserved in their original state and are protected against willful and malicious alterations.

It is important to note within the context of the law that documents are not just contracts and agreements one signs with third parties. Examples of what constitutes a document include all e-mails, project plans, timesheets, expense reports, budget reports, invoices, chargebacks, risk-assessment memos, meeting minutes, scope definitions and changes, project proposal and budget approvals, and milestone sign-offs.

Section 906: Corporate Responsibility for Financial Reports links representations made in Sections 302, 404, 409, and 802 by certified signing officers to provisions of the criminal act. Section 906 outlines specific penalties, including imprisonment and multimillion dollar fines, against certifying officers for financial reports that do not comply with Sarbanes-Oxley.

How Project Managers Can Comply with Internal Control Regulations

Project managers have two options for complying with and implementing effective internal controls. The first option is the traditional method of using manual processes to comply with a new law or methodology. The second option uses the compliance requirement as an opportunity to automate business processes.

Manual Compliance (Polling) Method

Traditionally, many companies comply with new regulations using the polling method, as follows:

- Hire consultants to understand the regulations and perform a gap analysis.
- Build spreadsheets, forms, and meeting-driven compliance-specific initiatives.
- Agree on a paper-based sign-off process or bring in a new workflow application dedicated to compliance and auditing.

This method requires constant, almost daily, and mechanical effort to establish and maintain compliance. The result is more administrative overhead and the associated higher costs.

Comply and Optimize Method

A more compelling alternative for compliance is the comply and optimize method. This course of action allows companies to automate their business processes with workflow software used enterprise wide that is instantly linked to the company's financial applications. That is the essence of Project Workforce Management that enables the organization to:

- Visually design, manage, and enforce the company's project, workforce, and financial processes.
- Validate data according to the company's policy at the point of entry.
- Audit all transactions and system activity.
- Design reports and executive dashboards to monitor operations and compliance.
- Track and audit all approvals and change requests.

With Project Workforce Management, executives and managers have access to real-time, dynamic, and consolidated reports on their operations. It is noticeably easier to analyze real-time, audited data on projects and portfolios than it is to manually consolidate multiple spreadsheet files to create static snapshots based on un-audited and unverifiable information.

What Project Workforce Management Does for Sarbanes-Oxley Compliance

Project Workforce Management facilitates compliance by providing:

- Cost accounting and interdepartmental chargebacks (for proper cost allocation)
- Scope management
- Project-cost estimation
- Risk reporting and assessment
- Issue tracking

How can a company's officers certify the financial statements if internal controls are paper- or spreadsheet-based? Or, worse, what happens if the organization operates multiple disconnected enterprise software applications, where administrative staff is asked to manually rekey or manually import/export data between such systems?

Quite simply, officers cannot and should not depend on error-prone and manual operational systems that can easily cause significant damage to their organizations and to their own careers. In worst-case scenarios, this type of weak corporate infrastructure may lead to mistakes, errors in judgment, and unreported criminal, fraudulent or unauthorized activity. To be able to rapidly report on the company's financials and any material changes, operational systems must provide real-time business information. This information must be collected in full compliance with all applicable regulations, including Sarbanes-Oxley.

Automating business processes is the key to establishing confidence in an organization. A process-managed enterprise:

- Has simultaneous and instant macro and micro views of its operations
- Can identify and correct mistakes more rapidly
- Incorporates predefined, centralized, institutionalized, and self-managed processes and procedures that automatically enforce compliance and governance
- Supports secure, role-based, and audited information systems
- Has substantially lower operating costs and administrative overhead

Project Workforce Management enables executives to collaborate in real time with all stakeholders including project-service delivery teams, project managers, and other executives, helping to preemptively identify and manage any potential trouble spots (Table 4.1). The system ensures that all work and spending is in compliance with Sarbanes-Oxley by providing:

- Executive dashboards and analysis reports that consolidate real-time views of the organization's projects, risks, issues, and performance.
- Management, routing, and auditing of all project, workforce, and financial processes.
- Validation at the point of entry. Any exceptions are highlighted to facilitate quick detection of any potential issues.
- Detailed reporting on all payable, billable, funded, and capitalized projects.
- Visibility and transparency for all transactions. The system tracks approvals and changes for all projects, budgets, costs, charges, and revenue.
- Full reporting of all system activity such as, logins, logouts, updates, deletions, and new entries.
- Work-policy control and communication.
- Automated approval of employee work, spending, and travel.
- Project and resource-based document management.
- Role-based security and data access.

SARBANES-OXLEY LAW	HOW PROJECT WORKFORCE MANAGEMENT FACILITATES COMPLIANCE
Section 302—Expanded Representation by Certifying Officers	Audited, process-managed, and effective internal controls allow the certifying officers to confidently sign the company's financial reports.
Section 404—Effectiveness of Internal Controls	Centralized, tracked, audited, and institutionalized project, workforce, and financial approval and change management processes.
	Work processes are automatically validated for compliance at the point of entry.
	Leads to verifiable data and effective internal controls that can be depended on.
Section 409—Rapid Reporting	Centralized and detailed work process information is used to report on and analyze the company's business in real time.
	The company is able to quickly report on its financial situation and any material changes on a quarterly or as-needed basis.
Section 802—Destruction, Alteration, or Falsification of Records	All system activity is audited.
	Any document or transaction changes are recorded and can be reported on; documents to preserve and audit include invoices, chargeback reports, timesheets, expense reports, status reports, and project artifacts such as scope change requests, project risk assessments and issues.
Section 906—Corporate Responsibility for Financial Reports	Helps certifying officers confidently report the company's financials on a timely basis.
	Detects questionable transactions and activities, protect company assets, and avoid trouble with the law.

Table 4.1   Sarbanes-Oxley and Project Workforce Management

Risks of Poor Governance:
Three Brief Case Studies

The risks of poor corporate governance have been laid bare in some very high-profile fraud cases and corporate governance failures. Sarbanes-Oxley regulations, had they been in place, could have informed investors of impending disaster, helped detect and prevent fraud in its initial phase, or at least provided investors with some warning signs.

Numerous fraudulent and illegal acts were committed and well publicized at Enron, WorldCom, and Arthur Andersen. For the purpose of illustrating the impact of Sarbanes-Oxley on a company's operations, the sections that follow highlight only portions of the criminal activity pertaining to effective internal controls.

Enron

No rapid reporting of material changes—off balance sheet accounting (violation of Section 409): Enron, for a very long time and as a standard business practice, routinely made risky investments in projects and businesses that had nothing to do with its core business. Many of these investments had implied liability and carried a substantial investment risk. However, Enron's financial statements and public filings did not reveal to its investors the extent of these liabilities and their potential impact on the company's financials and core business. In addition, the company did not disclose the fact that some of these investments had started to result in substantial losses. This is a violation of Section 409 on rapid reporting, which states that a business must report any material changes on a rapid and current basis. The unraveling of those investments and the related liabilities is what started the company's swift and downward spiral.

Poor revenue recognition controls (violation of Section 404): On February 20, 2001, Enron announced it had entered into a $1.3 billion, 15-year contract with an Indianapolis-based pharmaceutical company. Enron was to manage the supply of electricity and natural gas for that company's facilities in Indiana, as well as perform operations and maintenance on energy assets and related energy infrastructure upgrades that would increase energy efficiency at the facilities. The problem with the deal, however, was that Indiana had not yet deregulated its wholesale electricity market. Enron, therefore, could not yet provide the company with electricity. Enron, however, chose to forecast how much it would earn during the projected 10 years of the contract and valued the deal at approximately $600 million over a 10-year period. The company then began to recognize $60 million each year as realized revenue. Fraudulent and intentionally deceitful revenue recognition policy and revenue reporting is, of course, a violation of effective controls (Section 404).

WorldCom

Incorrect accounting of expenses and project types (violation of Section 404): In WorldCom's case, the company's revenue from its core business was starting to deteriorate due to competitive pricing pressures for long distance calls and the company's poor performance. To show continued profits, the company's management decided to reclassify certain projects. For example, WorldCom was spending millions every quarter to maintain its telecommunications network. Cost of such maintenance projects should be classified as an operating expense and reported as such in the company's income statement. WorldCom's management team decided to disguise its profit shortfalls every quarter by reclassifying some of these maintenance projects and capitalizing them. The cost of a capitalized project appeared as an asset on the company's balance sheet and only a fraction of the cost appeared as an amortized expense (depreciation) in the company's income statement. As a result, the company was able to substantially improve its profit picture.

WorldCom was also engaged in fraudulent project accounting, expense reporting, and asset identification, and lacked audited and verifiable interdepartmental chargeback controls (violation of Section 404). Furthermore, the company was not reporting its deteriorating profit picture (violation of Section 409), a material change in its business prospects.

Arthur Andersen

Destroying, altering and/or falsifying documents (violation of Section 802): Arthur Andersen's auditors committed several blatantly fraudulent acts. However, what led to their ultimate downfall and the reason the U.S. government decided to shutdown the company was the management team's intentional destruction of audit documents, e-mails, and memos related to the Enron file. A strict document-retention policy in compliance with Section 802, proper computer systems, and safeguarding procedures at Arthur Andersen would have prevented, or at least detected, the intentional destruction of documents that could have been used as evidence of fraud against Enron.

Company's auditor must attest in writing as to the effective internal controls of the company being audited (violation of section 404): Arthur Andersen, as the auditor of Enron, did not comment on that company's poor internal controls, risky investments, the misuse of Enron's assets, lack of transparent transactions, and the fraudulent activity it had been witness to.

NOTE

1. http://www.bizjournals.com/sanantonio/stories/2003/04/14/focus2.html.

5

Complying with Labor Laws and Accounting Regulations

I haven't committed a crime. What I did was fail to comply with the law.
—David N. Dinkins

As we move into the era of the flat world, one of the things that is making global commerce possible is what Bill Gates refers to as the "frictionless" economy; whereby the widespread availability of easily accessible, transparent information in the hands of buyers, sellers, and workers reduces prices, minimizes barriers, and increases the velocity at which business transactions can be done.

One big trend is pulling in the opposite direction: the increasing burden of compliance that is being placed on organizations. Increased compliance requirements are a result of a myriad of developments, ranging from the recent corporate scandals and ethics crises in the United States, to the increased regulatory presence of the European Union, to the need to do more reporting and be more vigilant in this age of worldwide terrorism and cyber crime.

The challenge for business organizations is to continue to operate with alacrity and precision to meet Gates's vision, while not being unduly burdened by increased compliance requirements. This chapter illustrates just a portion of the various labor laws and government and accounting regulations organizations must face, and discusses how companies can still be compliant while increasing their agility and performance in the flat world.

Automation, Compliance, and Complexity

As we illustrate in this chapter, the effects of compliance are far-reaching and complex. Every part of a company's management team and operations is touched by its requirements: human resources (HR) and workforce management, information technology (IT), product development, accounting

57

and finance, as well as project managers who may sit in any number of operational areas throughout the company.

To manage the increasing regulatory scrutiny, companies are turning to automated systems—even forcing "Late Adopters" and "Laggards" within their organizations to automate their processes. Without automated data collection, validation, and reporting, even the most fundamental compliance issues, such as Sarbanes-Oxley for publicly-traded companies, are a burden that could put any company out of business or force it to go private to avoid the burdens of reporting and oversight requirements.

However, some technologies introduce their own layers of needless complexity. Traditional information systems are typically focused on one set of business processes, for example, compliance management systems, workforce management systems, and project management systems. For the sake of compliance, companies are tempted to invest in and maintain multiple disconnected software applications—each sponsored by a different executive. For example:

- Labor compliance is sponsored by HR and payroll departments.
- Sarbanes-Oxley, generally accepted accounting principles (GAAP) revenue-recognition, and cost-accounting solutions are sponsored and championed by finance executives.
- Project management tools are sponsored by IT, engineering, or the project management offices.
- The billing system is sponsored by the professional services organization.

Companies that think and execute in a flat world must look beyond point solutions. Specialized project and workforce systems that only operate within one department or group cannot have the "reach" required to operate in a flat world. Furthermore, companies managing compliance cannot afford the layers of complexity brought on by integrating these solutions or designing custom data warehousing and analytics tools for on-demand reporting and audits. These additional burdens make the entire enterprise less nimble and more vulnerable to encounter fraud, errors, and compliance-related challenges.

Many organizations still solve many of their problems with short-term tools such as spreadsheets and custom-made applications, which silo data, duplicate effort, are prone to errors, and make the internal controls, compliance reporting, and auditing processes unmanageable.

High-performing companies are demanding true enterprise-wide project and workforce systems—and this is the promise of Project Workforce Management. Project Workforce Management not only brings together the far-reaching components that a project and service-driven organization needs to manage (people, projects, and processes), but it intrinsically helps them manage compliance. As a result, compliance can become the natural by-product of a well-run company instead of an added burden that slows down the company's critical functions.

Compliance laws are regional in nature. This chapter focuses primarily on North American compliance issues. Companies operating in Europe, Asia, and other regions can also address local compliance issues using the concepts and systems described here since all compliance initiatives have the same fundamental tracking, data validation, auditing, and reporting requirements.

U.S. Federal and Local Labor Laws

Labor laws dictate minimum wages, overtime pay, paid and unpaid leave standards, and fair labor practices. In the United States, federal laws provide a baseline for these regulations, and many states have more stringent laws of their own. In Canada, labor laws vary by province.

Here are some of the labor laws and labor compliance issues for employers to consider:

- The Fair Labor Standard Act (FLSA) establishes minimum rates of overtime pay for hourly workers. For employees who are eligible, the employer must pay 1.5 times the regular hourly rate for any hours worked over 40 in one week. Eligible employees are typically those in nonmanagerial or nonprofessional roles, but the requirements can be complex for some employers and specific rules apply in certain types of businesses such as restaurants, manufacturing plants, and construction companies.

- The Family Medical Leave Act (FMLA) provides eligible employees with up to 12 weeks of unpaid leave each year when a new son or daughter is born or adopted, or when the employee or a family member (spouse, child, or parent) of the employee requires care for a serious health condition. Employees who request FMLA may take leave in increments as small as one hour. Employee eligibility depends on tenure, number of hours worked, and the number of employees at the location(s) where the employee has worked.

- California and other states have their own wage laws such as overtime calculations when working more than eight hours per day, working on the weekend, and reporting for duty outside regular working hours.

In addition to labor laws, many companies have their own vacation policy and other paid-leave time rules. For example, employees may be allowed to accrue vacation time on a monthly basis depending on their seniority.

Challenges of Labor Law Compliance

Since labor laws vary from one location to another, companies with multiple work sites have to account for applicable labor laws in that region that may also apply to temporary workers. Here are just a few of the issues a company can face:

Which workers are eligible? Exempt employees, those ineligible for over-time, are usually white-collar workers such as executives, managers, professionals, and administrative staff. However, there are exceptions depending on industry and the type of work performed. For example, in California, there are exemptions from overtime laws for software workers (who have a certain amount of minimum base salary), outside salespeople, actors, and the crews of fishing boats, just to name a few.

Which tasks are eligible? For example, an employee who spends some time managing and working on a crew at a different location, may be in a "gray area" between exempt and nonexempt status, depending on the type of in-dustry and the definitions set forth in the state where the work is performed.

What rates and benefits apply? If an employee works at multiple jobs at varying rates in one period, any overtime hours must be paid at a weighted average rate. Also, workers who change job locations may be eligible for dif-ferent wages and different overtime pay in different states.

Project Workforce Management and Labor Laws

Time-tracking solutions and payroll systems that do not have compliance con-figuration tables built-in are not equipped to handle complex pay rules, nor do they have the front-end user interface to capture and validate the correct infor-mation at the point of entry. Traditionally, time data is first entered or trans-ferred into a spreadsheet, an application that does not automate labor compliance, or a custom-built program, and then an administrative assistant manually adjusts the overtime and leave time hours based on the employer's business rules. This approach can be flagged as a control weakness in addition to being a costly, error-prone, and tedious process. On average, HR and ac-counting staff spend one to two days per payroll cycle calculating and adjusting pay, evaluating paid and unpaid leave time eligibility, and processing paychecks.

Project Workforce Management automates these business rules to support labor law compliance in the following ways:

- Asserts that employees are compensated equitably and fairly based on the work performed. The use of differentiated time ensures that each time entry is attributed to the appropriate task, work location, rate, overtime, and leave-time regulations.

- Reduces the amount of time needed to calculate employee compensation. It also reduces the cost associated with payroll processing, accounting, and clerical resources required to perform these repetitive tasks.
- By keeping approved, audited, and centralized records, it reduces the number of disputes over wages from current and former employees. Thereby, it also reduces the expensive legal fees and fines that the government has established for employers found guilty of not paying employees their fair wages.

Generally Accepted Accounting Principles (GAAP) and Software Investments

In the United States, GAAP includes a Statement of Position (SOP) 98-1 that sets forth how companies must account for the software they buy or develop. Since, practically speaking, every company buys or develops software; SOP 98-1 has far-reaching effects for every company in the United States. GAAP guidance on software-development accounting is intended to standardize how companies:

- Report revenue earned through software development
- Expense or capitalize software development and acquisition costs
- Depreciate (tangible assets such as computer systems) or amortize (intangible assets such as software code) capitalized costs

This is important because expenses are fully and immediately realized on the company's income statement, while capitalized costs become assets on the company's balance sheet and are depreciated or amortized over time throughout what is agreed to be the "useful life" of the technology. For example, a $1 million investment in software expected to be useful for 10 years would appear as an asset on the balance sheet in year one, with offsetting expenses of $100,000 in that year and in the next nine.

In the absence of guidance, companies might make decisions to expense or capitalize costs based on differing criteria. For example, a highly profitable company might decide to expense all software development costs as incurred to offset income and lower taxes, while a less profitable or unprofitable company might decide to capitalize the same costs to improve its income statement in the short term. When companies invest a significant amount in technology development, these distinctions can meaningfully affect income statements and balance sheets.

GAAP guidance for software accounting is segmented into four categories:

1. Software an organization purchases or develops with the intent to lease, sell, or market to users external to the company; either as a complete product or service, or as part of one. For example, Microsoft develops a new version of Microsoft Word.

2. Software an organization uses internally in its research and development activities, as opposed to software that it uses internally to run its operations. For example, simulation software that helps an automotive company design more aerodynamic cars would be considered software used for research and development.

3. Software an organization develops under contractual arrangements for others; for example, a consulting firm builds an airline reservation system for a client under a fixed price contract.

4. Software developed or purchased for internal use; for example, a company develops software to help its finance department run more efficiently.

Challenges of GAAP SOP 98-1 Compliance

In a perfect world, software development projects and the developers themselves would stay within the boundaries of these four categories. But in real life, every company applies its talent and time to a combination of these activities.

For example, a professional services firm might use one developer's expertise to build a new section for its intranet, to build a time-and-expense reporting system for a client under contract, or to create a packaged software application for the firm to sell, or to build a scenario-modeling application to help the organization improve future IT development projects. Each of these projects is governed by a different accounting guideline. Moreover, each guideline recommends different expense and capitalization decisions depending on which stage of the development cycle the cost was incurred in and for which activity.

Clearly, not all software development activities can be accounted for in the same way, and companies must comply with a veritable alphabet soup of governing organizations, statements, pronouncements, and positions that guide when software development costs should be expensed or capitalized.

Within SOP 98-1, development costs to maintain an existing system are expensed, while development costs to upgrade the same system are capitalized. Travel expenses for a programmer to work with an outside vendor to write code in the application development stage can be capitalized, but if that same programmer travels to be part of a team helping to train new users, that cost must be expensed.

SOP 98-1 presents a complex compliance challenge because governance is nuanced by:

- The type of software development project; for example, new applications, system upgrades, maintenance, website work, or business process reengineering analysis

- The stage of development in which the cost is incurred: preliminary, application development, or post-implementation/operation
- Whether the cost is "material," meaning significant with respect to the organization's revenues and overall IT costs
- The useful life, or period over which the company expects to use the software

Project Workforce Management and GAAP SOP 98-1

Project Workforce Management's ability to account for differentiated time and expenses is key to its effectiveness in facilitating compliance with GAAP and SOP 98-1. Organizations must track all software development costs and activities by project, project stage, activity within the stage, and person. Organizations with these challenges are compelled to automate—subject to rules, policies, and internal controls—the marking of time entries, expense entries, and requisition items as capitalized or expensed.

Because the process of moving this time and expense data to accounting is automated, it is no longer cumbersome to allocate employee time and expenses to the appropriate line items on the income statement and balance sheet. And because the software projects and products are tracked, these amounts are correctly expensed, depreciated, or amortized, and none are overlooked as a result of data being siloed in separate systems or databases.

Government and Defense Contracts

The Defense Contract Audit Agency (DCAA) reviews contracts between contractors and the U.S. Department of Defense, as well as many other agencies of the U.S. government. Most audits of federal government contracts are performed by the DCAA.

DCAA's job is to ensure that costs billed to the contract are legitimate and allowable by the government. Under DCAA requirements, contractors must not only submit routine reports, such as detailed justification for contract billing; they must also produce on-demand responses to government auditors' requests for information. The DCAA's heaviest scrutiny falls on contracts with *cost-plus* or other cost-reimbursement provisions. Failure to comply has significant penalties, risks, and costs for contractors.

In general, to comply with DCAA standards, a contractor must:

- Be prepared for various types of audits, including potentially extensive pre-award proposal, timekeeping, and cost accounting system reviews.
- Use manual effort, if necessary, to compensate for any deficiencies in its accounting and reporting systems.

- Keep stringent timekeeping records that track employees' time on work activities.
- Maintain highly detailed, accurate accounting records of costs incurred, with accurate differentiation of direct and indirect costs.

Contractors who rely on piecing together information from disparate sources are at a competitive disadvantage. Inefficient procedures and poor controls typically leave these contractors ill-prepared for audits and vulnerable to a host of penalties and other consequences of noncompliance. However, for contractors with properly automated systems, DCAA compliance and audit preparation is a nondisruptive, routine process, because DCAA compliance is a by-product of their focus on Project Workforce Management.

Challenges of DCAA Compliance

DCAA compliance is particularly challenging for the following reasons:

- *You never know when you will be audited by the DCAA.* The timing and intensity of DCAA involvement depends on the type of contract awarded. For fixed-price contracts and time-and-material (T&M) rates, most of DCAA's auditing efforts take place during the proposal stage. For flexibly priced contracts, such as cost plus fixed fee, DCAA gets involved with the contractor as costs are incurred.
- *You never know what a DCAA audit will focus on.* The DCAA's "Fiscal 2007 Budget Estimates" describes more than a dozen different audits covering everything from proposal pricing and contractor stability to internal controls and termination claims. Audits can be pre-award or post-award— and some fit in both timeframes. Some audits are announced and some are unannounced.
- *Data collection can be burdensome.* At the pre-award stage, DCAA expects contractors to be prepared to back up their proposals with very detailed information, such as detailed schedules of labor and overhead rates used in the proposal. First-time government contractors need to gather, maintain, verify, compile, and report new types of data to government agencies—in the form of DCAA-compliant invoices, audit responses, or other reports.
- *Federal accounting standards pose new challenges.* As a condition of government contracting, many vendors must follow federal cost-accounting standards. Contracts and subcontracts not qualifying for any of several exemptions are subject to the cost-accounting standards, which involves the assignment, measurement, and allocation of costs. DCAA has the responsibility for reviewing contractors' implementation and compliance with the standards.

- *Inadequate compliance has many adverse consequences.* A government contractor is responsible for appropriately accounting for costs and for maintaining records, including providing supporting documentation to adequately demonstrate that costs claimed have been incurred, are allocable to the contract, and comply with applicable cost principles in this subpart and agency supplements. Auditors, or the contracting officer, may disallow all or part of a claimed cost that is inadequately supported. For deceitful claims, such as improper recording or misallocation of employee time, the penalties can be much more severe, including criminal charges, fines, loss of contract, and loss of standing as a Department of Defense (DoD) contractor.

Project Workforce Management and DCAA Compliance

Project Workforce Management enables and streamlines DCAA compliance in the following ways:

- *Differentiation for direct project costs:* Costs that apply directly to the DCAA project must be separated from overhead costs. Types of billable time and expenses must be defined explicitly on a per-entry basis. Here, the differentiated time and expense tracking aspect of Project Workforce Management is critical. Each task is applied correctly to the project, and every charge to the project is justified with detailed task-level information.
- *Time and expense recordkeeping deployed to employees:* According to DCAA requirements, every employee must record his or her own time, and do so daily. A differentiated time and expense system meets this requirement and provides an easy-to-use interface for time and expense collection. The system supports DCAA's requirements for explanations and approvals on any changes to the time and expense data, and split billing when the resource is shared, in other words, when work is being done for multiple contracts or projects.
- *Adherence to federal cost-accounting standards:* Because all costs of the project, down to the most minute detail, are recorded as the project is executed, adherence to cost-accounting standards is enforced and streamlined.
- *Controlled access to data:* Project Workforce Management includes authentication and role-based security that complies with DCAA requirements for format, history, aging, and lockout after multiple failed login attempts.
- *Immediate response to audits:* Perhaps the most compelling feature of Project Workforce Management for DCAA compliance is the ability to respond to unannounced DCAA audits without disrupting operations. Because all data from the project, workforce and financials are integrated

DCAA REQUIREMENT	PROJECT WORKFORCE MANAGEMENT SOLUTION
General	
Access to data must be controlled.	User authentication and role-based security that complies with DCAA requirements for format, history, aging, and lockout after multiple failed login attempts.
To substantiate costs, sufficient records must be retained three years after the final contract billing.	All data is stored in a central and secure database. Internal auditors can generate real-time reports on all government contracts and overhead costs.
Time and expense process includes a verifiable audit process for all changes and transaction entries.	Audit of all approvals, changes, entry deletions/creations; audit reports.
Time	
Every employee must record his or her own time charges.	Users login using secure passwords.
Time charges must be recorded daily.	Timesheets can be locked for previous days; system requires that the user enter a note to change any past entries.
Changes to time entries require an explanation by the employee and management approval.	Any change creates an audit event. Users and managers can be required to provide explanations for any modifications or corrections.
If the resource is shared, the time charges have to be split across multiple projects.	Split billing.
Costs	
Identify direct project costs versus overhead costs.	Define types of expenses and identify which ones are billable expenses. Provide appropriate access rights and enforce a note entry when changing data. Allow billable flag override on a per entry basis.
A verifiable process for identifying why an incurred expense is a direct cost.	Approval process for expense reporting and money charge entries.

Table 5.1   Project Workforce Management and DCAA Requirements

and accessible through a Web-based interface, audits can even be conducted remotely.

Table 5.1 summarizes how Project Workforce Management meets specific DCAA requirements.

Scientific Research and Exploratory Development

To encourage innovation and stimulate research and development activity, many countries such as the United States, Canada, and the United Kingdom provide a scientific research and exploratory development (SR&ED) program. This type of program offers significant investment tax credits to businesses of any size and in any sector that conduct research, develop new, improved, or technologically advanced products or processes within that jurisdiction.

In the case of the Canadian SR&ED program, a Canadian-controlled private corporation (CCPC) can earn an investment tax credit (ITC) of 35 percent up to the first $2 million of qualified expenditures, and 20 percent on any excess amount. (For CCPCs, part of the ITC may be fully refundable in cash.) Other Canadian corporations, proprietorships, partnerships, and trusts can earn an ITC of 20 percent of qualified expenditures.

Companies can receive refunds for work undertaken that qualifies as scientific research and experimental development. Work is considered SR&ED if:

- It is conducted to overcome one or more technological problems.
- It includes trials, experiments, or analyses to solve these problems.
- The organization conducting the work requires experience or technologies not commonly available to solve these problems.
- The work will result in a technological advancement. Even if the attempts prove unsuccessful, the work may still qualify.

Eligible work may be done either by the company claiming SR&ED credits or by a contractor. Allowable expenditures for SR&ED typically include:

- Salaries and wages of employees who were directly engaged in SR&ED
- Cost of materials consumed or transformed in the prosecution of SR&ED
- SR&ED contracts performed on the company's behalf
- Lease costs for buildings used substantially (90 percent) or primarily (50 percent) for SR&ED
- Overhead applied to SR&ED

- Third-party payments applied to SR&ED
- Capital expenditures applied to SR&ED

Challenges of the Scientific Research and Exploratory Development Claim Process

The extensiveness of the SR&ED claim process—including the filing of forms and both the technical and financial reviews—is daunting to many businesses. In fact, the program is underused—relatively few of the businesses that are eligible for benefits even undertake the process. Some of the major challenges for businesses are described next:

- *Planning work as SR&ED:* One of the biggest challenges in preparing an SR&ED claim is the gathering of the documentation that substantiates the work as SR&ED from the beginning. Businesses must have a specific problem to solve, and then document the ways in which they went about solving it.
- *Qualifications of personnel:* Companies who make SR&ED claims need up-to-date records of the skills, education, and experience of all employees who might contribute to the objectives of an SR&ED project, so they may claim all the wage and salary expenditures to which they are entitled to and to expedite the review process.
- *Time reporting and other financial information:* Financial reviewers look closely at the timesheets of SR&ED workers and the amount of time attributed to SR&ED work. Companies who plan to file SR&ED claims need a reliable and accurate time-reporting system that allows them to allocate time and tasks to specific projects, so that all eligible SR&ED work can be accounted and reported.
- *Data collection:* Several types of information reported in an SR&ED review may, in the absence of a centralized management system, become stored throughout a large number of disparate word-processing documents, spreadsheets, other computer files, and paper records; for example: timesheets, expense reports, purchases, project objectives and hypotheses, project planned versus actual budgets, project timelines, milestones, and progress (e.g., Gantt charts), status reports, minutes of meetings, resource-allocation records, job descriptions, project journals and lab notes, experimental and technological trials, test results, and conclusions.

As a whole, this body of data can be unwieldy to the point of making an SR&ED review time consuming, costly, and perhaps even impractical. Large collections of separate documents, especially when stored by many different people and on different computers, as well as the lack of security often result in discrepancies between what is reported in the payroll system, the accounting system, and multiple versions of SR&ED-related documents and spreadsheets. Discrepancies of this type during an R&D audit process can result in substantial claim adjustments and a significantly prolonged audit where each and every entry and record keeping policy is challenged and questioned.

Project Workforce Management and Scientific Research and Exploratory Development

Project Workforce management greatly simplifies SR&ED compliance in the following ways:

- *Project initiation:* A well-defined project charter and review process is required to substantiate the claim that a project qualifies as SR&ED. Project Workforce Management standardizes and automates the process of reviewing and approving new SR&ED projects. It provides a platform for creating, sharing, and approving the project charter and objectives; gathering supporting documentation and research; and providing a foundation that will keep the project on track and true to its objectives.

- *Project definition:* This phase consists of creating a Work Breakdown Structure (WBS) that defines portfolios, projects, tasks, phases, and milestones. At this phase of the planning process, it is critical to identify which components of the WBS will be eligible for SR&ED benefits. This can be accomplished easily within the Project Workforce Management solution.

- *Resource allocation and skill matching:* SR&ED Technical Reviewers verify whether or not the people assigned to SR&ED tasks are qualified to perform those tasks. Therefore, it is important to have employee skills and experience, job descriptions, and project/position skill requirements on record. Project Workforce Management provides a central database of this information for full-time, part-time and outsourced resources. It also automates the matching of people to project positions based on skills and availability.

- *Time and expense tracking:* Accurate and reliable time and expense tracking is critical to a smooth SR&ED audit. Not only records must be complete from the beginning of the project, but in many cases individual line items must be attributable to qualified SR&ED. Project Workforce Management provides detailed reporting capabilities to all of the participants of a project, including accounting, HR, managers, and every skilled resource.

- *Project scope and risk management:* A workflow-based ProjectWorkforce Management system automates the scope-change and risk-management process, and records all changes in project scope as they occur. At SR&ED review time, project leaders can then substantiate why the deviations occurred, and whether or not any unplanned work (and related costs) qualifies as SR&ED. Scientific research and exploratory development auditors also look at project risks to see what issues were encountered and how they were handled as the project is executed and new information becomes available. An important criterion for eligibility of a project is its risk factors; if the project is low risk, then it is probably not eligible for an SR&ED claim.

- *Reporting and analytics:* Because it is an enterprise system, Project Workforce Management collects, consolidates, and reports information in real time from anywhere in the world. Not only are SR&ED line items ready at review time, but managers and executives can get an accurate snapshot of SR&ED-eligible expenditures at any time, through executive dashboards, reporting, and analytics.

Project Workforce Management Simplifies Compliance

Today's companies can find themselves between two opposing forces: the emergence of a flat world, and the complexities of compliance to even the most fundamental and mandatory laws and regulations; such as labor laws and GAAP. While one force demands simplicity and speed, the other can appear to make simplicity and agility impossible.

Automation of information systems is the natural outcome of the collision of these forces, and Project Workforce Management is the automation solution for project and service-based businesses that face these compliance issues.

The components of Project Workforce Management clearly solve major compliance challenges:

- *Time and expense tracking:* Differentiated time is critical to compliance. Task-level data rolls up to support labor law issues, the time and expenses for software development, and all activities that could impact DCAA audits, SR&ED eligibility, and other similar compliance matters. Differentiated time and expenses are recorded by person, project, project phase, activity, and task. What's more, the collection of data is Web-enabled, so it is deployed directly to each timekeeper.
- *Cost and revenue accounting:* Whenever required, adherence to federal cost-accounting standards is built-in to the system and easily supportable in reports and audits. Expenditures are automatically expensed or capitalized according to GAAP. The system formalizes and enforces a revenue accounting and recognition policy in compliance with regulations.
- *Workforce planning:* Workers are utilized correctly, according to their competencies and availability, and in accordance with regulations. Project Workforce Management optimally schedules the workforce by locating

the most qualified and available resources to fill specific roles and accomplish specific tasks on a project.

- *Project process management:* Project Workforce Management enables better management of project processes, including project initiation, risk and issue reporting, as well as scope control using policy-based, enforced best practices. In the case of SR&ED, Project Workforce Management establishes the necessary foundation and documentation to qualify a project for tax credits.

- *Analytics:* For required reports and audits, Project Workforce Management provides instant access to critical information. Audits—especially unannounced ones—do not disrupt operations. It also provides a consolidated, real-time, and dynamic view of the company's projects, processes, and workforce with a special emphasis on reporting the financial perspective of projects.

Moreover, as laws and guidelines change, an automated Project Workforce Management system provides the flexibility to adapt to change quickly.

INFORMATION AND KNOWLEDGE: FRINGE BENEFITS OF COMPLIANCE. In his quintessential guide to personal and financial success *Think and Grow Rich* (New York: Tarcher/Penguin Group, 2005), Napoleon Hill tells the story of an entrepreneur who gained unprecedented success in the insurance industry through a lesson he learned by failing in the gold mining business. In his younger days, this man had failed to turn a profit in his gold mining company because he had given up in dismay, not realizing that he had stopped his drills just three feet from striking one of the richest gold veins later to be found in California. Never again did he let himself "stop three feet from gold."

What business managers, working to comply with a host of laws and regulations, may not realize is that they, too, might be stopping "three feet from gold." For within the data needed to comply with these laws and regulations is also the intelligence to improve business operations and competitiveness.

Forward-thinking organizations drill through compliance issues with this "gold" in mind. By successfully implementing the processes that compliance demands of them, they are actually gaining the agility and responsiveness that will lead them to a flat world.

PART II

Project Workforce Management

6

Organization and Work Breakdown Structures

A mountain of evidence shows that 85 to 90 percent of errors originate in the organization's structure, system or process. Yet all too many executives look for who rather than what went wrong.

—Jim Clemmer[1]

Organization and work modeling is one of the fundamental building blocks of a Project Workforce Management system. The work breakdown structure (WBS) defines work elements and the organization breakdown structure (OBS) organizes the resources that perform the work. Time and expense entries, charges, risks, issues, documents, and any other workflow entries are associated with OBS and WBS items.

Without Project Workforce Management, companies maintain parts of the OBS and WBS in many different systems. For example, the master list of projects is maintained in a project management application; the master list of users and groups is maintained in the company's enterprise resource planning (ERP) or human resources (HR) system; while the list of customers is maintained in a customer relationship management (CRM) application. Project Workforce Management coexists and integrates with all of these systems using the OBS/WBS structure, and links the information from these different systems. Figure 6.1 illustrates sample organization and work breakdown structures and the relationship between them.

As presented in Figure 6.2, there are three major benefits for carefully defining and managing your company's OBS/WBS: strategic, tactical, and financial. The discussion that follows describes each of these benefits in more detail.

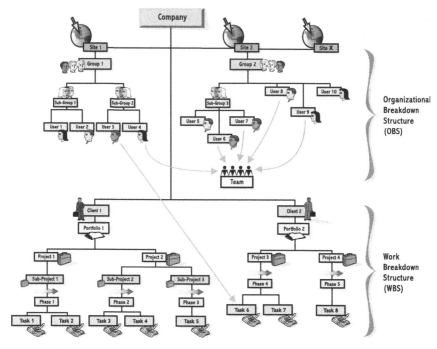

Figure 6.1   Sample Organization and Work Breakdown Structures

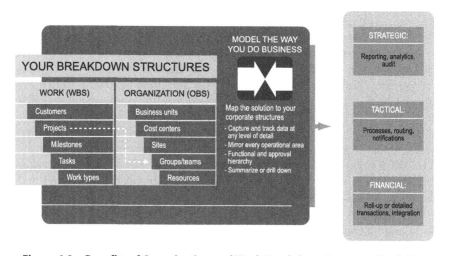

Figure 6.2   Benefits of Organization and Work Breakdown Structure Modeling

Strategic

Real-time reporting and analytics is the most critical reason for investing in a Project Workforce Management system. Leveraging the OBS and WBS reports provide detailed or summarized information with the possibility for drilling up/down for more in-depth analysis.

Tactical

In addition to setting budgets and limits, notification can be triggered based on thresholds and rules when certain events occur. For example, a notification e-mail can be triggered when any of the billable projects in the Billable Projects subfolder of the WBS reaches 80 percent of scheduled work being completed, or a notification e-mail is triggered when any of the software projects in the Software Projects subfolder reaches 75 percent of budgeted cost.

The user can quickly navigate the company's OBS/WBS hierarchy to define budgets and limits, as well as cost and revenue rates. Also, with role-based data security for OBS/WBS, you can limit access to the customer and project list, so that only a certain business unit, group, team, or user can view it. Implementing data security and setting budgets, limits and rates is much more cumbersome when the user has to work with flat unlinked lists or multiple disconnected systems.

Financial

Due to the hierarchical and linked nature of the OBS and WBS, project time, expense, cost, and billing information can be rolled up (summarized) into cost centers, business units, or resource groups; or, it can be drilled down to the desired level of detail (see Figure 6.3).

OBS and WBS structures are very similar conceptually to a file system's folder/subfolder/file hierarchy model. Information is organized in a hierarchy similar to folders in a file system. The folder/subfolder paradigm allows quick mass changes to a hierarchy of project and workforce elements. For example, you can group items under the same folder and collectively manage their security, budgets, limits, and other attributes.

This chapter describes the benefits of using OBS and WBS for project and workforce management. It also provides guidelines that can help organizations during their OBS and WBS business modeling process.

Organization Breakdown Structure

OBS consists of the hierarchy of the company's business units, sites, groups, subgroups, teams, and users. While a deep OBS substantially improves analysis

Time and Expenses by Project

Year	Quarter	Projects 01	Users	Payable Time Amount	Payable Expenses	New Total
2006	Q1	DEV Projects#1	Andrew, Dixon	$260,000.00	$11,375.00	$271,375.00
			Jay, Adams	$97,500.00	$13,000.00	$110,500.00
			Max, Benson	$97,500.00	$13,000.00	$110,500.00
			Total	$455,000.00	$37,375.00	$492,375.00
		DEV Projects#2		$455,000.00	$37,375.00	$492,375.00
		DEV Projects#3		$455,000.00	$37,375.00	$492,375.00

Time and Expenses by Business Unit

	Business Units	Users	Payable Time Amount	Payable Expenses	New Total
Q2	Development	Andrew, Dixon	$6,668,000.00	$282,620.70	$6,950,620.00
Q3		Jay, Adams	$1,122,000.00	$187,000.00	$1,309,000.00
Q4		Max, Benson	$2,928,097.82	$334,100.00	$3,262,197.82
Total		Jim, Green	$280,500.00	$187,000.00	$467,500.00
		John, Simpson	$699,847.79	$37,400.00	$737,247.79
		Kevin, Kennedy	$1,122,000.00	$187,000.00	$1,309,000.00
		Mandy, Johnson	$1,122,000.00	$187,000.00	$1,309,000.00
		Marty, Lambert	$1,122,000.00	$187,000.00	$1,309,000.00
		Dimitri, Ivanov	$2,919,847.77	$333,400.00	$3,253,247.77
		Paul, Philips	$74,800.00	$23,620.70	$98,420.70
		Toby, Nixon	$74,800.00	$37,400.00	$112,200.00
		Total	$18,133,893.38	$1,983,541.40	$20,117,434.78
Grand Total			$18,133,893.38	$1,983,541.40	$20,117,434.78

Figure 6.3   Sample OBS/WBS Time and Expense Report

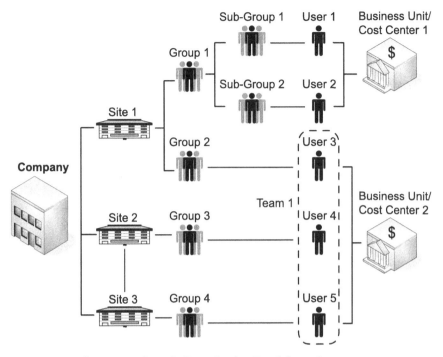

Figure 6.4 Sample Organization Breakdown Structure

and reporting, an OBS that is too deep takes longer to create and maintain. Also, it becomes more cumbersome for administrators to manage data security, associations, budgets, limits, and rates. A shallower OBS is much easier to maintain but reduces the amount of detail that is available in reports and analytics (see Figure 6.4). Each company must strike the right balance of OBS richness versus simplicity for its unique needs. The OBS is a corporate structure managed by the Project Workforce Management system administrator.

Work Breakdown Structure

The WBS consists of the hierarchy of the company's customers, portfolios, projects, subprojects, work types, and tasks. If the WBS is too deep, then it takes longer and gets more cumbersome for users to choose the right activities to work on. A deep WBS substantially improves analysis and reporting. A shallower WBS is much easier to maintain but reduces the amount of detail that is available in reports and analytics. Each company must strike the right balance of WBS richness versus simplicity for its unique needs (see Figure 6.5).

The higher levels of WBS (customers, portfolios, and engagements) are treated as a corporate structure managed by the Project Management Office

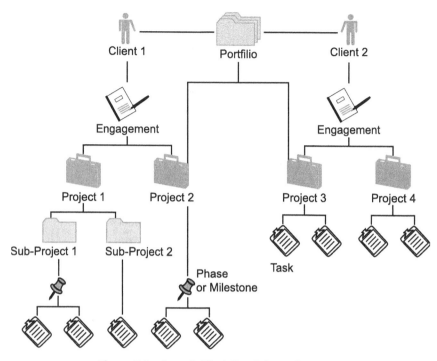

Figure 6.5 Sample Work Breakdown Structure

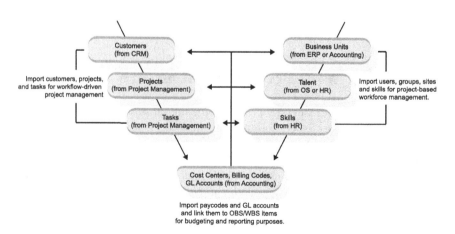

Figure 6.6 Building Blocks of Organization and Work Breakdown Structures

(PMO) and the Project Workforce Management system administrator. The more detailed lower level parts of the WBS (projects, tasks, milestones) are managed by project managers.

Integration

Figure 6.6 shows how OBS and WBS elements can be linked to other enterprise systems. Project Workforce Management imports and links customer, project, employee, human resources, payroll, and billing information as the building blocks for OBS/WBS. For more information, see Chapter 20.

NOTE

1. http://www.expertmagazine.com/artman/publish/article_830.shtml.

7

The Workflow Foundation

It's all about consistency. That's the way it has been forever. You can win the battles, but it doesn't matter unless you win the war.

—Jeremy Mayfield

E-mail and spreadsheets are so easy to use that most of us assume that they are an efficient way of organizing and recording work. Similarly, the personal contact we get from meetings gives us the feeling that they are the most effective way to collaborate.

However, in a company with more than just a handful of employees, the number of times requests are forwarded and escalated, the number of follow-ups, and the repetition of questions can easily add up to tremendous hidden costs, as well as frustration for employees, suppliers, and customers. E-mails, meetings, and conversations cannot be classified, sorted, and analyzed by project, task, or a resource group for tracking, auditing, and reporting purposes. Completing a work process requires that various people follow a predefined procedure, track their time and budgets, and capture all project information. These goals cannot be achieved cost effectively without using software that is specifically designed to manage work processes. The lack of a well-defined structure for guiding people through processes results in redundancies, inefficiencies, and mistakes.

The feature of Project Workforce Management that addresses these problems—and makes Project Workforce Management different from other solutions—is its *workflow foundation*. The workflow foundation drives, manages, and streamlines the flow of all project, workforce, and financial processes.

The workflow foundation automates many everyday work processes. This process automation enables executives to securely collaborate in real time with every member of the management team and all project contributors. Workflows also reduce the need for written procedures, follow-ups, and meetings. Training new staff on corporate policies and best practices is

83

much faster and easier with self-service workflows and visually designed processes that guide new employees along the way—all of which leads to a significant reduction in mistakes, repetitive work, and administrative overhead.

A workflow management system completely defines, manages, and executes business processes using software. The sequence and progression of the work process is driven by the computer representation of the workflow logic. In an organization in which all staff is experienced and accustomed to the common way of doing things, problems may have become *invisible*. As long as the procedures don't change and the staff remembers them, this flow may continue without a glitch. However, in today's fast-changing business environment, even companies with well-established business models and processes need to reexamine, redefine, and reengineer themselves constantly to remain efficient and competitive—this means *doing things differently.*

Traditional methods of documentation and staff training run the risk of having newly defined rules, policies, and methods that are not well understood or followed. Resistance to change might emerge because the staff is used to doing things the old way. These problems are only amplified in today's fragmented and remote workforce, where employees and project contributors can be anywhere, and in a highly regulated environment where companies face new compliance challenges. If a standard enterprise wide workflow system is used to manage projects, which is also linked to financials, and if that same workflow system guides the workforce through the proper steps to enforce the policies as well as audit the activities, then the results will be more predictable.

This chapter describes the workflow foundation in detail and explains how workflow concepts, when applied to project management, workforce management, and financial reporting, provide an organization with an effective and predictable strategy for operational control.

Process Driven Project Management

More and more businesses are starting to realize that a workflow system is applicable across their entire organization to manage any business process related to project and service delivery. The same solution can address the process automation needs of any project type including any information technology (IT), shared service, product development, or billable projects: CIO Magazine's Research on Process Driven Project Management:

> The findings quantified distinctions between IT shops that live for the average and the few that take *process leadership* seriously. *Elite IT performers* weren't just two or three times better than median performers—they *were seven or eight times better.* High performers—roughly 13 percent of the 98 sampled—contributed on average *eight times more projects, four and a half times more applications and software, four*

and a half times more IT services, and seven times more business IT changes. They implemented 14 more changes with half the failure rate. [1]

An important difference between Project Workforce Management solutions and traditional project management is that the entire project/service delivery cycle is automated, controlled and audited using a workflow system. A graphical workflow interface provides visual definition, control, tracking and auditing of approvals, routing, role-based assignments and notifications. All Project Workforce Management processes are automated using the same user interface, concepts, and business logic. By leveraging the same visual framework, users experience a consistent and intuitive interface that is easy to learn and use to manage any project and workforce related business process.

What Is a Workflow?

A workflow is a structured way of defining and automating procedures and processes within an organization. When a workflow is implemented using software (versus, for example, defining it in a document and communicating it using e-mail), it guides all the individuals that participate in the process and enables them to record their activities at every phase of their involvement.

Figure 7.1 illustrates a simple workflow that includes a few steps that are common to many processes. A workflow can consist of two or more states

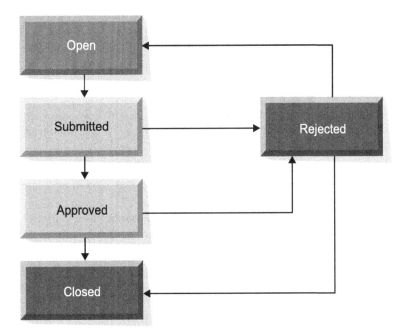

Figure 7.1   A Simple Workflow

(also called activities), such as the blocks in the illustration. It usually has a well-defined initial state and one or more final states. The process flows from one state to another; this is called a transition. Different roles or individuals are assigned to each state with certain privileges to take the process to the next step (i.e., change the state) or reassign it to another role or individual. A state may make transition into another state by user action or automatically depending on the conditions that have been set.

In summary, a workflow system provides:

- Work items, a to-do list
- An entry form that represents the task
- A graphical representation of the workflow
- A process that guides the user through the steps in the workflow
- A mechanism to assign, search, and report on the work items

Workflows, Human Business Process Management, and Enterprise Application Integration Business Process Management

Workflow management is also referred to as human business process management (BPM). Human BPM is focused primarily on the automation of human-centric business processes (such as issue tracking, timesheet and expense management, risk assessment) while Enterprise Application Integration (EAI) BPM tends to automate business processes that are designed to integrate enterprise applications (such as connecting salesforce.com to SAP).

Human Business Process Management
- Requires people to get work done by interacting with a workflow application that provides to-do lists, work assignments, alerts, and notifications.
- Has participants that are mostly individuals who collaborate on work processes using the system lists and queues or interact directly.
- Can have long process duration (for example, a task stays in someone's to-do list without any action).
- Automates workflows that are created to manage business purposes (for example, a customer reports a problem or an employee submits an expense report).
- Almost always requires integration with an enterprise application (for example, timesheet data is exported to a payroll system; approved expense reports are sent to accounting as accounts payable).
- Has limited application integration capabilities.

Enterprise Application Integration Business Process Management

- Is used to create application connectors using Web Services:
  - —Transform and map data between different applications using XML.
  - —The connection can be transactional (the entire process succeeds or the data is rolled back to its original state) or a simple nontransactional data update.
- Participants are usually one or more enterprise applications or IT systems.
- Is used by IT to build integrations.
- Humans are involved only if there are exceptions (for example, the automated export to SAP fails and an administrator is notified to take action).
- Processes execute quickly since there is no human action required and are usually simpler in terms of their flow than a human work process (less participants involved).

The workflow concepts described here are primarily focused on human BPM.

Which Work Processes Need Workflows?

Any nontrivial project, workforce, or financial process needs to be workflow managed. Project Workforce Management groups work processes based on their main usage area:

- *Customer:* Applies to a professional service organization or revenue-generating departments.
- *Project:* Applies to product development, IT, billable, and nonbillable project and service delivery teams.
- *Workforce:* System of record is the employee (includes any consultants).
- *Financial:* System of record is a combination of customer, project, task, employee, or resource group for which the work is done, expenses incurred, and items purchased.

Project initiation, scope change, risk assessment, and issue tracking are some of the key project processes that must be managed in any project. The widely known and rapidly growing Project Management Body of Knowledge (PMBOK) guide[2] and certifications discuss the administration of these work processes as part of the project execution phase. However, the templates and solutions in PMBOK focus on capturing and documenting such events rather than the workflow to manage and institutionalize these project processes from start to finish. Treating these events as workflow-driven processes (in addition to treating them as documents and templates) provides visibility and

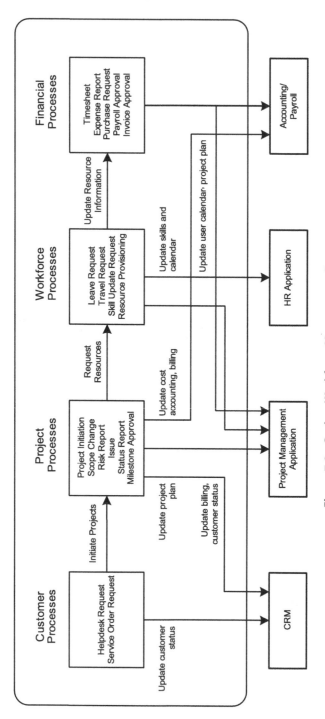

Figure 7.2 Project Workforce Management Processes

transparency into their status at any stage. In fact, there is no mention of the need for a common standards-based workflow engine to manage all project, workforce, and financial processes. A more fundamental approach to work process management is required and it is the only way a company can achieve the consistency, automated compliance, transparency, and execution excellence that is so vital for any organization today.

The main Project Workforce Management processes, their interactions with each other and other enterprise software systems are shown in Figure 7.2. Project- and service-driven businesses run on processes as shown in Table 7.1.

Customer Processes

Customer processes include workflows such as helpdesk issues and service requests (see Figure 7.3). Customer processes are designed to ensure that service level agreements (SLAs) and the company's customer management policies are tracked, enforced, and monitored. They also connect the sales team and executives to the project/service delivery teams. For example, an account executive can view a report of any outstanding issues and the status of current projects before calling a customer to probe for potential business opportunities.

Project Processes

Project processes include project initiation, scope change, and risk reporting. They are designed to streamline project execution, manage change,

CUSTOMER MANAGEMENT	PROJECT MANAGEMENT	WORKFORCE MANAGEMENT	FINANCIAL MANAGEMENT
Service request	Project initiation	Leave request	Timesheet
Helpdesk	Scope change request	Travel request	Expense report
Order management	Risk report	Skill update request	Purchase request
RFP management	Status report	Resource request	Payroll approval
Sales order approval	Issue problems	Training request	Invoice approval
	Milestone approval	Hiring	Accounts payable and receivable
	Pipeline management	Termination	Regulatory and compliance management

Table 7.1 Project Workforce Processes

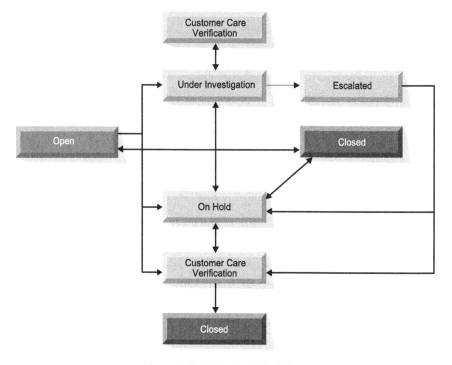

Figure 7.3   Helpdesk Workflow

audit all project activity, and connect project management to financials (see Figure 7.4).

Workforce Processes

Workforce processes include resource provisioning (such as preparations for a new hire), resource requires, leave requests, and skill update requests. They are designed to optimize resource utilization and capacity planning as well as to connect human resources to project and finance teams (see Figure 7.5).

Financial Processes

Financial processes include timesheet and expense report tracking and billing. These processes are designed to track costs and revenues associated with any work performed and to connect financial processes to project management and workforce management (Figure 7.6).

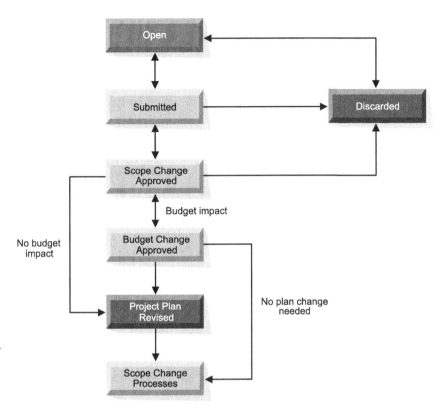

Figure 7.4   Scope Change Workflow

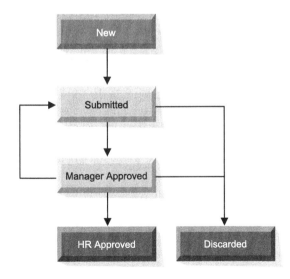

Figure 7.5   Skill Update Request Workflow

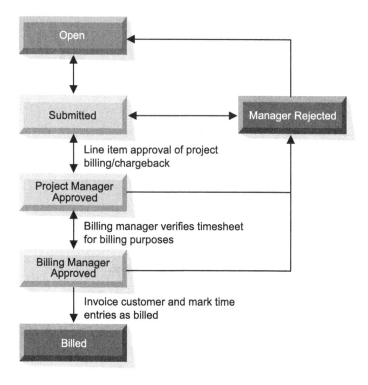

Figure 7.6   Billable Timesheet Approval Workflow

Other Workflows and How They Fit

Defect tracking (also known as "bug tracking" in the software industry) is one of the essential tools in engineering, research and development (R&D), or construction firms, and in any other organization that develops products or delivers projects. Figure 7.7 illustrates a simple defect tracking workflow. This workflow will most likely be treated as a project workflow since defects are reported for a specific project or product.

Documents may require an approval process; for example, sending a response for a completed request for a proposal to a customer. For compliance and auditing purposes, companies frequently need document approval workflows that maintain various versions of a document, store the comments of the people involved in the cycle, and control access rights. Figure 7.8 shows an example of a document approval workflow. Document approval would be considered a customer process if the document is for a customer; a project

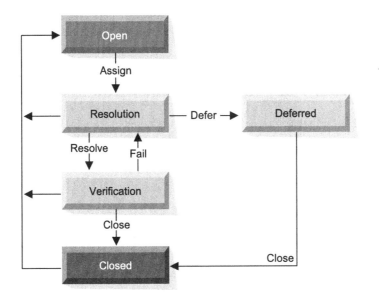

Figure 7.7   Defect Tracking Workflow

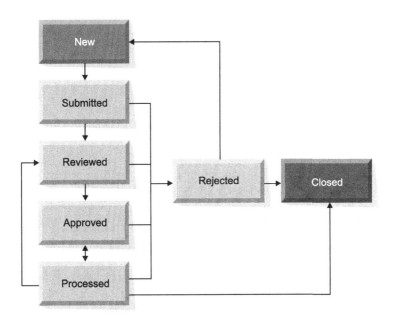

Figure 7.8   Document Approval Workflow

process if it is for a project, a financial process if it is for regulatory compliance, and so on. Therefore, its nature very much depends on the document's ultimate consumers.

Main Components of a Workflow System

Table 7.2 describes the most important components of a workflow system. A workflow system used to automate people-, project-, and financial-related processes has the following capabilities.

Departmental Workflows

Classify and sort workflows by department since different types of workflows are designed and used by each department. For example, sales team, service organization, IT, engineering, R&D, billing, and other departments have their own set of workflows.

Roles

Roles define functionality and data access privileges in a workflow system. For example, managers need the ability to assign issues to team members, or a CFO may need to approve purchase requests of a certain amount. Roles are also used by the system to send notifications to a group of users based on predefined conditions. For example, an organization may want to notify critical issues reported after hours to on-call users who have the responsibility of supporting such customers.

Creating Queries

Queries search the database for workflow entries that match certain criteria such as the workflow entry:

- Has priority equal to, less than, or greater than a certain priority level
- Is of a certain type, such as scope change request, project issue, risk report, and so on
- Is created or originated by certain individuals or customers
- Is in a specific state, such as open, deferred, or rejected
- Is assigned to certain users, roles, or teams
- Is associated to a project or task
- Was created within a date range
- Contains certain keywords in the workflow entry text
- Certain values are set for user-defined fields

COMPONENT	DESCRIPTION
Process modeler/designer	Graphically design and model the work process. Define the workflow's states and transitions including start, end, sink, and intermediate states.
Roles	Define end users, group managers, project managers, administrators, and other roles for access to workflow entry, approval, and processing actions.
Security	Specify which users and resource groups can access various types of workflows; also define field level and state-dependent security for the workflow's data.
Form designer	Visually design the end-user forms that can be customized without any programming on a per workflow basis
Rule engine	Define rules such as escalations (e.g., if a workflow entry stays in a certain state for too long), conditional routing (e.g., if the expense report is greater than $5,000 send it to second level approval), and other pre- or poststate or transition processing.
Queue/workflow management	Display the user's current queue of workflow entries to work on. Depending on their access rights, users can see their work list, the list of the work that has been created or assigned to others (in case of a manager), and all workflow entries (in case of an administrator).
Notifications	Send notifications by e-mail, cell phone, or pager based on predefined conditions, such as certain events or inactivity.
Analysis and reporting	Report on the status of various work processes (what work is outstanding, what is late, etc.), audit of any workflow activity and access to real-time analytics for fast decision making.
Activity monitoring	Monitor workflow queues for bottlenecks and performance problems. Ensure optimal throughput at all stages of the workflow and generate benchmarks and utilization reports.

Table 7.2   Components of a Workflow System

95

Visualizing the Flow

It is essential for users to visualize the workflow's diagram including transitions and the overall process flow. The graphic representation of a workflow (such as any of the workflow diagrams in this chapter) helps end users understand a workflow entry's status, path, and progress; and visually explains the processes and roles to all participants. A picture is indeed worth a thousand words; without a visual representation, it is much harder to design a workflow and to communicate it.

Handling Exceptions—Conditional Routing

Escalation rules can be defined for any work process to notify process managers when certain workflow entries are neglected and make sure they are handled in a timely manner. The following are some examples:

- An SLA has been established between the customer and the company. Workflow software can be used to ensure that all issues are resolved within the guidelines of the SLA. For example, a priority 1 issue has to be looked at within 24 hours of being reported. Workflow software escalates the issue to a manager if there has been no activity on the reported issue within 12 hours of creation.
- If a deadline is about to be reached and a request has not reached a final state, then the request is escalated to a designated person(s) prior to the deadline.
- When a budget is exceeded for work related to a workflow entry, the assigned user and the manager receive a notification of the exception.

Organization and work breakdown structures[3] simplify the definition and automation of escalation rules. For example, if a priority 1 issue is not responded to in one business day then escalate it to the support manager; if timesheet is not completed by Friday at 5 P.M. then escalate it to the user's group manager; if scope change impacts the project schedule then escalate it to the project manager, and if it impacts the budget escalate it to the CFO.

Assignments and Notifications

An assignment rule is logic that automatically assigns a task to a specific role or user when a workflow reaches a given state. Depending on the severity or urgency of the matter, different methods of notification can be used to inform users of their new assignments. For example, if the state of a workflow requires emergency attention, the assignee could receive a text message by cell phone; otherwise, a simple e-mail or notification on a work dashboard is sufficient.

Organization and work breakdown structures are instrumental for setting up assignments and notifications, because they define the relationships between people and groups. Effective assignment rules are closely based on these structures. For example, automatically assign all IBM projects' issues to the IBM Support Group, assign all small customer projects to the online execution team.

Parallel and Sequential Processes

Many processes do not have to occur sequentially. Workflow systems support the concept of a *subworkflow* as a transition from a given state. The following are examples of subworkflows and their applications:

- When any one reaches any final state in the subworkflow, transition to the next state. For example, multiple assistants receive a request to send a package; any of them who is available can send the package and the request is marked as completed.
- Specific subworkflows must be completed before the next state can be reached. For example, project proposal needs to be approved by at least the CEO and the CFO; COO's approval is optional.
- If one or more of the subsequent states fail, transition to another state. For example, project proposal needs to be approved by at least the CEO and the CFO. COO approval is optional; however, if the COO rejects, then the project has been rejected.
- All the subworkflows must be completed successfully before the next state is reached (for example, project proposal must be approved by the CEO, the CFO, and the COO).

Configurable Workflow

A company is likely to quickly outgrow the feature set and template processes offered out-of-the-box by the workflow system. Allowing users to define their own workflows, user-defined fields, form design, triggers, notifications, and roles makes the application configurable enough to adapt to the company's changing needs without custom programming.

Linked Flows

One type of workflow can often trigger the creation of or activity in other linked workflows. For example, when a service visit work process is completed, the system can create a billing workflow so that an invoice is prepared and sent to the customer for the service order, or a risk report workflow entry results in one or more scope change requests that are initiated to address the reported risk. Workflows can also be nested; for example, a support issue can create an escalation issue, and when the escalation is resolved, the original support workflow entry is closed.

Customer Access

Customers can have access to the workflow processes in a controlled manner so that they can see the status of their projects and requests. Self-service access to the workflow's dashboards, reports, and even the workflow entries themselves, creates a valuable opportunity for customers to collaborate closely with the company. This self-service facility avoids repetitive questions, unproductive status inquiry calls, and allows customers to report and track issues and requests at their own convenience.

Process Risk Management

Operational risk is defined as the probability that one or more processes will either fail or consume excessive resources. These deficiencies then lead to inconsistent performance, higher costs, loss of business opportunities, or lower revenue. Operational risk is an inherent property of any business process; however, quantifying the risk's financial cost is difficult.

To manage process risk, the company should:

- Systematically identify operational risks in every business process,
- Document the source of the risk,
- Estimate the risk's financial consequences (quantify the cost of the risk),
- Determine cost effective measures to mitigate the risk, and
- Incorporate risk management in the design of the business process.

The workflow system's exception management features (such as conditional routing, alerts, and notifications) as well as a well-designed business process can substantially reduce or at least contain operational risk.

Workflow Drives Project Workforce Management

Change is here to stay; user-configurable workflows continuously align Project Workforce Management processes with your evolving and current business needs. The benefits of workflow-driven Project Workforce Management are:

- *Reduced dependency on IT:* Define work policy validated at point of entry, change approval routes and roles, and add/remove fields and notifications without the need for custom programming, and without involving any IT resources.

- *Lower maintenance costs:* Workflow-driven software immediately adapts to your needs as your organization and work structures, policies, and processes change.

- *Self-service portals with visual feedback:* Provides users with the self-services, queries, and work lists they need to answer their most common questions, such as: Who is looking at my project request (or issue, expense report, etc.) now? What is the process for initiating a project? Who rejected my timesheet and why?

- *Standard-based approach to managing business project processes:* Makes it simpler to extend the same platform to automate and standardize more project and workforce processes. For example, a company can start by automating their timesheet approval process then use the same workflow engine to automate expense reports, billing approval, leave requests, skill update requests, and scope changes.

- *Quickly identify and implement best practices:* It is much easier to establish and collaborate on best practices across the organization, including the partial or complete implementation of project management methodologies such as PMBOK or PRINCE.

- *Ensured compliance, auditing, and reporting:* Addresses both sides of the compliance challenge. First, processes are designed and modeled to be compliant with regulations. Second, auditing and controls enforce the compliance processes. Workflow-driven software provides reporting and analysis of all data changes, deletions, creations, approvals, and rejections—increasing corporate accountability, reducing risk, and facilitating compliance with regulations and process improvement initiatives such as Sarbanes-Oxley, Defense Contract Audit Agency (DCAA), IT Infrastructure Library (ITIL), Capability Maturity Model Integration (CMMI), and Six Sigma.

Workflow Reports

A few sample workflow reports are illustrated in Figure 7.9. Project, workforce, and financial workflow entries linked to organization and work breakdown

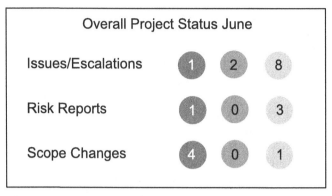

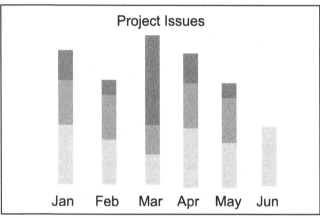

Figure 7.9   Sample Workflow Charts

structures provide a powerful foundation for creating insightful reports and answering some key executive questions such as:

- Which projects have too many scope changes?
- Which resources are always late with their timesheets or expense reports?
- What types of issues keep reoccurring?
- Which business unit is taking on the highest risk projects?
- What resource group has the highest productivity rate?

And many more such questions can be answered in real-time using a common workflow platform that connects workflows, organization and work breakdown structures and project financials in one data source. See Chapter 19, "Reporting and Dashboards," for a more detailed description of project workforce reports and dashboard examples.

NOTES

1. From a study cited in *CIO Magazine,* "It's All About the Execution" November 15, 2006.
2. For more information visit www.pmi.org.
3. See Chapter 6, "Organization and Work Breakdown Structures."

8

Initiating Projects

To believe with certainty we must begin with doubting.
—King Stanislaus

A considerable amount of energy and effort is centered on project execution and final delivery. However, the more time and energy that is invested in the project initiation phase, the more likely it is that fewer problems will occur when the project is underway.

Project initiation is the definition of a standard corporate-wide policy and process to approve projects. The initiation process typically includes a business case review, feasibility study, risk assessment, and budget plan including high-level goals—all with the intention of getting the approval of management, customers, and other stakeholders to fund and launch the project.

Today, many companies still use manual, paper, or e-mail-based processes to approve new projects. Teams request project and activity codes by e-mail, telephone, or fax. The process is cumbersome and time consuming not only for the approver but also for the teams and departments that have to execute the project. Additionally, once the project is launched, project teams lack the centralized collaborative infrastructure required for a successful project launch and consistent status reporting.

The process of initiating projects is different in every department, depending on the type of work, each executive's management habits, or the department's relationship with the executive committee. After a few months, no one can quickly determine who approved a project; what justified the project; or what changes have been made to the project's budget, schedule, scope, or objectives. Without a centralized and audited system for project initiation, questionable projects are far more likely to receive funding. Without a clear report of how and why projects are approved or rejected, no one can be held accountable when a project fails or is not funded when it should have been. Furthermore, without tools for properly auditing and archiving project-related documentation, such as status reports and milestone sign-offs, companies are in danger of accused of inadequate corporate governance controls (see Chapter 4).

Manual processes lead to the following challenges in a project- or service-driven firm:

- Good projects may not get funded, or bad projects may continue to be funded, due to deficient project initiation controls and inconsistent processes.
- Slow setup of project and team work environments delays new project launch.
- Lack of a central location to store project information makes it much more difficult, if not impossible, to conduct compliance audits or real-time project status analysis.
- The blizzard of e-mails, documents, spreadsheets, and paper is overwhelming for the people who support project or service delivery.
- Coordinating the launch of projects executed by distributed teams in dozens of sites is difficult.

Investing in a project initiation solution helps the organization overcome these challenges.

Automating the Project Initiation Process

A project initiation process streamlines project proposal management and approval, organizes project information, automates compliance tasks, and enhances team collaboration. Benefits of an automated project initiation solution are:

- Streamlines new project requirements and information gathering; automates administrative tasks necessary for project set up
- Standardizes processes for project and activity code requests and approvals
- Closes the information gaps early by formalizing project launch; integrates project set up with other enterprise software solutions such as customer relationship management (CRM), project and resource planning
- Identifies and communicates project engagement deliverables and resources
- Reduces time spent on audit preparation and other compliance related activities
- Streamlines the project and activity code creation process
- Lowers overall costs of project and service delivery due to standardization and coordination
- Enhances team productivity by helping to avoid misunderstandings

Project Initiation Workflow

Many professionals think of project initiation as some sort of analysis effort, such as assessment, feasibility study, or business case development. According to Project Management Institute (PMI), this type of analysis effort is a separate project (with its own project charter) that provides the information needed to make a decision about initiating a new project. However, as depicted in Figure 8.1, in the

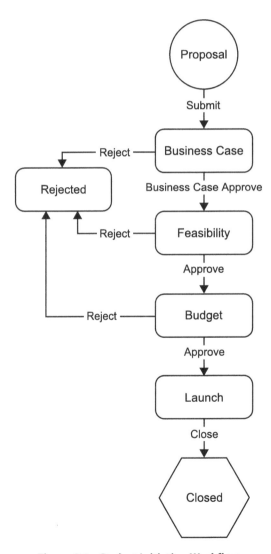

Figure 8.1   Project Initiation Workflow

context of Project Workforce Management, project initiation is actually a work-flow that establishes a framework for taking on a new project. It is assumed that the person who is submitting the initiation request has sufficient information to propose the new project for review and approval.

Project Initiation Stages

A best-practice project initiation template process is described in this chapter. Every business and industry has its own particular project initiation requirements; the information and process presented here can be tailored to fit your specific business needs.

PROPOSAL STAGE. The project initiation form (Figure 8.2) requires specific information for any project proposal, including project manager, stakeholders, budget, business case, and feasibility considerations. Various stakeholders such as executives, the finance team, and project managers can approve or reject the proposed project depending on your project initiation process. A project is initiated if, and only if, its business case, feasibility, and budget are approved by all stakeholders.

In the proposal stage, you intend to propose a new project. The proposal has to follow your organization's predefined project proposal checklist and policy.

A project proposal checklist includes:

- Project name and summary of the project
- Customer (internal or external) information
- Business case or strategic fit and assumptions
- Project objectives, benefits, and scope definition
- Identify project sponsors
- Proposed project manager
- Acceptance and success criteria
- Preliminary project plan, resource requirements, and timeline
- Preliminary work breakdown structure, estimates, milestones, and deliverables
- Individual roles and responsibilities
- Resource, equipment, and material requirements
- Quality assurance plan
- Risk management plan
  — Risks if project is not approved
  — Risks that can impact the project (result in failure, budget, and schedule overruns)
- Supporting documents

General Information

Project Name:*	
Portfolio:	
Business Unit:	
Project Manager:	
Project Sponsor:	
Project Description:	
Business Case:	

Project Information

Planned Start Date:*		Planned End Date:	
Technical Lead:			
Business Analyst:			
Summary of Project Scope:			
Business Impact:			
Business Risk Level:			
Project Artifacts Location:			

Financial Information

Project Code: _____

Pricing Structure:*   Time & Material ◯   Fixed Bid ◯   Expenses ◯

Hourly Rate: _____   Expense Type: _____
(if applicable)   (if applicable)

Budget Approved?:* Yes ◯   No ◯

Est. Labor Budget: $_____   Est. Expenses Budget: $_____

Revenue Period: _____   Cost Center: _____

Figure 8.2   Sample Project Initiation Form

BUSINESS CASE REVIEW STAGE. The project initiation workflow routes the proposal to the appropriate decision maker(s) who need to review and approve the business case. Depending on your policy, the business case may require approval from one or more individuals; if multiple individuals are involved, the approvals can occur sequentially or in parallel. The reviewer(s) can completely reject the proposal, or push it back to the person who made the proposal requesting additional information.

FEASIBILITY OR READINESS STUDY. Once the business case has been approved, a designated individual or group of individuals must assess the project's feasibility. For an information technology (IT) project, the feasibility state would be owned by the CTO or CIO. For a billable project, the readiness study would be conducted by the vice president of professional services or another designated executive. For a product or research and development proposal, the CTO or vice president of engineering will assess the project's feasibility.

Feasibility analysis includes an assessment of the project's resource requirements to determine whether the organization has the resources available to execute the project, as well as an evaluation of the project's risks to decide whether they are manageable. The proposal can be rejected at this stage or sent back to the person who made the proposal requesting additional information.

BUDGET APPROVAL STAGE. Following the business case review and feasibility study, the budget approval stage is usually assigned to a financial executive, such as a CFO, or someone with budget authority, such as a COO. The reviewer looks at the project's timeline, cost and resource estimates as well as the cash flow implications, and decides whether to approve and secure the required funding.

LAUNCH OR EXECUTION STAGE. At this point, the project is tentatively approved. The project sponsors and managers have to make the final preparations for launching the project. Activities include:

- *Project plan:* Using the preliminary project plan, the project manager builds the project's work breakdown structure and cost estimates. If there are any scope changes that impact business fit or budget, then send the proposal back for approval.
- *Quality assurance plan:* Define and communicate the plan that will ensure the project will be delivered at the expected quality level and error rates.
- *Individual roles and responsibilities:* Define and communicate the project management team roles, status reporting hierarchy, and stakeholder involvement as well as responsibilities. Status reports must specifically mention milestones reached, completed deliverables, and percentage completion of major tasks compared to baseline estimates.

- *Project log book:* This is an online time-stamped journal of all project activity from project start to end. It provides a quick snapshot of project activities and current status. The log is also useful for analysis and audit of what has gone right or wrong with the project at any given point.
- *Audit trail:* A list of all project activity, changes, and approvals. The audit trail is similar to the project log, but is presented as a report and is available in searchable and filtered format.
- *Minutes:* Maintain a record of all internal and external meetings and communications.
- *Project close report:* Plan for a report that assesses the benefits and results at project close compared to baseline targets.
- *Tools and methods:* Agree on methods and tools to execute the project including documentation and reporting standards that everyone has to comply with.
- *Reporting cycle:* Agree on reporting frequency, format, and process between project members and stakeholders.

The Role of Project Initiation

Too many projects get funded based on incomplete assumptions, false expectations, and favoritism. Chapter 18, "Project Prioritization and Selection," explains how a company can incorporate a rigorous and systematic approach to project selection and prioritization. Project prioritization and selection is often considered an integral part of the project initiation process. A combination of the concepts and tools presented in that chapter in conjunction with the project initiation processes described here will substantially enhance your ability to approve and fund only the best projects.

As the first step in the project and service delivery lifecycle, the initiation process formally authorizes a project to begin, and links a project to the plan, the work, and the strategic objectives of the organization. Because these links are critical to a project's success, the initiation process may be repeated during project execution when there is a significant scope change, newly discovered risks, or other circumstances that make it desirable to redefine, reauthorize, or recalibrate the project.

Projects must be aligned with the organization's strategic direction. The project initiation and scope-change processes help ensure this alignment is enforced throughout the project lifecycle. Establishing a formal project initiation process, which is fully integrated with your Project Workforce Management and CRM systems, ensures that only the best-fit projects get funding, and the required due diligence, preparation, and set-up work has been done long before any project gets staffed and starts costing the company time and money.

9

Workforce Planning

One cannot buy, rent or hire more time. The supply of time is totally inelastic. No matter how high the demand, the supply will not go up. There is no price for it. Time is totally perishable and cannot be stored. Yesterday's time is gone forever, and will never come back. Time is always in short supply. There is no substitute for time. Everything requires time. All work takes place in, and uses up time. Yet most people take for granted this unique, irreplaceable and necessary resource.

—Peter F. Drucker

There is an old adage that says business is like a car; it won't run by itself except downhill. Yet, when it comes to arguably the most important element of business—human capital—many enterprises are not fully in the driver's seat. They use outdated top-down manual systems, or simple spreadsheets, to get the right people to the right place at the right time.

For a project-driven or professional services organization, human capital is king. It is essential to have an enterprise-oriented, 360-degree view of talent. It is even more important to involve your project workforce in the planning, allocation, and tracking processes, so that the best people with the most appropriate skills are always working on the most critical projects.

In a talent-tight environment, workforce planning can help project-driven organizations allocate, manage, and forecast critical human capital across the enterprise. Specifically, workforce planning enables organizations to: (1) ensure long-term capacity and demand planning; (2) account for differentiated time in an era of distributed teams and project centric work; and (3) comply with regulatory requirements including Sarbanes-Oxley.

Companies that fail to treat workforce planning strategically open themselves up to tangible and costly business risks. Inefficient processes and unstructured behavior run rampant when resources are not utilized at optimal capacities. Collaboration is less than ideal, billing cycles are lengthy, project status is based on outdated information, and project costs are not managed—or

111

even known—with certainty. A nonoptimized workforce can spell lost revenue, lost profit, nonmotivated employees, and disappointed customers.

Workforce planning reveals how organizations can:

- Manage to deliver projects on time and within budget.
- Provide an environment for collaborative optimization of a project workforce.
- Ensure that proper resources are in place to deliver projects.
- Ensure an optimal and trained resource pool.
- Effectively report on project information in real time.
- Ensure employees focus on core responsibilities rather than administrative tasks.
- Efficiently manage the life cycle of a service or project engagement.

This chapter describes how savvy organizations are using workforce planning—which includes the processes of allocating, managing, and forecasting human capital from a strategic perspective across the enterprise. Workforce planning tools use behind-the-scenes intelligence to align shifts in demand with the existing and potential supply of human capital. For organizations that depend heavily on people, workforce planning is fast becoming the "hidden force" that spells the difference between market participation and market *leadership*.

When You Need Workforce Planning

You need workforce planning if:[1]

- If you are a project-driven and/or professional services firm
- When your organization spans across buildings, campuses, regions, time zones, and countries
- When employees no longer work face-to-face with their peers
- When your organization has geographically distributed project, process, or service delivery teams
- When your project workforce reaches 50 or more, or when your billable (client-facing) workforce reaches 30 people or more
- When the demand for resources is fulfilled by multiple sources—centralized, dispersed, and external resources

Benefits of Workforce Planning

There are a number of key benefits of workforce planning including:

- Increased employee productivity through more focused work
- Increased employee collaboration to deliver projects and service clients

- Provides a uniform method for governing resource allocation
- More opportunities due to improved resource management
- More effective resource utilization and retention
- Captures all project-related costs quickly and accurately
- Streamlines business processes so that clients can be serviced more efficiently
- Improves client satisfaction due to quicker and optimized project staffing
- Improves reporting capabilities for more effective decision-making
- Improves management of project portfolios, resource allocation and utilization, project status and cost reporting, and billing

In *Living on the Fault Line* (New York: Collins, 1st edition, 2002), market strategist and consultant Geoff Moore suggests that organizations can create a sustainable competitive advantage—first by understanding that there has been a radical shift in what constitutes a "scarce resource," and then by putting today's scarce resources to better use than their competitors do. Moore observes that in the Industrial Age, the scarcest resource was financial capital; today the scarcest resources are time, talent, and management attention.

Much has been written about the looming talent shortage that is being driven by retiring baby boomers and other factors. This trend makes it imperative to keep employees motivated and productive by continually anticipating and correcting gaps between future demands and current skills, so that people—and the business—are developed to their full potential.

Long-Term Competency and Capacity Planning

In 2001, the U.S. government identified "strategic human capital management" as a "high risk" area and launched a Workforce Planning initiative. Studies showed 31 percent of the overall federal workforce, 53 percent of workers in supervisory positions, and 65 percent of senior executives were eligible to retire within five years. In its "Major Management Challenges and Program Risks" report, the U.S. General Accounting Office noted that downsizing and hiring freezes, conducted without the insights of workforce planning, had "eroded the ability of many agencies . . . to perform their missions."

A 2004 study conducted across IBM customers revealed that companies in the private sector are not doing any better. Sixty percent of the 456 respondents said they do not believe they have the organizational structure, internal capabilities, and leadership resources to meet their goals. One CEO observed, "Our style has been based on industrial relations, not human relations," and another commented, "There are hyper-growth requirements and there is a war for talent."[2]

Account for Differentiated Time in an Era of Distributed Teams and Project-Centric Work

Prioritizing, assigning, and auditing the way human capital is allocated within an organization has become increasingly complicated with the shift to a services economy.

Enterprises must adjust to increasing fragmentation of their workforces into "subject matter expertise" delivered by specialized workers both inside and outside the organization. While only a short while ago just a small fraction of an enterprise's work was formed around projects and differentiated time, today about half of the work is, and experts expect this trend to continue.

Complying with Regulatory Requirements

Workforce planning helps the company to specifically address the forecasting and capacity planning aspects of effective internal controls.

Need for Workforce Planning

Table 9.1 summarizes the economic and organizational shifts driving the need for workforce planning.

FROM . . .	TO . . .
Focus on cutting costs	Focus on accelerating growth
Product economy	Services economy
Extended enterprise	Fragmented enterprise
Static workforce	Project workforce
Undifferentiated time	Differentiated time
Organization-centric thinking	Project-centric thinking
HR "owning" workforce development	Line of business "owning" workforce development
Focus on employee	Focus on aligning employees, projects, and customers
Minimum disclosure	Regulatory scrutiny requiring a detailed accounting of time
Regular place of work	Mobile, virtual place of work

Table 9.1   Economic and Organizational Shifts Driving the
Need for Workforce Planning

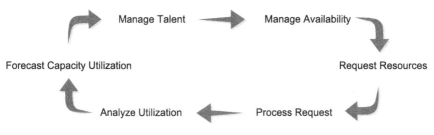

Figure 9.1   The Workforce Planning Cycle

Workforce Planning Cycle

Workforce Planning is an iterative discipline that guides an organization through the cycle of managing and deploying talent, to analyzing current and forecasted utilization. Workforce planning solutions address the core issue of using time, talent, and management attention to create a sustainable competitive advantage.

Continued movement through the workforce planning cycle, as shown in Figure 9.1, drives organizations to optimize their use of time and talent, and gives management insight into any necessary corrective actions. Organizations committed to this discipline create a strategic advantage. Accounting for and optimizing time for a project workforce places greater demands on the systems used to manage how the right people get to the right places at the right times.

Considerations in Deploying Workforce Planning

Organizations addressing these shifts by deploying workforce planning should keep the following considerations in mind to gain the most advantage from the system:

1. *Eliminate "stovepipes" and view your entire organization as a shared project workforce.* Workforce planning systems deliver the greatest impact when they are used enterprise-wide to illuminate skills, expertise, coverage areas, depth, risk exposure, and subject matter expertise. In many organizations without workforce planning, informal buddy systems lead managers to choose their favorite people for project and service teams, leaving many other capable people underutilized.

   While these informal systems give the most aggressive managers what they need, the organization as a whole gets an incomplete picture of the relative strengths and weaknesses of its workforce, and cannot fully understand or control utilization risks. It also has no way of knowing if the most appropriate talent is assigned to the right customers on the highest priority projects to maximize revenue and profitability for the company overall. Managers may encourage knowledge gaps and territorial information to keep the best resources for their specific projects.

Using a workforce planning system enables an organization to see the entire employee base as a *shared project workforce*. Talent, customer requirements, and projects across lines of business can be interrelated so that skills can be transferred and human capital redeployed in ways that benefit the organization as a whole.

2. *Make workforce planning bidirectional and collaborative.* The best workforce planning processes are built bottom-up, but also depend heavily on solid communication of strategic objectives from the executive suite down. For this reason, representatives across different lines of business and from varying responsibility levels should collaborate on identifying the needs of the organization before outlining requirements and selecting a system.

Line-of-business owners, managers, and individual contributors all need to understand the strategic and operational priorities of the company, sales forecasts, changes in product and service lines, changes in customer composition and requirements, launches or divestitures of business units, and capital investments that will impact productivity and demands for human capital.

The workforce planning system should encourage employee participation, such as the ability to input and update current skills, rank work interests, and identify training needs based on this information. Managers should be able to estimate voluntary and involuntary turnover, model different time/cost/utilization scenarios based on various resource assignments, and have access to the information required to justify training and hiring decisions. The line-of-business owners should be able to ensure that processes for requesting and assigning talent, accounting for time, executing projects, and billing customers are followed. Executives should receive the reports they need for compliance records, as well as guide the strategic growth of each business unit.

A collaborative planning system lets users make easy *real-time* changes to processes, workflow patterns, talent assignments, and reports, as usage drives better understanding of how to optimize the system. For example, some systems automatically change the way talent requests and assignments are routed for approval, based on changes users make to a workflow. Figure 9.2 illustrates different approval processes that could be involved when a project manager and a resource manager collaborate to request, approve, and book resources.

Project managers can request specific resources or *generic resources* to work on their projects. A generic resource is a frequently used role, skill set or user profile such as a System Analyst, Database Administrator,

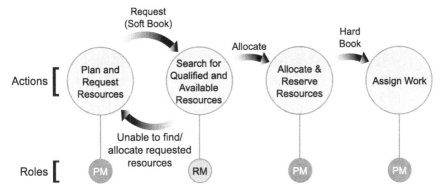

Figure 9.2   Scenario: Project Manager Soft Books Specific Resources

or Loan Officer. A generic resource allows you to specify the type of resource you need without asking for specific employees or consultants (Figure 9.3).

3. *Model demand and supply—measure gaps and plan to fill them.* Workforce Planning systems translate into measurable competitive advantages when users tap them to answer questions such as. "Do we have the right mix of talent to meet both current and shifting project demands, and account for future growth? Are billable resources being used in an optimal way? Can project costs be managed more effectively? Is there a better way to deploy our resources? Can billing cycles be shortened to reduce accounts receivable and increase in cash flow?"

The best systems help users "strengthen the people pipeline." They should help users anticipate how upstream changes in business objectives, projects, and service portfolios translate into needs for downstream resource availability, expertise, proficiency, skills, and experience types.

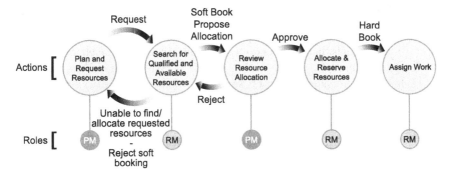

Figure 9.3   Scenario: Project Manager Approves Proposed Resources

They also help users neutrally assess the most appropriate sources to fulfill demand, whether it is from the internal resource pool, new hires or external service providers.

The Workforce Planning system must have the analytic horsepower to model demand and supply, and to identify gaps in best practices for deploying talent, managing costs, and optimizing the revenue cycle. Systems that make it easy for managers to model "if/then" scenarios encourage them to consider alternatives for aligning talent, projects, and customers; to examine cost/time trade-offs; and to change project priorities as business conditions or customer requirements change. Reports can also enable managers to pinpoint potential problems and make corrections before they impact customers. For example, managers can justify the return on investment for hiring or training talent, and in serving emerging trends in customer demand.

4. *Close the "intelligence loop" from the back office to the front office.* Workforce planning helps tie operations to business strategy, and gives executives the information they need to ensure human capital is being used in ways that best support the organization's growth and profitability.

These systems provide the intelligence that the executives need to align resources with market opportunities, and to identify and overcome business threats, such as an aging workforce, a changing skill-base due to changing market demands, and changes in compliance requirements. They also provide the information needed to continuously improve how resources are requested and allocated and how training, hiring, and outsourcing decisions are made.

Executive dashboard capabilities highlight at-a-glance information such as budget use by a business unit, project alignment with the company's strategy and priorities, budgeted hours and costs versus actual hours and costs, as well as other variances that might threaten the business if not corrected.

5. *Understand your scalability and flexibility needs.* Organizations in change-oriented and fast-moving industries, subject to evolving regulations, should consider systems that enable easy, real-time alterations to processes, workflows, and reports. The solution should be designed with intuitive tools that enable nonprogrammers to make these changes. Most organizations also will do well to consider a system that enables a modular implementation approach, such as the ability to automate one service line or business unit at a time.

Managing Resource Requests

Project Workforce Management's underlying workflow system is used for resource request approval, routing, notification, and assignment steps within the

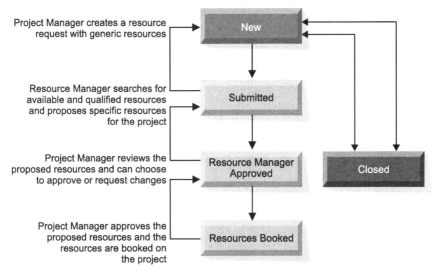

Figure 9.4   Sample Request Workflow

workforce planning process. The workflow is configured or new workflows are designed and implemented without any programming using the workflow modeling tool. This capability allows companies to configure the application to support their current processes or reconfigure them as they evolve without expensive customization. A sample resource request workflow is shown in Figure 9.4.

Resource managers request resources using a request form. The request form includes the project manager's desired specific or generic resources, a high level timeline for the project's resource requirements, and guidelines for processing the request such as urgency, importance of skill versus availability matching and other search factors. Managers can propose alternative plans in case the original plan is not fulfilled.

Power of Collaborative Workforce Planning

Collaborative workforce planning solutions integrate workforce information and processes from across the enterprise—such as payroll, project management, human resources, and customer relationship management—to deliver strategic insights that drive better business decisions.

The following capabilities make the workforce planning system more collaborative for the enterprise:

- *A system of record that combines the customer, the project, and the workforce:* This system of record reveals the interplay among these elements,

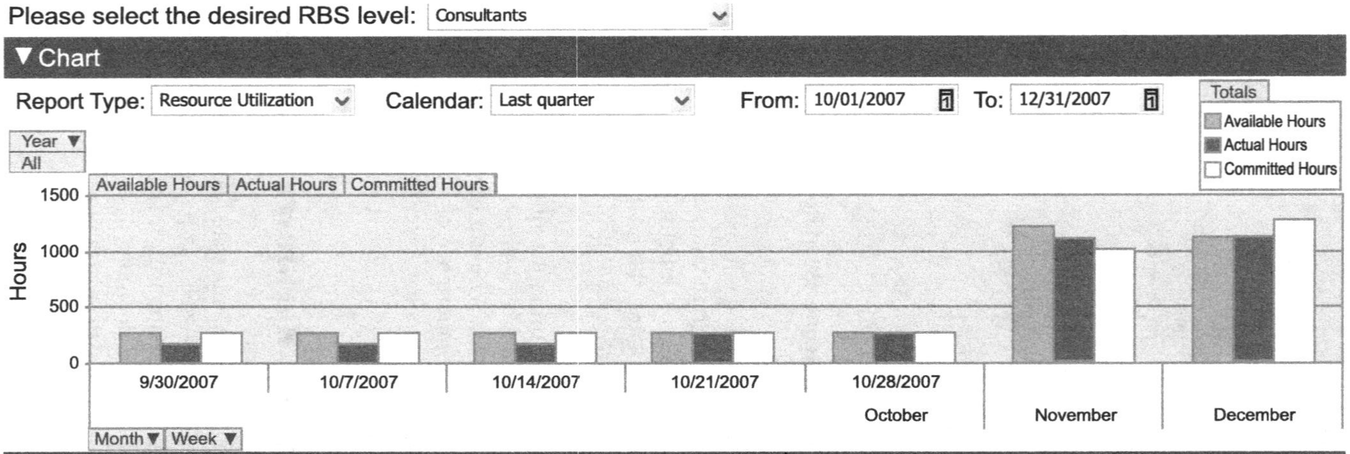

Please select the desired RBS level: Consultants

▼ Chart

Report Type: Resource Utilization   Calendar: Last quarter   From: 10/01/2007   To: 12/31/2007

Year ▼
All

Available Hours | Actual Hours | Committed Hours

Totals
- Available Hours
- Actual Hours
- Committed Hours

Month ▼ | Week ▼

▼ Grid

Year ▼	Months ▼	Weeks ▼		Available Hours	Actual Hours	Committed Hours	Utilization Ratio	Forecasted ($)	Actual ($)	Consumed (%)
All	⊟ Oct	9/30/2007	+I	280.00	160.00	280.00	57%	9,800.00	5,600.00	57
		10/7/2007	+I	280.00	160.00	280.00	57%	9,800.00	5,600.00	57
		10/14/2007	+I	280.00	160.00	280.00	57%	9,800.00	5,600.00	57
		10/21/2007	+I	280.00	280.00	280.00	100%	9,800.00	9,800.00	100
		10/28/2007	+I	280.00	280.00	280.00	100%	9,800.00	9,800.00	100
	⊞ Nov		+I	1,132.00	1,200.00	1,100.00	97%	38,500.00	42,000.00	109
	⊞ Dec		+I	1,176.00	1,176.00	1,232.00	100%	43,120.00	41,160.00	96
	Grand Total			3,808.00	3,416.00	3,732.00	90%	130,620.00	119,560.00	92

▼ Cost Allocation Summary

Figure 9.5   Sample Resource Utilization Report

120

enables managers to optimize human capital allocations in ways that balance project profitability, customer satisfaction, and company priorities.

- *A workflow engine that is intuitive and adapts to your business processes:* A visual model of the underlying workflow for requesting resources, approval, routing, notification, and assignment makes it easy for users to adapt the system to their business processes. A system that includes best practices templates gives users a head-start in designing their workflows.

- *Score-based resource matching:* Find *the most qualified resources based on configurable and flexible search criteria.* A resource query result that shows a match score for each resource in response to a search by a variety of matching criteria—including skills, proficiency, availability, interest, previous client or industry experience, similar project experience, previous project performance, cost, location, and willingness to travel—simplifies aligning projects, customers, and talent. The search results show hours available, hours requested, current backlog of requests for each resource in the results page, along with a score based on the candidates' search criteria match ranking and the importance placed on various search options including skills, availability, and cost.

- *An enterprise resource pool to show a complete view of resources:* Look for a system that enables you to create a robust skills database that combines skills, proficiency, experience, interests, travel preferences, and other variables into a skill set that can be assigned to a role or a person.

- *Analytics to create actionable intelligence:* Analytics tools help management understand resource availability, allocations, forecasts (see a sample resource utilization report in Figure 9.5), operational variances, and human capital utilization across the organization and at more granular levels, such as by business unit, workgroup, or resource type.

NOTES

1. Gartner Research Note G00129674, September 2005, and based on our observations of the needs of the project workforce.
2. Source: http://www-5.ibm.com/se/news/publications/IBM_CEO_04_Survey_All_F2.pdf.

10

Project Planning

Plans are nothing; planning is everything.
—Dwight D. Eisenhower

Any nontrivial project needs a plan—especially if it requires the completion of multiple tasks and the collaboration of multiple resources. Project plans vary from simple—with a few tasks and one or two milestones—to complex—with dozens of subprojects, hundreds of tasks, many milestones, and numerous contributors in multiple locations and time zones. An enterprise project planning tool has to be both simple enough for people to use and scalable enough to handle any type of project.

This chapter describes the basic elements of project planning, and explains how it interacts with the workforce planning and time and expense tracking components of Project Workforce Management.

We also introduce earned value reports, which measure the true value created during project execution at any given point in time. The combination of planning, tracking, and estimating work on a collaborative basis provides the foundation for analyzing earned value. Workflow-driven budgets, estimates to complete, and status reporting are also valuable metrics that Project Workforce Management provides for keeping projects on track and on budget throughout their life cycles.

What Constitutes Project Planning

Project planning is an element of project management focused on detailed scheduling of tasks and resource assignments. A project plan starts with a project requirements document and scope definition, both of which are prepared during the project initiation process (see Chapter 8, "Initiating Projects"). Using these initial documents, a project planner determines what tasks are necessary to execute the project and their dependencies (also known as the project's work

123

PWBS chart Gantt chart	Graphically draw the project plan, including any task dependencies, by visually adjusting task durations and priorities and by linking tasks to each other.
RBS chart resource assignment	Import project teams and assign resources to tasks. The RBS chart shows the resources and their task lists for resource assignment and planning.
Earned value report Budget and status reports Cost and revenue reports	View real-time project earned value, project status, budget, and cost/revenue reports. The reports can be configured to include your specific project tracking metrics.
Integration	Project plan is integrated with Project Workforce Management. Create a plan, assign resources, and track it with the time and expense tracking module. View planned versus actual work at any time.

Table 10.1   Main Components of a Project Planning Tool

breakdown structure). The planner then estimates the duration of each task. The tasks, durations, and dependencies form the project plan. This step can be standardized by using project templates that define the starting work breakdown structure for the project. Gantt tools are used to graphically manage the project plan. Once the initial plan is available, the project manager assigns resources to the tasks (known as resource assignment). Following this step, the costs of each task can be estimated. The project plan can be changed to achieve the most optimal resource usage, to account for resource availability, or to reduce costs while still achieving the project's deadlines and objectives.

Project planning is important for longer projects that consist of many tasks and involve many resources; shorter or more straightforward projects may not require any formal planning at all. Table 10.1 describes the most important components of a project planning tool.

Role of Project Planning

Project planning plays a pivotal role in the Project Workforce Management process. When a project requires planning, the plan is used to accomplish the following:

- The project manager creates and submits a staff request to the resource manager to find and book the required resources.
- On approval of the request, the project manager builds a project team and assigns the work to team members.

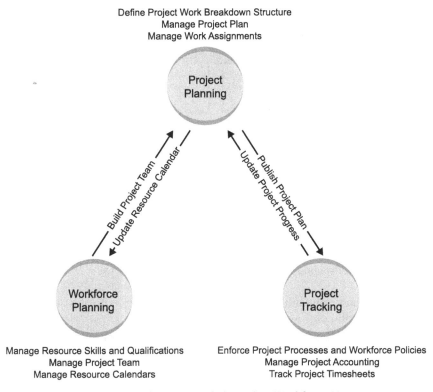

Define Project Work Breakdown Structure
Manage Project Plan
Manage Work Assignments

Project
Planning

Build Project Team
Update Resource Calendar

Publish Project Plan
Update Project Progress

Workforce
Planning

Project
Tracking

Manage Resource Skills and Qualifications
Manage Project Team
Manage Resource Calendars

Enforce Project Processes and Workforce Policies
Manage Project Accounting
Track Project Timesheets

Figure 10.1   Project Planning's Role in Project Workforce Management

- The plan and the assignments are published to the time and expense tracking system (for project tracking) so that project contributors can see what they need to work on, to report on their actual effort, and to communicate what part of the work has been completed.

Figure 10.1 illustrates the connections between project planning, workforce planning, and project tracking within the overall Project Workforce Management methodology.

Project Work Breakdown Structure Chart

Project Work Breakdown Structure (PWBS) is a grouping of the project's work elements, such as tasks and milestones, that outlines the total project scope (see Figure 10.2). Each descending level in the PWBS represents an increasingly detailed definition of the project. Note that the PWBS defines project-specific work elements and should not be confused with the company's work breakdown structure (WBS) that describes the company's work structures and model (see Chapter 6, "Organization and Work Breakdown Structures"). The PWBS is

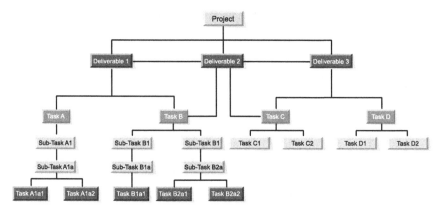

Figure 10.2   Sample Project Work Breakdown Structure

a subset of the enterprise WBS that defines a project's specific and detailed structures. A well-planned PWBS allows project managers to:

- Define and communicate the total scope of the project to all stakeholders and contributors.
- Create a solid foundation for building a good project plan; a well-designed PWBS makes it much easier to plan resources and estimate the work.
- Break down each of the planned outcomes (the root nodes of a PWBS) into detailed actions that can be planned and assigned to resources.

For a planning application to simplify a project planner's work, its foundation must revolve around displaying and editing the project work breakdown structure.

Gantt Tools

A Gantt chart (see Figure 10.3) displays the project work breakdown structure including task dependencies, any scheduling constraints, the duration of each task, and the percentage of the task that is completed. Its purpose is to help the

ID	Task Name	Start	End	Duration	Sep 2001										
					16	17	18	19	20	21	22	23	24	25	26
1	Task 1	9/17/2001	9/21/2001	5d											
2	Task 2	9/24/2001	9/26/2001	3d											
3	Task 3	9/17/2001	9/19/2001	3d											
4															

Figure 10.3   Sample Gantt Chart

project team visualize and understand the project's major activities, milestones, and current status. Bars with arrows between each major activity illustrate the timeline that is required from the start of a new activity to its completion. Gantt charts can also display additional information, such as the actual hours worked on each task.

RBS Chart

Resource breakdown structure (RBS) is a list of personnel displayed in a hierarchical structure (Figure 10.4). Resource breakdown structure is a subset of the organization breakdown structure (OBS). While the OBS includes corporate structure-related elements such as sites (offices) and business units, the RBS displays a hierarchy of the functional groups (departments) within the organization, the resources in each group, and their job functions—such as the individual's title, skill sets, and roles.

CRITICAL PATH. The *critical path* is the shortest distance from project start to completion. In Figure 10.5, Task 1 and Task 3 are on the critical path. The critical path identifies which tasks have zero slack. If any of the tasks on the critical path are delayed, they will cause the project to be delayed. A project planning tool can calculate and display the project's critical path in real-time. The critical path takes into account the logical dependencies between tasks and enables managers to modify the plan, activity start and end dates, and resource allocations to optimize the project schedule.[1]

Project Team

Once the specific resources or the types of skills required have been identified, the project manager makes a formal request to book the resources. The process of requesting and assigning resources involves several considerations such as

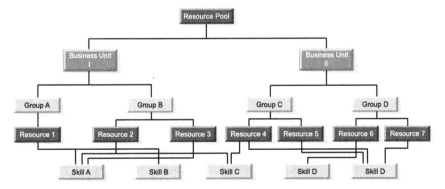

Figure 10.4   Sample RBS Chart

ID	Task Name	Start	Finish	Duration	Feb 2007					Mar 2007				Apr 2007					
					1/28	2/4	2/11	2/18	2/25	3/4	3/11	3/18	3/25	4/1	4/8	4/15	4/22	4/29	5/6
1	Task 1	1/29/2007	2/8/2007	9d															
2	Task 2	2/19/2007	3/5/2007	11d															
3	Task 3	2/12/2007	5/2/2007	58d															
4	Task 4	3/6/2007	3/21/2007	12d															
5	Task 5	3/22/2007	4/18/2007	20d															

Figure 10.5   A Critical Path Example

skills, prior experience, personal interests, costs, and availability (see Chapter 9, "Workforce Planning").

The Project Team is the team of resources who contribute to the project in some way. For example, in the case of a software project, the project manager, business analysts, developers, and quality assurance testers would all be Project Team members. The Project Team is created by selecting resources from the company's RBS.

Resource Assignment

Resource Assignment is the process of determining what people, materials, or equipment—and what quantities of each—are required to carry out a project. Project and resource managers have to identify, document, and assign project roles and responsibilities, and communicate them to the Project Team. Roles and responsibilities may be assigned to individuals, groups, or teams. Prior to acquiring the resources needed for a project, the project manager must first assess what skills are required to perform the project tasks, and where in the project's timeline will those skills be required.

To identify what resources are required to complete a given project, a project manager has several options available, such as reviewing the plan of a completed project of a similar nature, using pre-established best practice templates designed by the company for similar projects, or assessing the work and creating an initial project plan that is iteratively improved as the project is executed.

Earned Value

Cost and schedule are two critical factors that greatly impact the success of projects. To manage project costs and schedules effectively, project managers need a methodology, and tracking metrics that provide reliable project status reporting at every phase of the execution. Earned value (EV) was first used in

1967 by the U.S. Military as a means of project control and performance analysis. Now earned value analysis (EVA) is recognized as a best practice and is mandated by many government agencies and large corporations. In project management, this value is earned as activities are completed.

Earned value analysis provides a project manager with consistent and precise indicators and warning signs in the early stages of the project. These indicators can be used to forecast the actual budget needed to complete the project within the defined parameters. If the final forecasted results are unacceptable to management, steps can be taken early on to alter the final requirements.

The attributes of earned value are threefold. Earned value:

1. Is a uniform unit of measurement for progress at the project level or for any subelement of the project, defined based on the PWBS.
2. Is a consistent method for analysis of any project progress and performance. It can be used as a key performance indicator to accurately compare and measure performance of projects across the organization.
3. Can be used as the basis of cost performance analysis of any project.

The traditional units used to measure earned value include hours worked and cost. For labor-intensive projects, hours worked can be considered adequate for earned value analysis. For a more accurate earned value analysis that reflects the true costs of the project, it is recommended to include all project-related costs as part of the base budget and all actual costs of work performed, including labor rates, subcontractor costs, and overhead.

Earned value provides an accurate indication of cost and schedule variance while a project is in progress. Simply comparing planned and actual costs is not sufficient because these numbers by themselves do not compare the percentage of work completed to the percentage of the planned costs expended. For example, a project that is under budget may give the impression that it is in good condition, but it may fall behind schedule because not enough work is being done. Only by analyzing the earned value for the project can you determine the true status of the project (see Figure 10.6).

Benefits of Earned Value

Earned value provides simple but powerful answers to many questions such as:

- How much is it really costing us to earn every project milestone?
- How much is it going to cost to finish the project based on current progress?
- When is the project going to finish?
- Exactly where are we now?
- What are our problem areas? And why?
- How does this project compare with other projects?

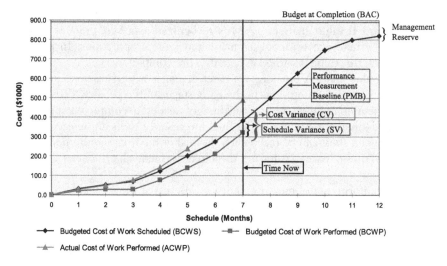

Figure 10.6   Earned Value Graph

Earned value analysis includes several indicators that are used to answer these questions. Below is a list of the most common EVA indicators:

- *Budgeted cost of work scheduled (BCWS):* The planned costs of tasks scheduled to be performed during any given period in the project cycle.
- *Budgeted cost of work performed (BCWP):* The planned costs of tasks or parts of tasks that were accomplished during any given period in the project cycle.
- *Actual cost of work performed (ACWP):* The actual costs incurred for performing planned work during a given period in the project cycle.
- *Estimate-to-complete (ETC):* The estimate of cost to complete task from the current point in time independent of the BCWS.
- *Budget at completion (BAC):* The full budget for the project, which is usually equal to the BCWS.
- *Cost variance (CV):* The difference between the budgeted cost of completed tasks and the actual cost incurred (CV = BCWP − ACWP).
- *Schedule variance (SV):* The difference between the budgeted cost of completed tasks and the scheduled cost (SV = BCWP − BCWS).
- *Cost performance index (CPI):* The relationship between the actual costs versus the budgeted costs for tasks that have been completed (BCWP/ACWP). A CPI greater than 1 indicates under run cost.
- *Schedule performance index (SPI):* The relationship between the tasks that have been completed versus the tasks scheduled to be completed

(BCWP/BCWS). An SPI greater than 1 indicates that the project is ahead of schedule.

- *Independent estimate at completion (IEAC):* Projected final cost of the project based on performance so far. Can be forecast using the formula: IEAC = BAC/CPI.
- *Independent schedule at completion (ISAC):* Projected duration of the project based on performance so far. Can be forecast using the formula: ISAC = Schedule/SPI.
- *To-complete performance index (TCPI):* TCPI = (Budget − BCWP)/ (EAC − ACWP) where EAC is the estimated amount to spend.

Steps for Accurate Project Earned Value Analysis

1. *Define scope of the work and establish PWBS.* The most critical and most challenging requirement of employing EVA is to define the project's total work scope. This task is difficult for any project, and particularly so for product development, software, and information technology (IT) projects. Yet, without a defined scope that represents 100 percent of the planned work, there is no way to measure the project's performance definitively.

   Project work breakdown structure is the most efficient way to define the scope of the work—it is the roadmap for analyzing the project's progress and performance. It breaks the projects into small and well-defined tasks that are easier to estimate and manage than larger packages of work. Project work breakdown structure also provides a multilevel structure for analyzing the project at varying degrees of detail. From a well-defined PWBS, earned value can be measured at various levels of the PWBS such as phases and milestones.

   To properly manage a detailed PWBS, project managers need project planning and tracking tools capable of visually defining and managing the PWBS with unlimited levels of hierarchy.

2. *Allocate resources and define budgets for each PWBS element.* An accurate EVA depends on a project budget that is not only accurate, but includes enough detail for each element of the PWBS so that partial comparisons of budgeted costs and actual costs are meaningful. Therefore, managers must budget costs for each element of the PWBS, and keep the detailed budget updated as the scope of the project changes.

   For some projects, it is appropriate to track budgets based on hours worked and ignore the dollar amounts associated with the work. For others, it may make more sense to track the number of hours required, and multiply by an average rate per hour to determine the dollar budget. Project planning and tracking tools provide flexible budget tracking based on the type of work performed, skills required, resource cost, and project or client negotiated rates. In addition to labor costs, managers can budget for time, expenses, material, and capital expenditures.

3. *Track the actual cost of work performed.* After defining the PWBS structure and allocating resources for each element, it is important to track the actual cost of work performed against each PWBS element. Accurate and up-to-date actual tracking is essential for precise and timely EV analysis. The project tracking tool must have the following capabilities:

   - Ability for project managers to assign tasks to project contributors; project contributors should be able to quickly see their schedules and tasks.
   - Timesheet interface that reflects the PWBS and resource assignments; each resource must be able to view their time-scaled work assignments and enter actual effort against the assigned task.
   - An easy and efficient way to track time, expenses, and materials for each PWBS element.
   - Approval process for all time and expense entries.
   - Ability to accurately track labor costs.
   - Full integration with project planning to update the project plan and progress; plan can be updated in real time or only after time and expense are approved.

4. *Track the actual work performed.* Tracking the cost of work performed is only meaningful if it is accompanied by a measurement of the amount of work performed for that cost. Using a project tracking tool, scheduled tasks are reported as started, completed, or in progress, as appropriate. The percentage complete of unfinished activities must also be reported for an accurate EVA.

   For physical work, it is usually easy to determine the percentage of work completed. For example, if 100 widgets are to be produced, and 30 are completed to date, then the task is 30 percent complete. For product development, software development, or an IT project, actual work is not as easy to measure. For example, if a programmer is performing a task budgeted at 100 hours, has completed 50 hours, but only reports being 20 percent done, it is difficult to estimate the actual progress of the project. Two methods can be employed to assess the percentage complete for these types of projects:

   - Report percent complete according to completed milestones within the activity. For example, the milestone "Complete Design Document" might be broken down as follows: preliminary research complete, 20 percent; first draft complete, 40 percent; team reviews submitted, 70 percent; final approval, 100 percent. The key in defining this kind of rule is that each milestone is discrete, and its criterion for achievement is clear and specific.

- Report an estimate-to-complete (ETC), which consists of the best estimate of the actual amount of work remaining rather than the amount of work performed. This is very effective for large projects where implementation plans change frequently, or when work performed faces great uncertainty due to the type of work or technology used. The ETC method relies heavily on the easy and fast collaboration among team members and project managers, so that they can obtain accurate and timely estimates of the work remaining and actual work performed.

Earned Value Analysis Examples

Based on the defined budget, cost, and actual work performed, a project manager can use the EVA to provide an indication of the project status. The examples that follow show how EVA can answer questions about the project status easily and accurately.

For the examples, we use the following assumptions:

RES1 is a software designer and costs $80/hour.

RES2 is a software designer and.costs $100/hour.

USING EVA TO DETERMINE WHERE YOU ARE.   There are many ways to measure cost. For example, we could measure actual money spent. However, it is common in a work environment to measure cost in terms of *labor*—that is, in work hours or work days spent. Thus the budget for a project could be $30,000 or it could be 300 labor hours, and the amount spent so far could be $4,500 or it might be 45 labor hours. EVA can be used with any unit of measure, but it is important to decide which one to use. The level of detail available to track project cost is usually dependent on the project-tracking tool used. For example:

A task called "Module Design" has a BCWS of 20 days @ 8 hours per day, and the work is split equally between RES1 and RES2.

After five days of work on the project, the recorded actuals from the project tracking tool are as follows:
- RES1 has missed one day of work on the project due to an emergency on another project.
- Based on the milestones reached for RES1 it was determined that he has accomplished 45 percent of the overall work scheduled.
- RES2 has worked all five days on the project.
- RES2 encountered problems with one of the tools used and estimates that he will require two additional days to complete the task (ETC Method).
- Based on this information provided RES2 has performed $5/12 = 42$ percent of the work scheduled.

INDICATOR	CALCULATION	COMMENT
BCWS	$5 \times 8 \times \$80 + 5 \times 8 \times \$100 = \$7,200$	
BCWP	$(0.45 \times 80) \times \$80 + (0.42 \times 80) \times \$100 = \$6,240$	
ACWP	$32 \times \$80 + 40 \times \$100 = \$6,560$	
SV	BCWP − BCWS = 6,240 − \$7,200	The project is behind schedule.
SPI	BCWP / BCWS = 0.87	The project is running at 87% of the planned schedule.
CV	BCWP − ACWP = −320	The project is \$320 over budget even though less work than schedule was done by RES1.
CPI	BCWP / ACWP = 0.95	The project is over budget by about 5%.

Table 10.2   Earned Value Analysis Example

EVA based on this information is shown in Table 10.2.

FORECAST SCHEDULE AND COST VARIANCE.   EVA can be used to forecast the total cost and schedule for the project based on the information calculated previously. Using the example above, the measures are used to estimate the cost and schedule at the end of the project (see Table 10.3).

A LATE PROJECT.   Once it has been determined that a project is behind schedule or over budget, the next question is usually: Can something be done to get back on track? The TCPI is an indication of how the team must perform for the duration of the project in order to meet the desired cost goal. If TCPI is

INDICATOR	CALCULATION	COMMENT
BAC	$10 \times 8 \times 80 + 10 \times 8 \times 100 = \$14,400$	Budget at completion.
IEAC	BAC/CPI = \$16,552	Estimated budget at project completion based on project performance so far.
VAC	BAC − IEAC = −\$2,152	Budget variance at end of project if performance is maintained.
ISAC	Schedule/SPI = 160/0.95 = 168.5	The project is behind schedule.

Table 10.3   Schedule and Cost Valiance Example

greater than 1, the team must perform better than planned in order to meet the goal; and if it's less than 1 you can get by with performing under the plan.

TCPI compares the amount of work remaining with the budget remaining to spend. The remaining work is calculated based on the difference between our initial budgeted cost for work scheduled and budgeted cost for work performed. The budget left to spend is the difference between the budget approved and actual cost spent of performing the work. It is at this point where upper management reviews project budget and deliverables and modifies either one or both in order to achieve a TCPI value close to 1.

In the previous example, suppose you want to finish at exactly $14,400 budget:

$$TCPI = \frac{(14,400 - 6,240)}{(14,400 - 6,560)} = 1.04$$

This means that the team must perform at 104 percent of the originally planned performance in order to achieve this goal, that is, 4 percent higher performance than originally planned.

Budget and Status Reports

All projects, large or small, usually require a formal budget. Both time and cost budgets are extremely important for any project. Without a formal budget it is very difficult for the project manager to control the project's scope and manage change.

Project Budget

When a budget is defined, it should be broken down into labor and non-labor costs including any travel, services, capital expenditure (equipment) and material costs. Table 10.4 shows the potential difference (or delta) between a project's original budget, its current estimate, and its actuals.

A planning tool allows the project manager to compare budgets, estimates and actuals for individual tasks, milestones or the total project. A notification

	BUDGET	ESTIMATE	ACTUAL	BUDGET	ESTIMATE
Time (hours)	100	85	90	−10	−5
Cost ($)	10,000	8,500	9,000	−1,000	−500

Table 10.4   Sample Project Budget Report

system automatically informs the project manager, either by e-mail or other means, if the project's total budget or a task's budget has been exceeded. Integration with a timesheet system enables the project manager to suspend some tasks or the entire project if a budget has been exceeded. Also, rules can be defined in the workflow engine to automatically suspend tasks (see Chapter 7, "The Workflow Foundation").

Progress Reporting

There are several ways in which project contributors can report on their progress and communicate with project managers. Here are three main mechanisms project contributors use to report on their progress:

1. *Effort tracking:* Project planning tools are often integrated with an enterprise timesheet management system (see Chapter 11, "Enterprise Timesheet Management"). The timesheet system tracks time for the entire company for all planned and unplanned project work, nonproject work, and paid or unpaid leave time. Project planning should integrate with the timesheet system as follows:

   • Once a project plan is created and resources are assigned to tasks, the plan is sent to the timesheet system.

   • Project contributors see their assignments on their timesheets when they log in so they know what to work on.

   • Project contributors enter the amount of work done (also known as actual work or effort) in every timesheet period (weekly, bi-weekly, etc. depending on the company's policies).

   • The plan is automatically updated so that the project manager can determine whether the project is on track and to make schedule, budget, or scope adjustments as necessary.

2. *Estimate to complete:* Having team members provide an estimate to complete for each major activity or deliverable is an invaluable tool for the project manager. By evaluating a team member's ETC for every project task, a project manager can evaluate whether the project's budget and schedule are on track, or whether any plan changes are necessary.

   Allowing each member of the team to specify the amount of time they estimate to complete a task ensures that the project manager has the information needed to update the project's budget and schedule. The ETC can be turned on or off on a per-task basis since the project manager may not want to allow schedule deviations for certain tasks.

   Here is an example of an ETC communication:

   • The project manager has allocated 20 hours for Task ABC to John.

   • John works 10 hours on the task but he says he needs another 30 hours to complete the work. He uses the ETC field for Task ABC in order to communicate this. Therefore, he is only 25 percent done.

- The project manager can decide to revise the task's end date to give John more time to complete the work, assign part of the work to someone else, or ask John to work harder and keep the same end date.

3. *Status reports:* Together, timesheets and ETC do a good job of tracking effort and percentage complete on a per-task basis. This information is the basis of EVA explained earlier in the chapter. In addition, most project managers want to see a written weekly or monthly status report by project managers that summarizes in words:

- What was accomplished in the last week
- What the plans are for the following week
- Comments on any yellow or red flag tasks or subprojects
- Concerns, obstacles, or challenges that the project contributor needs help with

   Status reports, if consistent at all, are usually e-mails, spreadsheets, or another decentralized forms of documentation. Critical project insight may be lost when project status reporting is managed this way. Status reports can be automated using the Project Workforce Management's workflow engine. With a workflow engine, status reporting is a consistent, audited, and dependable process:

- Status reports are automatically created based on the company's template and pushed to project contributors for the status report cycle (example every week).
- The project contributor completes the status report.
- The status reports are automatically routed by the workflow system to project managers.
- The workflow system alerts any users who are late submitting their status reports.
- Project managers review the status reports and follow up as necessary.
- All status reports are maintained in a searchable centralized database. Management and auditors have full access to all project status reports for any audit or review exercise.

Schedule Management Techniques

Project managers use various types of schedule management techniques, each having a specific purpose. The most commonly used schedule management techniques are the milestone schedule and the deliverable schedule.

Milestone Schedule

A milestone schedule is created by the project team and the customer to evaluate progress toward the final objective. This schedule helps the team by defining the sequence of the project's major milestones and the time in which they need to be completed. Milestone schedules are a good way of tracking and getting paid for billable projects.

Milestones are recorded on the project timeline, between the first milestone, which is the project start date, and the last milestone, which is the project finish date. It is strongly recommended that the number of major milestones in a given project timeline be kept to 10 or less.

Deliverable Schedule

A deliverable schedule facilitates the transition of a deliverable from one team or person to another. It shows the sequence of deliverables to be created, from first to last, and who is accountable for meeting the completion dates for each deliverable. Deliverable schedules are a good way of tracking product development, research, and development as well as IT projects, especially when a large number of project contributors and teams are involved.

Typically, a deliverable is depicted as a subproject of the main project. Each deliverable can be further broken down to show the activities that need to be performed by various resources in order to complete the deliverable.

NOTE

1. Taking into account resource availability and forecasting accuracy constraints can improve critical path analysis. Look for books on critical chain project management.

11

Enterprise Timesheet Management

Time is the scarcest resource and unless it is managed nothing else can be managed.

—Peter F. Drucker

Labor represents the number one cost for most businesses. Because of the impact that labor costs have on the bottom line, and the inherent complexities of managing and recording the work needs and habits of people, streamlining a company's timesheet processes can have a large and immediate positive impact on the company's return on investment.

Enterprise timesheet management reduces compliance costs and administrative overhead, improves project visibility, accelerates billing, tracks performance, and enhances decision making by providing dependable real-time cost and billing analysis. But despite the benefits, automation of the timesheet management cycle must be approached carefully so that its adoption is accepted by the entire organization.

This chapter explains the benefits of automating timesheet management and describes its main characteristics including the timesheet management cycle, approval workflows, and integration points with other enterprise software systems.

What Is Enterprise Timesheet Management?

Enterprise timesheet management is the process of centralizing and streamlining timesheet processes for all work done in the entire company, including any planned and unplanned project work, nonproject work, and paid or unpaid leave. A timesheet system results in immediate efficiencies, improved work analysis, and financial visibility. It also ensures compliance with governance,

139

labor, and accounting regulations. Tracking of work performed for other business units or billable projects provides the necessary information for effective cost allocation and performance and resource utilization analysis.

Enterprise timesheet management is more than just a time and attendance system that links to payroll. It provides the means to ensure work is accurately tracked, costs are allocated to the appropriate projects and cost objectives, and projects are delivered on time and within budget. Project and service-oriented organizations experience tremendous benefits by capturing accurate and relevant cost and billing information in a timely and efficient manner. A timesheet system drastically reduces administrative tasks and paper-intensive procedures, and avoids the heavy maintenance and training costs associated with multiple disconnected or custom-built timesheet systems.

Project- and service-oriented organizations are constantly challenged to improve worker productivity. For example, a business unit that delivers billable services tries to minimize bench time (the amount of time that billable resources are not assigned to billable work); or an IT department tries to stay within its annual budget even while it is flooded with new projects and scope change requests.

Many of the difficulties in improving productivity are caused when necessary information for making decisions is not collected, is collected but not available with the sufficient level of detail, is inconsistent, or all of these. Managers of each department need direct and real-time access to their groups' timesheets in order to be able to track internal costs and calculate billing or chargeback information. For these reasons, management teams often require functionality well beyond what a departmental or custom-built time and attendance solution can provide.

All organizations should track work against two major reporting structures. First, the organization must define who does the work—which is referred to as the organizational breakdown structure (OBS). Second, the organization should define the nature of the work being done, and for whom it is being done, known as the work breakdown structure (WBS; see Chapter 6, "Organization and Work Breakdown Structures"). In essence, a company needs to organize, track, analyze, and manage all its time information using the OBS and WBS. Tracking time against the OBS and WBS elements is also known as accounting for *differentiated time* (see Chapter 1, "The Rise of the Project Workforce").

Timesheet Management Requirements

As shown in Figure 11.1, enterprise timesheet management addresses the following requirements:

- *Labor law compliance:* Provides automatic compliance with state and federal labor laws as it relates to work hours, overtime, and leave time management

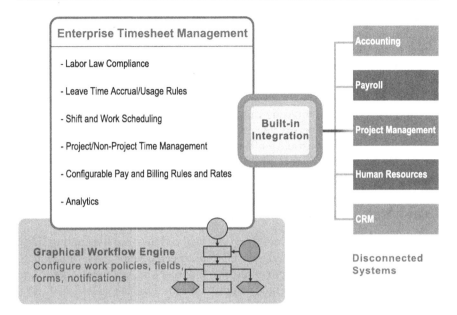

Figure 11.1   Enterprise Timesheet Management

- *Leave time accrual:* Calculates paid and unpaid leave time eligibility and accrues paid leave time based on the company's policies
- *Shift and work scheduling:* Manages shifts and work schedules so that managers and employees can collaborate on what to work on next
- *Project and nonproject time management:* Tracks all types of work whether it is billable or not including any project work or nonproject work, as well as any paid and unpaid leave time
- *Configurable pay and billing rules and rates:* Calculates the cost and billing of every single time entry for reporting and billing purposes, taking into account a variety of compensation and billing scenarios (fixed, hourly, milestone based, etc.)
- *Time and labor analytics:* Provides reports and analytics so that management can evaluate performance and identify areas to be improved

In addition, the timesheet system integrates with other enterprise applications so that project and resource cost and billing information is managed and maintained in a single data source and yet shared enterprise-wide.

Differentiated Time Equals Activity-Based Costing

Differentiated time, also referred to as activity-based costing (ABC), is the foundation of an enterprise timesheet system. Activity-based costing tracks work at the activity level, providing the lowest level of detail necessary to capture all the required information about the work being performed. A timesheet system allows association of generic work types to projects in order to create a task (in some businesses, projects are called accounts and tasks are referred to as activities or jobs). Tasks are assigned to employees and consultants for work tracking purposes.

The major challenge in using this functionality is to balance the benefits a detailed ABC provides versus the associated overhead. Too many levels of detail will create an administrative effort far outweighing the benefits. However, your organization may have compliance or other requirements that make capturing more detailed information a necessity.

Labor Law Compliance

As described in Chapter 5, "Complying with Labor Laws and Accounting Regulations," there are several federal and state-specific labor laws with which every company must comply. An enterprise timesheet management system can be configured to track and enforce compliance with these laws.

These laws describe minimum wage guidelines, regular and overtime pay rules, and paid/unpaid leave time accrual and usage. The sections that follow outline how enterprise timesheet management supports these regulations.

PAID/UNPAID LEAVE TIME ACCRUAL AND USAGE RULES. Timesheet management systems (Figure 11.2) have a leave management component that allows the company to define and enforce the company's paid and unpaid leave time (also known as paid time off; PTO) accrual and usage rules. Leave management affords these benefits:

- Minimizes the company's exposure to liability and employee grievances related to leave time
- Reduces costs associated to unauthorized leave time

Timesheet of: John Doe	Week of: 02/27/2007							
Leave Time Balances:								
Vacation: 80 hrs		Sick Leave: 16 hrs				Personal Days: 8 hrs		
Task Name	Sun 27	Mon 28	Tue 29	Wed 30	Thu 31	Fri 1	Sat 2	Total:
Preliminary Investigation Stage								
Evaluate Market	4	3	2					9
Analyse the Competition		5	6					11
Sub Total	4	8	8					20
Non-Working Time								
Personal Day					8			8
Sick leave						8		8
Unpaid Leave	4							4
Sub Total	4				8	8		20
Total for week	8	8	8	8	8			40

Figure 11.2   Leave Time Reporting

- Frees managers to focus on their core responsibilities by automating leave-related administrative activities

The main functions of a leave management system include:

- Manage paid and unpaid leave.
- Calculate accruals and leave balances based on various criteria including resource type, seniority, and other factors.
- Provide employees with self-service dashboards and reports so they can see their leave balances for themselves.
- Set alerts if leave balances reach certain predetermined thresholds.
- Provide a configurable leave request approval form, workflow, and notifications.
- Update employee's availability and timesheet based on an approved leave request.
- Use leave time reports to analyze, identify, and forecast absence trends and patterns.
- Automatically update user timesheets and availability based on their regional holidays.

The following two examples show how leave management controls leave time accrual and usage:

1. *Vacation:* The company's vacation rule is as follows: Eight hours of vacation is earned for every 200 hours of service and vacation must be used in multiples of eight hours (full days). Therefore, employees will automatically accumulate vacation time based on this rule, and they will not be able to enter vacation time in their timesheets in any increments other than the full eight hours.

2. *Sick leave:* The company grants every employee three paid sick leave days per year (assuming eight work hours per day). The sick leave bank is reset to zero each year, and any unused sick leave days are paid as a bonus. Therefore, employees can enter a maximum of 24 hours of paid sick leave on their timesheets; any hours above this threshold will be automatically counted as unpaid leave.

Shift Work Scheduling

Organizations are increasingly operating on a 24/7 schedule. A poorly devised shift plan can lead to inadequate coverage, stressed and overworked employees, and lower customer satisfaction. The planning challenge becomes even more complicated as the number of shift workers grows from tens to hundreds or thousands of employees. Frequently, workers operate in multiple time zones and regions, each having unique vacation and holiday requirements. Schedules can also become complicated when a company must accommodate part-time or seasonal workers (Figure 11.3).

Traditional project management systems and related concepts[1] are designed to serve the needs of project workers; therefore, they do not provide any capabilities to handle nonexempt employees. Companies that employ nonexempt and part-time workers must either develop a custom timesheet program, or invest in a workforce management application that is disconnected from the project management system. Shift and work scheduling component of a Project Workforce Management system addresses these shift planning and scheduling challenges.

Main benefits of treating time and attendance management as an integral part of Project Workforce Management are:

- It provides a single enterprise-wide system to track employee availability, skills, work time, pay, project and nonproject work, paid and unpaid leave, leave requests, expense reports, billing, and other project, workforce and financial related work processes.

- It centralizes real-time reporting and analysis of all work across multiple resource groups.

In addition to these, a time and attendance system offers its own set of measurable benefits to the organization:

- Reduces payroll preparation time by 80 percent (American Payroll Association).

- Reduces time misappropriation (e.g., long lunches, early departures, late arrivals) that accounts for up to 4.08 hours per week (American Payroll Association).

Period start: 01/17/2007

Vacation: 80 hrs				Sick Leave: 16 hrs		
Mon 01/17	Tue 01/18	Wed 01/19	Thu 01/20	Fri 01/21	Sat 01/22	Sun 01/23

− Client	Project	Task	From	To	Duration
Internal	Administration	Regular Time	9:00	12:00	3:00
Internal	Administration	Wellness	12:30	14:00	1:30
Internal	Administration	Shared	14:00	15:00	1:00
Internal ▼	Administration ▼	Regular Time ▼			

− Read-Only Summary View	Mon 01/17	Tue 01/18	Wed 01/19	Thu 01/20	Fri 01/21	Sat 01/22	Sun 01/23	Total
Regular Time	3:00	3:00						00:00
Wellness	1:30	3:30						00:00
Shared	1:00	3:00						00:00
− Leave Time								
Leave W/O Pay (411)								00:00
Total Time	05:30	08:00	00:00	00:00	00:00	00:00	00:00	13:30
Worked Schedule Total Time	08:00	08:00	08:00	08:00	08:00	00:00	00:00	40:00

Figure 11.3   Shift Work Entry

- Automatically detects and indicates tardiness, absenteeism, and erroneous entries.
- Reduces average timesheet review time by 80 percent. (Average timesheet review takes six minutes. With automated policy validation and exception highlighting, configurable workflows, time is reduced to one minute.)

The main features to expect from a time and attendance system are as follows:

- Defines rotating or repeated employee schedules and shifts, with strict or flexible attendance rules, breaks, premiums, and overtime policies.
- Employees are forced to work on specific shifts or can choose a shift.
- Automatic time entries for the employee based on the employee's shifts and schedule; employee can make changes as necessary.
- Ability for managers to see the employee's scheduled shifts and any exceptions before approval; approval is automated for timesheets that have no exceptions.
- Built-in conformance with state and federal labor laws such as California wage laws, Fair Labor Standards Act (FLSA), and Family Medical Leave Act (FMLA). (See Chapter 5, "Complying with Labor Laws and Accounting Regulations.")
- Visual definition of the company's time reporting policy, including minimum and maximum work days, overtime rules, shifts, premiums, and paid/unpaid leave time usage; the system enforces the rules at the point of entry.

Project/Nonproject Time Management

For project workers, the timesheet system integrates with project planning tools to import the list of work assignments (Table 11.1). Employees enter time against the detailed tasks assigned to them and use Estimated Time to Complete[2] to collaborate with the project manager if any plan adjustments are necessary. Any nonproject work such as meetings, interviews, administrative work, training leave time, and other tasks are also reported using the same timesheet system.

Configurable Pay Rules and Rates

An enterprise timesheet system is the company's central cost-accounting and detailed, project-level revenue tracking system. It is therefore necessary to be able to specify the company's pay and billing rules including any special bonus or payment arrangements. Timesheet systems support various types of pay rules including hourly, daily, fixed (salaried) pay rules. Timesheet systems that

RESOURCE	ETC	TIME (HOURS)				
		MON	TUE	WED	THU	FRI
Project: A	4	4	5	6	5	24
Analysis	4				3	
Meeting with customer		2	3			
Issue resolution		2	2	6	2	
Project: B	5	4	8	4	2	23
Research	4	2	4			
Issue 512		1				
Issue 322		1	2	2	2	
Fit to business	1		2	2		

Table 11.1   A Sample Timesheet With Project Line Items

incorporate time and attendance capabilities also support overtime, shift, and premium pay for nonexempt workers.

Since the same timesheet solution is being used to track billing, enterprise timesheet systems support the variety of billing rules and scenarios that you find in companies offering professional services (see Chapter 14, "Billing, Chargeback, and Invoicing").

Analytics

Analytics provides managers with instant resource group and project status reports. For example, a group manager can quickly find out how much vacation has been taken by the group over the past year and how much remains unused (Table 11.2). A billing manager can get a report of the billable hours for last month and project managers can find out how much time has been spent on their projects. Reports can be simple two-dimensional text reports or consist of pie charts, bar charts, and/or other forms of graphics. Time reports can also be embedded in various executive dashboards.

Other Requirements

Other notable timesheet management requirements are as follows:

- *Multiple timesheet views:* How timesheets are presented to employees in one department may be different from another since there are various

RESOURCE	PERIOD	STATUS	TIME (HOURS)		
			REGULAR	BILLABLE	LEAVE
Group: Engineering					
John Murphy	01/29/2007 to 02/04/2007	Completed	40	40	0
Zack Norman	01/29/2007 to 02/04/2007	Completed	35	20	8
Jessy Thompson	02/04/2007 to 02/11/2007	Open	20	10	0
Group: Sales					
Patrick Wong	01/29/2007 to 02/04/2007	Completed	40	0	0
Adrian Stevenson	01/29/2007 to 02/04/2007	Completed	40	0	8
Jack Wu	01/29/2007 to 02/04/2007	Completed	40	0	0
Orlando Jones	01/29/2007 to 02/04/2007	Completed	40	0	0

Table 11.2   Sample Timesheet Manager Report

types of resource groups in any organization (see Today's Workforce section that follows for more information). The timesheet system should allow the company to configure the timesheet view for every resource group. For example, administrative staff may be asked to enter leave time only, since their regular work is on the same repetitive administrative tasks.

- *Multiple notes and note enforcement policy:* Depending on the company's timesheet management policy and various timekeeping regulations, the employee or manager may be required to enter a note when a time entry is modified.

- *Postperiod close adjustments:* One of the most difficult manual tasks is to correct errors in past timesheets that may impact employee pay, paid overtime calculations, billing, and leave time accrual. Timesheet systems that support postperiod close adjustments will automatically make the necessary adjustments.

- *Management by exception:* Timesheets that always have the same tasks can be automatically approved. Managers will be asked to approve timesheets only if they have any exceptions such as leave time entries or any unusual work patterns.

Enterprise Timesheet Management Cycle

The timesheet management life cycle (Figure 11.4) outlines how work and nonwork time is tracked, reported, approved, and processed. The process is briefly described as follows:

- Employees, consultants, and field workers enter time; the system validates the timesheet at the point of entry based on the company's policies.
- The timesheet is sent to the designated person(s) for approval/review.
- Once approved, the timesheet is forwarded to payroll/accounting for processing.
- If any billable work is done, the time entries are reported to the billing manager for invoicing purposes.
- Project plans and schedules are updated to reflect the actual work done; project managers can measure earned value and actual project performance.
- Detailed or summary cost, as well as billing information, is exported to the accounting system for financial reporting.

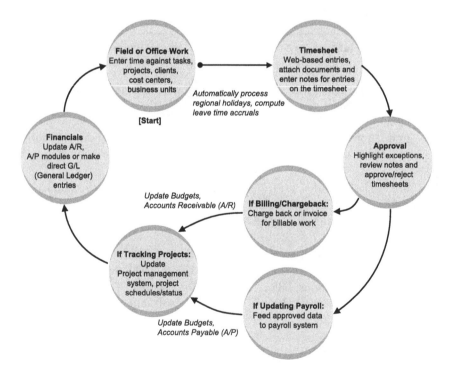

Figure 11.4   Timesheet Management Cycle

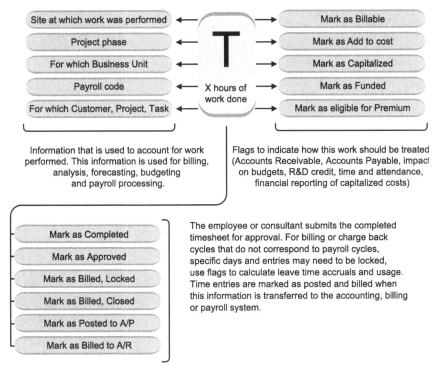

Figure 11.5   A Time Entry

- Project cost allocation, resource performance, billing, and time information is made available for inclusion in executive dashboards, reports, and for real-time analysis.

The Time Entry

Figure 11.5 shows the many different attributes and information that are linked to a time entry. Behind the scenes, an enterprise timesheet management system is tracking this information so that payroll, billing, cost allocation, project tracking, and reporting can occur in real time.

Today's Workforce

In any project- or service-oriented organization there are many different types of resource groups, each one having its own unique timesheet approval process requirements. A typical arrangement of resource groups is shown in Figure 11.6.

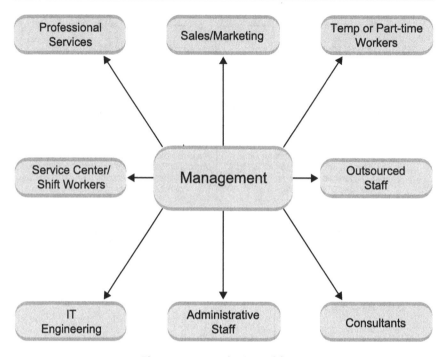

Figure 11.6   Today's Workforce

- *Engineering or IT department:* This group is usually made up of exempt employees who work on a variety of projects. Their time is typically tracked as a percentage of the day they spend on various projects, not in terms of hours.
- *Professional services team:* This team performs billable services that generate revenues. Its time is usually tracked in 5- or 15-minute increments against projects (or engagements). Practically every minute of work must be accounted for and justified.
- *Administrative staff:* These workers do the same type of work day in and day out. They enter time against no more than three to four different categories, such as General Admin, Data Entry, Payroll Admin, or Accounting. Their timesheets are usually managed by exception, meaning managers only have to verify their timesheets for leave time entries. Administrative workers are typically nonexempt employees who get paid overtime as defined by federal and state laws.
- *Service center representatives/shift workers:* This group of workers has an elaborate compensation plan that includes different hourly rates depending on the shift, a premium pay for after hour or weekend service, on call

time if they are asked to carry a cell phone when away from work, and overtime pay for exceeding the hours as defined in the standard work week. Shift workers enter time against their scheduled shifts and, using their timesheet interface, can change shifts as appropriate.

- *Outsourced staff:* In the most typical scenario, the outsourced partner agrees to provide qualified resources based on an hourly, daily, weekly, or monthly rate with an agreed on minimum and maximum number of hours of work. In this case, every outsourced resource must enter time against the projects or tasks he/she is working on, so that the company can track costs, efficiency, and progress. Outsourced workers would not be eligible for any type of paid leave time, and their timesheets should be configured to display only eligible projects and tasks.
- *Consultants:* Hired on a contract basis and paid on an hourly, daily, or a fixed-cost basis, consultants are usually required to submit detailed timesheets and are not eligible for any paid leave.
- *Temporary or part-time workers:* May or may not be entitled to vacation and overtime pay, depending on their exempt/non-exempt status and the number of hours they work per week. Timesheets for such workers must be configured to accommodate for the shorter work week and leave time accrual, and usage rules if these apply.
- *Sales/marketing and executives:* These groups are usually exempt employees who are working on a variety of sales, marketing, and operational related tasks but are generally not doing project work. Their timesheets are usually managed by exception, meaning managers only have to verify their timesheets for leave time entries.

Timesheet Management Workflows

Timesheet Approval

The timesheet approval workflow (Figure 11.7) uses the same business process foundation described in Chapter 7, "The Workflow Foundation," and tracks timesheets from creation to end. The graphical workflow allows the company to define states, transitions, and roles that control the business process. Each state can be assigned to multiple or alternate approvers. The company can create several workflows to accommodate the diverse needs of its various resource groups and business units. For example, a different timesheet workflow would be used to track a professional services unit (to formally approve billable work), another for engineering (line item approval of project chargeback), and yet another for administrative staff (a simple nonproject based timesheet approval process mostly focused on managing leave time and exceptions).

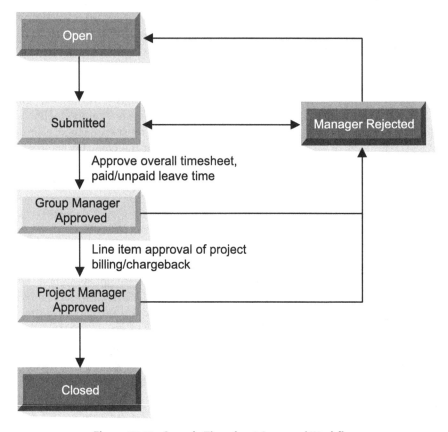

Figure 11.7   Sample Timesheet Approval Workflow

Line Item Approval

Often, project managers are sharing resources with managers of other projects. Each manager approves or rejects time entries at the task level—also known as *line item approval*—but project managers can only approve the line items that belong to their respective projects.

Leave Request

The leave request workflow automates the leave request and approval processes. Employees have access to a leave request form that they can complete and submit online. The form asks the employee to specify the reason for the leave (vacation, sick leave, or other reason), whether it is a paid or unpaid leave, an explanation for the request and the departure and return dates. If the

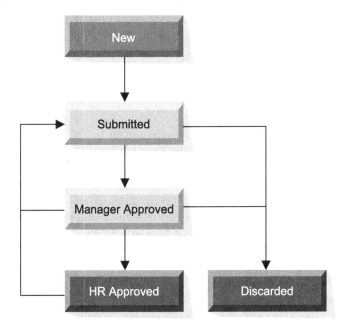

Figure 11.8   Sample Leave Request Workflow

manager and human resource representative approve the request (the workflow shown in Figure 11.8 may include as many approvers as the company requires), the employee's timesheet is automatically completed on their behalf for
the leave time. The employee's availability is also updated in his or her calendar
so that no work is assigned while the employee is away. Appropriate notifications are sent to anyone who needs to know about the employee's absence.

Integration

An enterprise timesheet management system can integrate with many other
mission-critical applications. For more detailed information, see Chapter 20,
"Integration." The following is a brief overview of integration points with a
timesheet system:

- *Integration with workforce planning:* A workforce planning system is
  used to book resources against projects. Resource plans can be automatically imported into employee timesheets as assignments or task filters so
  that employees can see their project assignments. Also, regular, paid, and
  unpaid leave time entered in timesheets can update resource availability
  and utilization rates for future performance measurements and capacity
  planning.

- *Integration with project planning:* A project planning system is used to create a detailed project plan down to the task level; resources are then assigned to perform those tasks. The assignments can be automatically imported into the timesheet system so that employees can see their detailed task assignments. As actual work is completed, the project plan is updated from the timesheet data, and project managers can evaluate planned versus actual work.

- *Integration with payroll:* Timesheet data can be fed into payroll using either associated pay codes or pure time entries. This depends on which system (the timesheet or the payroll system) is calculating the actual pay, based on pay rules.

- *Integration with billing:* Timesheet data can be fed into the billing system. The system can export either billable amounts associated to billing codes or pure time entries. This depends on which system (the timesheet or the billing system) is calculating the actual billing amounts, based on billing rules.

- *Integration with accounting:* Time entries can update accounts payable data as costs that are applied to one or more cost centers. Likewise, time entries that represent billable hours can also update accounts receivable data for revenue centers. The timesheet system can also be used to calculate work in progress (billable work done but not yet billed) and export this information to the accounting system for financial reporting purposes.

- *Integration with customer relationship management:* Account executives can check the status of a billable project to see how much work has been done, how much of the project has been billed, and what work remains to be done.

NOTES

1. Project Management Body of Knowledge (PMBOK) (*source:* www.pmi.org).
2. See Chapter 10, "Project Planning."

12

Travel and Entertainment and Expense Management

Beware of the little expenses; a small leak will sink a great ship.
—Benjamin Franklin

Most (75%) organizations are still using a process that is highly manual. Due to the high transaction volume and manual nature of the process, noncompliance and outright fraud can fall between the cracks. Indirect costs account for approximately 20%–30% of an organization's total expenses. Of that, 30% is "rogue" spending. These are the likely areas where fraud or unsupported activity can be found.[1]

Travel and entertainment (T&E) expenses is the second largest cost for most companies after labor; however, expense control procedures are often extremely labor-intensive due to the lack of effective tools and disconnected solutions. Project deliverables and budgets can be severely impacted if expenses are mismanaged or misallocated. Streamlining expense reporting and control processes can bring substantial benefits to an organization by reducing the amount of administrative tasks, automating repetitive paper-intensive processes, allocating costs, expediting billing, and providing enterprise-wide expense reporting and analysis. Even a small gain in expense management efficiency can have enormous benefits and a positive impact on an organization's top and bottom line.

Expense management is complex in today's flat world due to a number of factors. Globalization means that more companies must manage expenses in multiple currencies and tax jurisdictions. Most workers—many who travel to various countries to perform project-based work—capture expenses in spreadsheets or custom systems. Expense reporting is error prone because spreadsheets and even handwritten expense reports are verified by clerks, rekeyed into other systems or spreadsheets, and sent to accounting for reimbursement and financial reporting.

155

In a professional services firm, the situation is aggravated further because both billable and nonbillable expenses for fixed-cost projects can represent a major portion of the total project costs. These costs need to be properly tracked and billed.

The collection and approval of expense reports is not the only difficulty. In a nonautomated system, it is difficult or impossible to implement limits and preset amounts (per diems). It is also labor-intensive to track and report on past expenses. Sharing expense data with other systems (such as project management) presents further challenges. In most cases, the proper gathering of this information is simply neglected, because the cost of compilation is too high. Exchanging information with other applications is accomplished by the manual rekeying of data, which is not only a resource-intensive task, but it also greatly increases the probability of error.

Whether a company is tracking billable costs or has established a budget for spending by project, expenses must be classified correctly and allocated to the right projects so that project managers can control costs and better forecast future spending trends.

Automation Benefits

Some of the quantitative benefits associated with expense report automation include:

- The average cost to manually process an expense report is approximately $40, and can be as high as $80 for some organizations.[2] An automated solution can reduce expense-processing costs by at least 40 percent and possibly as high as 90 percent.
- The second-largest corporate expense today is travel and entertainment.
- The Hackett Group has found that on average a corporation processes 20,000 expense reports for every $1 billion in revenue.[3]
- American Express Consulting Services revealed that the average expense report costs more than $36 and can take up to 18 days to process. This cost represents 3 to 15 percent over the total T&E budget.[4]
- *CFO* magazine's annual selling, general, and administration (SG&A) survey concluded that for most organizations, cutting just $1 of operational costs could have the same impact on the bottom line as increasing the revenue by $13.[5]

The manual processing of expense reports is inefficient, results in redundant data entry, and it is also highly prone to human error. Every expense-reporting process that a company streamlines can dramatically reduce the costs of data entry, administration, reimbursement, and approval (see Figure 12.1 and Table 12.1).

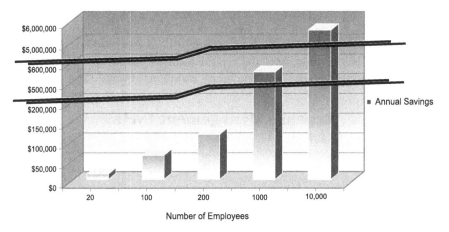

Figure 12.1   Annual Savings from Expense Automation

Number of employees submitting expense reports	20	50	100	200	1,000	10,000
Number of expense reports annually (assuming one each month)	240	600	1,200	2,400	12,000	120,000
Total administrative cost savings[a,c]	$6,852	$17,130	$34,260	$68,520	$342,600	$3,426,000
Total productivity cost savings[b,c]	$4,000	$10,000	$20,000	$40,000	$200,000	$2,000,000
Total actual cost savings annually	$10,852	$27,130	$54,260	$108,520	$542,600	$5,426,000

[a] The average cost savings per expense report processed is $28.55, which is calculated as $36.46 (the average cost per expense report processed without automation) minus $7.91 (the best-in-class cost per expense report processed with automation).

[b] The average productivity savings per expense report is 40 minutes, which is calculated as 55 minutes (the average processing time per expense report) minus 15 minutes (best-in-class processing time per expense report). Every employee saves 40 minutes × 12/60 = 8 hours per employee/year. Assuming an annual average salary of $50,000/50 weeks/40 hours = $25/hour.

[c] Rusty Carpenter, David Marcus, and Alan Sandusky, 2001 American Express Travel Related Services Co, June 2001.

Table 12.1   Cost Savings from Mechanizing Expense Reports

An expense management system provides strict controls over direct and indirect costs. Organizational expense policies are enforced at the point of entry and are an integral part of the expense reporting, approval, and reimbursement processes. Table 12.1 presents the typical savings that can be expected by mechanizing expense report creation for organizations of various sizes.

Expense Management Cycle

The expense management life cycle (Figure 12.2) outlines how expenses are tracked, reported, approved, and processed. The process is briefly described as follows:

1. Employees, consultants, and field workers create and submit expense reports; the system validates the report at the point of entry based on corporate policies. Workers are able to import credit card transactions automatically to reduce manual entry.
2. The expense report is sent to the designated person(s) for approval/review.

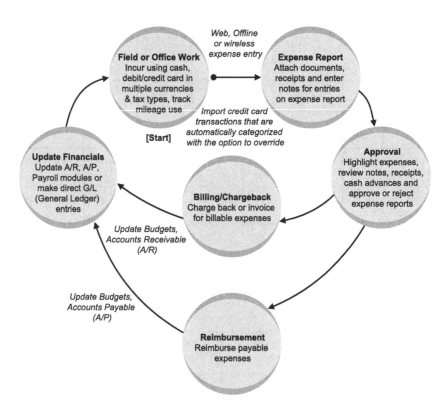

Figure 12.2   Expense Management Cycle

3. Once approved, the expense report is forwarded to payroll/accounting for processing.
4. If there are any billable expenses, the expense entries are reported to the billing manager for invoicing purposes.
5. Detailed or summary cost as well as billing information is exported to the accounting system's accounts receivable (A/R) and accounts payable (A/P) for financial reporting.
6. Project billing and expense information is made available for inclusion in executive dashboards, reports, and for real-time analysis.

Users of the expense reporting system have access rights based on their roles in the review and approval process. Typical roles include standard users who submit their expense reports, managers who approve them, and administrators who set up and manage the entire process.

An Expense Entry

Figure 12.3 shows the many different attributes and information that are linked to an expense entry. Behind the scenes, an enterprise expense management system

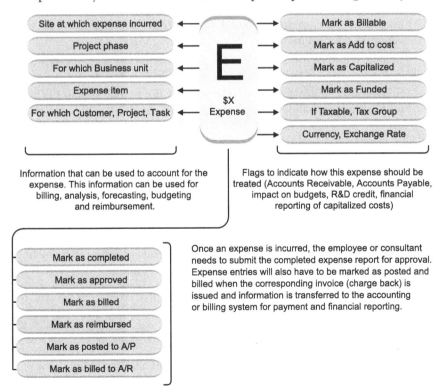

Figure 12.3   An Expense Entry

is tracking this information so that expense reimbursement, billing, cost allocation, project tracking, and reporting can occur in real time.

The expense item specifies the category to which the cost should be charged to. Expense items are classified into several categories for analysis and reporting purposes. Some examples include travel, entertainment, mileage, equipment purchases (hardware, software), office supplies, training, and cash advance. In each case, different types of information must be collected and specific business rules applied. For example, in the case of mileage, information such as destination and distance must be specified and each company may have its own policy on mileage rates and allowances that is automatically applied and verified at the point entry.

Expense Management Workflows

The following are some of the typical expense approval workflows:

- There are multiple levels of approval for expense reports depending on the resource, type of expenses, and amounts. For example, for travel expenses, the first-level information technology manager may be authorized to approve amounts under $1,000, but for larger amounts a second level of approval is required.
- Billable expenses for the last month are sent to the customer for approval.
- Automatic approval of certain types of expenses, such as VPN access and fixed monthly mileage amount, is handled by the system without the need for human approval (see Figure 12.4).

The expense approval workflow can be configured to accommodate these scenarios. In fact, different expense approval workflows can be created to accommodate the specialized needs of various business units. For example, the professional services unit would have a more elaborate expense approval process, since it involves billing expenses to the client, while the workflow used by internal nonbillable resources that travel for training and support would be simpler.

Expense approval workflows support various forms of notification such as dashboards, e-mail and cell phone (as appropriate). A notification is sent if an expense report needs to be approved or has been escalated if the original approval request has not been processed.

Line Item Approval

Often, an expense report includes expenses incurred against multiple projects. Each manager approves or rejects expense entries for their project—also

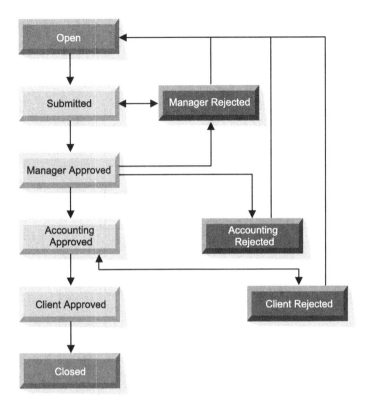

Figure 12.4   Sample Expense Approval Workflow

known as *line item approval*—but only for those line items that belong to their respective projects.

Travel Request Workflow

Because of the apparently simple nature of a travel request, many organizations use e-mail and spreadsheets to execute them. However, considering all the conditions and events that are associated with a travel request, a structured and automated means of processing such requests ensures better accuracy and efficiency (see Figure 12.5).

Typically, approval is required prior to making travel arrangements. Then the requestor reviews and confirms the options, the itinerary, and other details. Here are some of the travel-related data that needs to be captured:

- *Airline:* A company may have preferred airlines. An expense management system can suggest or enforce a specific carrier for certain destinations.

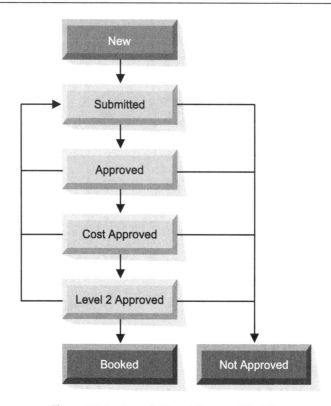

Figure 12.5   Sample Travel Request Workflow

- *Class:* Using business class or first class may be reserved only for executives, or altogether prohibited. The software can ensure that unauthorized employees do not make such a request.
- *Destination:* Indicate destination city and airport.
- *Rental:* Whether a car rental is required when arriving at the destination.
- *Cash advance:* Employees can request a cash advance in a specified currency.

Once a travel request is approved, the requestor's calendar and timesheet can be updated automatically, and an expense report can also be created and auto-populated with the approved travel details, rental, cash advance, and hotel costs.

Multiple Currency and Tax Jurisdictions

Companies with operations that span international borders need more than just the ability to select a currency for the amounts they spend. In some situations, an employee lives in one country (currency A), the base currency of the company is in a different denomination (currency B), and he or she incurs expenses while traveling to a customer's site in another country (currency C). In this scenario, the employee wants to be reimbursed in his or her own currency (A), the customer company wants to be billed in their local currency (C), and the company needs to keep track of all costs in its main currency (B). An enterprise expense tracking system with powerful reporting is required to manage these conversions and transactions.

Furthermore, a multinational corporation operating in several countries is likely to have set up a multicompany accounting system. The concepts of company and site (or location) are used to identify these operating entities and associate a base currency to each. Expenses related to each company can be processed based on the preferences set for the company, independent of the rest of the organization.

As for taxes, by capturing the tax information at data entry time (which is automatically reverse-calculated when the employee enters the gross amount for taxable expenses), the corporation can easily calculate and manage taxes corresponding to the location where each expense was incurred.

Corporate Policy Compliance

With the right business intelligence reporting system, managers can identify patterns in purchased items, preferred suppliers, and other spending trends. It enables them to forecast future spending, establish cost-saving agreements with suppliers, and monitor employee compliance with corporate policies. For example, by running reports on the destinations to which employees travel, a manager can negotiate a deal with a certain airline that serves the frequently traveled destinations. Not only would such an arrangement reduce travel expenses but it would also save time for the travel planner who would otherwise have to shop for the best fare for every travel request.

Using queries, managers can identify expenses, projects, and employee spending habits that may require a closer examination. For example, you can run a query to review travel and entertainment expenses of a business unit to identify any unnecessary spending.

Integration with Accounting Systems

Providing easy-to-use expense data entry and collection is an important aspect of overall expense report automation. However, proper processing of this data at the back end; sending reimbursement information to accounts payable and billing information to accounts receivable is also critical for total elimination of data rekeying.

Expense entries are linked to an expense type that in turn is linked to a general ledger in the accounting system. This association eliminates the need for the employee or the accounting staff to manually classify each expense item. Using attributes, the expense tracking system also automatically capitalizes (classified as a balance sheet item) or expenses (classified as income statement item) each expense entry.

Offline Expense Reports

Commonly, an employee will return to the office, especially after a long trip, with numerous expense slips and an urgent need to submit multiple expense reports and receive reimbursement. But frequently, slips are lost, and some do not have the date or the amounts written on them (typical of taxi receipts). The accounting employee then has to spend additional time trying to make sense out of a large pile of paper. Needless to say, this is a waste of the employee's time—not to mention a frustration.

The frustration, delays, and inaccuracies caused by this situation have negative impacts on the company:

- Expenses that need to be billed to the customer are submitted later, thus postponing billing and collection.
- The number of expense reports to be approved by managers tends to spike from time to time; therefore, the manager has less time to spend on verification, which increases the chance for invalid expenses to go unnoticed.
- Credit card payments become due, and in the absence of corresponding expense reports, they are typically paid without verification. When the expense report does become available, it creates a backlog of data entry and corrections.

With offline expense entry, employees can enter expenses on a daily basis while off site, or even on the plane home, without the need to connect to corporate servers.

NOTES

1. Metagroup Report on T&E and SOX, July 2004.
2. Rusty Carpenter, David Marcus, and Alan Sandusky, 2001 American Express Travel Related Services Co, June 2001.
3. Hackett Benchmarking & Research; part of Answerthink.
4. See note 2.
5. Randy Myers, survey by Exult Process Intelligence Center, December 2000 issue, pp. 66–80, CFO Publishing Corp.

Budgeting and Cost Accounting

In spite of an abundance of tools and competent team members, a high number of projects fail, and an even greater number are "challenged" projects. Challenged projects are over budget or over schedule—or both. These projects do not meet their original objectives, but just keep going until someone gets tired of them and pulls the plug.

In this chapter, we assert that systematic cost allocation and budget tracking can prevent projects from going bad by creating instant accountability, making it difficult to hide poorly performing projects, and facilitating problem detection early on. With these capabilities, companies can terminate bad projects sooner or take corrective action to save them.

Allocating costs to specific resource groups can have a positive impact for any company that has the option to outsource parts of or entire projects. To help you plan a cost accounting approach, this chapter explains the distinction between direct and indirect costs, capitalized and expensed projects, how to set up limits and notifications to manage budget consumption, and how budget tracking tools and techniques are used to control project costs. Also, the concept of budget rollups is introduced as a control tool that fits particularly well with hierarchical organization and work breakdown structures.

What Is Cost Allocation?

Cost allocation enables you to accurately measure the true cost and the return on investment of every resource group, project, and initiative; whether it is billable or not. Without cost allocation, a company treats the costs associated with all initiatives and business units as "general and administrative" expenses, making it impossible for management to determine which investments and resource groups are making money, meeting budget objectives, or executing effectively. Here are some grave numbers that show the severity of the cost allocation and budgeting problem.

63 percent of projects were delivered behind schedule and 45 percent went over budget.
—Standish Group report "Chaos: A recipe for success," 2001[1]

Outright failures of projects have declined from 40% to 23% during the past five years, but challenged projects swelled from 33% to 49% in the same period. That's bad because challenged projects often are more painful than projects that simply fail. And they are often just failures-in-waiting; dallying dismally until the patience (or the money) for getting them right runs out.
—*CIO* magazine, "The Secret to Software Success," July 2001[2]

These statistics and the threats described in Chapter 3, "Project Governance," show that projects can get in trouble very quickly in a variety of ways. This chapter describes cost accounting and budgeting techniques to use in your organization, describes how to account for various types of costs, and explains how to measure cost variances. The chapter concludes by illustrating how your organization can keep projects under control and meet or exceed expectations by accounting for costs in real-time, budgeting, analyzing earned value, setting hard spending limits, and using notifications.

When business units provide services for other business units or third parties, interdepartmental billing, and chargeback is used to allocate costs and measure performance (see Chapter 14, "Billing, Chargeback, and Invoicing").

Cost Rule Rate Engine

The rate engine is a software module designed to calculate the cost and billing of work performed. In the context of Project Workforce Management, the same rating engine is used to manage both cost and billing rules, since there are many similarities between these systems. Rate information is used to generate the following:

- Cost, revenue, profit/loss reports, graphs, and charts
- Invoices, payroll, and accounts payable data
- Analysis reports that allow users to drill up to summarize and drill down to the details to pinpoint strengths, problem areas, and inefficiencies

Rate engines support various cost tracking types, such as the hourly, daily, and fixed rates defined in the work breakdown structure (WBS) or in the organization breakdown structure (OBS). See Chapter 14, "Billing, Chargeback, and Invoicing," for a detailed discussion of billing rules and scenarios.

Direct and Indirect Costs

All costs, both direct and indirect, must ultimately be associated with specific projects. If all or part of a cost cannot be allocated to a specific project, then it must be allocated to a cost objective. Cost allocation is particularly important when a project is funded, such as a government contract or a project that qualifies for research and development (R&D) credits (see Chapter 5, "Complying with Labor Laws and Accounting Regulations," for more information). Figure 13.1 illustrates a sample cost breakdown by project chart.

Direct cost is any work or spending that is done for a specific project. Examples of direct costs are:

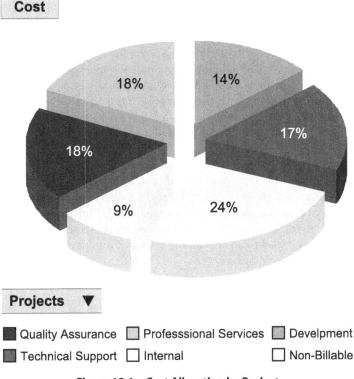

Figure 13.1   Cost Allocation by Project

- Specialized training for electricians to meet the contract's requirements
- Leasing costs of a truck used only for work at the contract's job site

Indirect costs are costs that cannot be associated directly to a specific project. Indirect costs benefit multiple projects or cost objectives. Common categories of indirect costs include general administration (accounting, payroll, purchasing, etc.), sponsored project overhead, general business travel, plant operation and maintenance, departmental administration expenses, and depreciation or use allowance for buildings and equipment. Examples of specific indirect costs are:

- Company-sponsored training not related to a specific contract
- Leasing costs of a multi-use corporate truck
- Computer equipment and software that is used to manage the office

Capitalized Costs Versus Expenses

Capitalizing or expensing software purchases and software development costs was explained in Chapter 5, "Complying with Labor Laws and Accounting Regulations." The same concepts described in that chapter apply to other types of spending.

For example, an oil pipeline company that spends millions of dollars annually to maintain and repair its oil pipes must allocate all associated costs to projects that are expensed. Ultimately, the maintenance and repair projects appear as line items in the company's income statement. However, if the company invests in building a new pipeline, then the project is a capital investment. Eventually, the capitalized portion appears as a line item on the company's balance sheet, and the depreciated portion appears as an expense on the company's income statement.

When a project is initiated,[3] the finance team must decide whether to classify it as a capital or expense project, and then associate the project to the appropriate general ledger accounts. One project may have several phases, some of which may be capitalized and others expensed. A Project Workforce Management system tracks all capital or expensed project costs and phases. The cost information is exported to an accounting system using general ledger transactions for financial reporting.

Budgets and Baselines

A baseline is an initial estimated cost and schedule. It is the value or condition against which all future measurements are compared to. It is a point of reference. In project management there are three baselines: schedule baselines,

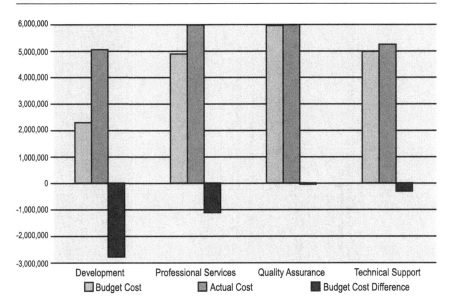

Figure 13.2 Budget to Actual Report

cost baselines, and scope baselines. The combination of all three is referred to as the *Performance Measurement Baseline*. Establishing a baseline is the formal end of the project planning process and the beginning of project execution. As a project's scope or schedule changes, a project's baseline can be updated to account for those changes; thus creating multiple project baselines.

Project managers must track the progress of tasks, costs, and time against the baseline(s), and use repeatable procedures to gather data, assess earned value, and report project status to all stakeholders.

Cost variance is the difference between the estimated cost of an activity and the actual cost of that activity. In earned value analysis, it is the budgeted cost of work performed less the actual cost of work performed (see Figure 13.2).

As work is performed, it is "earned" on the same basis as it was planned, in dollars and/or other units such as work hours. Planned value, compared with earned value, measures the dollar volume of work planned versus the equivalent dollar volume of work accomplished (see Figure 13.3). For more information on earned value analysis, see Chapter 10, "Project Planning."

Limits and Notifications

Managers may want to be automatically notified when certain thresholds are met. Managers may also want to restrict the submitted hours against a project

#	Task Name	Start	Actual Start	Finish	Duration	Actual Work	Complete %
1	Phase 1 - Planning	Thu 2/1/07	Thu 2/1/07	Mon 2/12/07	8 days	48 hrs	60%
2	Requirements Gathering	Thu 2/1/07	Thu 2/1/07	Wed 2/7/07	5 days	40 hrs	100%
3	Specification Document	Tue 2/6/07	Tue 2/6/07	Wed 2/7/07	2 days	8 hrs	50%
4	Client Meeting	Thu 2/8/07	NA	Mon 2/12/07	3 days	0 hrs	0%
5	PHASE 1 Complete	Mon 2/12/07	NA	Mon 2/12/07	0 days	0 hrs	0%
6	Phase 2 - Development	Tue 2/13/07	NA	Mon 2/12/07	20 days	0 hrs	0%
7	GUI Development	Tue 2/13/07	NA	Mon 2/26/07	10 days	0 hrs	0%
8	Core Development	Tue 2/13/07	NA	Mon 2/26/07	10 days	0 hrs	0%
9	DB Development	Tue 2/13/07	NA	Mon 3/5/07	15 days	0 hrs	0%
10	Reports Development	Tue 3/6/07	NA	Mon 3/12/07	5 days	0 hrs	0%
11	PHASE 2 Complete	Mon 3/12/07	NA	Mon 3/12/07	0 days	0 hrs	0%
12	Phase 3 - QA	Tue 2/27/07	NA	Fri 3/16/07	14 days	0 hrs	0%
13	GUI Testing	Tue 2/27/07	NA	Mon 3/5/07	5 days	0 hrs	0%
14	Core Testing	Tue 2/27/07	NA	Mon 3/5/07	5 days	0 hrs	0%
15	DB Testing	Tue 3/6/07	NA	Thu 3/8/07	3 days	0 hrs	0%
16	Reports Testing	Tue 3/13/07	NA	Fri 3/16/07	4 days	0 hrs	0%
17	PHASE 3 Complete	Fri 3/16/07	NA	Fri 3/16/07	0 days	0 hrs	0%
18	Phase 4 - Implementation	Mon 3/19/07	NA	Fri 3/30/07	10 days	0 hrs	0%
19	Server Install	Mon 3/19/07	NA	Wed 3/21/07	3 days	0 hrs	0%
20	Configuration	Thu 3/22/07	NA	Fri 3/30/07	7 days	0 hrs	0%
21	PHASE 4 Complete	Fri 3/30/07	NA	Fri 3/30/07	0 days	0 hrs	0%
22	PROJECT COMPLETE	Fri 3/30/07	NA	Fri 3/30/07	0 days	0 hrs	0%

Figure 13.3   Schedule Variance Report

170

or task to not exceed the budgeted hours. For example, if a budget has been set for Project ABC at 100 hours and the threshold notification has been set at 75 percent, then once 75 hours of work have been reported for Project ABC, an e-mail is sent to the project manager advising him or her of the milestone. If the Project ABC has been restricted to budgeted hours, then once 100 hours have been reported for the project, no more time entries will be allowed against that project. Some companies may also want to autosuspend a project once certain limits and thresholds have been reached.

Budget Rollup

With a hierarchical organization and work breakdown structure,[4] it is possible to set up budgets for detailed line items and then roll them up as necessary for summary budget control and reporting. Both time in hours and time in dollars (based on pay rules), along with expense budgets, can be defined and rolled up independently for any part of the organization and work breakdown structures. Here is an example using the East Coast Advertising Portfolio shown below. We assume the following budgets have been defined as in Table 13.1.

PROJECT	BUDGET CODE
East Coast Advertising Portfolio	100
New York Projects	100100
Project NY1	1001001
Project NY2	1001002
Boston Projects	100200
Project BO1	1002001
Project BO2	1002002
Project NY1	$50,000
Project NY2	$30,000
Project BO1	$10,000
Project BO2	$15,000

Table 13.1   East Coast Advertising Portfolio

The following information is made available without any manual effort:

- Rollup budget to East Coast Advertising Portfolio level for a total of $105,000, to Boston Projects level for a total of $25,000, and so on.
- Set a notification on New York Projects: if 75 percent of the total budget ($60,000) has been consumed then notify the manager.
- Set a limit of $100,000 on the total budget and suspend the whole project the moment the limit has been reached.

NOTES

1. *Source:* http://www.ijikm.org/Volume1/IJIKMv1p023-036Furumo03.pdf.
2. *Source:* http://www.cio.com/archive/070101/secret.html.
3. See Chapter 8, "Initiating Projects."
4. See Chapter 6, "Organization and Work Breakdown Structures."

14

Billing, Chargeback, and Invoicing

Experts often possess more data than judgment.

—Colin Powell

Internal service departments (such as information technology, IT) and professional services organizations are remarkably similar in many ways. They both:

- Provide services or execute projects for their customers (IT's customers are essentially the organization's other business units).
- Have to account, in detail, for all work performed and any project spending so that:
  - —For IT, cost is allocated to the appropriate business units, the IT budget is justified, and performance is measured.
  - —For professional services, customers are invoiced, and pay for the billable work and expenses incurred; and billable utilization rates are tracked and measured.
- Are constantly asked to do more with less, such as having less bench time for resources (better capacity planning) and a smaller administration team (commonly referred to as nonproject overhead).

Because of these similarities, and to gain efficiencies from them, Project Workforce Management treats internal billing (chargebacks) and external billing (invoicing clients) largely in the same way.

Although the project management and workforce management disciplines rarely mention invoicing—let alone describe how they are related to delivering and reporting on external projects—every piece of data that appears on an invoice or chargeback report is the result of information that is available from one of these systems. Project Workforce Management treats project management,

173

workforce management, and cost and revenue accounting as a unified and integrated set of concepts, disciplines, and methodologies. Unlike traditional project management systems, invoicing—a business critical function—is a core component of Project Workforce Management.

This chapter describes how automated billing and invoicing, based on best practices, stimulates cash flow, increases revenue generation opportunity, improves employee and customer satisfaction, and reduces costs. Here we describe the tools and processes that both IT and professional services groups can use to account for billable work and expenses, and we explore the challenges and benefits of automating the chargeback and invoicing processes.

Billing Requirements

Billing Rule Engine

As described in Chapter 13, "Budgeting and Cost Accounting," the rate engine is a software module that is designed to calculate the cost and billing of work performed. In a Project Workforce Management system, the same rate engine is used to manage both cost and billing rules, since cost accounting and billing systems have very similar requirements.

Rate engines support multiple pay and billing rules such as hourly, daily, and fixed rates defined in the work breakdown structure (WBS) or organization breakdown structure (OBS). The sections that follow introduce the main concepts, techniques, and tools required to automate and successfully manage billing in your organization.

Rate Precedence

Most projects and resources have standard billing rates. However, the standard billing rates may not apply to a specific customer, project, or task. *Rate precedence* allows an organization to define standard rates for resources, customers, projects, and tasks, and to override them on a case-by-case basis when necessary. Consider the following examples:

- Charge customer Acme $75 per hour for all consulting services. However, if Joe works on Acme Project XYZ, then charge $100 per hour.
- Charge customers $150 for standard accounting services. However, charge $250 per hour for any tax, audit, or transfer pricing work.

Maintaining History

Keeping track of rate changes is a reporting and auditing necessity; otherwise cost, revenue, and profit/loss reports that span rate changes will be inaccurate.

DATE INTERVAL	RATE RULE ($/HOUR)
January 1999 to March 2000	65
April 2000 to December 2000	70
December 2000 and onward*	75
*This rate will remain in effect until a new rate entry is created.	

Table 14.1   Jeff Jones' Rate History

Rate history can be maintained by ensuring that every billing rule has a specific start and end date, and that rates are captured against the time entries themselves. Consider the example in Table 14.1.

Marking and Managing Entries

Work performed, expenses incurred, and charges (project overhead, discounts, and other charges) can be billable and/or payable. If an entry is billable, then its amount is considered as revenue (if it is invoiced to a customer) or a chargeback (if it is charged to another business unit).

If an entry is marked as payable, then it is considered a cost and is eventually paid through payroll (for services) or treated as accounts payable. Entries that have been processed are marked as "billed" and/or "paid," and will not appear in subsequent payable and receivable queries, thus preventing any double charging or double counting.

Project Overhead

In addition to tracking cost and billing of a specific project, a project accounting system supports the tracking of project overhead. Project overhead can be incurred in monetary or hourly units. For example, project overhead could be recorded in the form of 200 hours of administrative overhead for every three months of project-related work, or $10,000 of administrative fees for each month of project work. The charges can be one time, recurring, or based on criteria determined by the company and the customer.

Nonproject Work

Nonproject work must also be accounted for, so that a single system is used for cost accounting and billing. Nonproject work can include administrative activities and charges, time spent in meetings, training, interviewing, and other off-project activities.

Nonrecurring Charges

Project execution often includes the occurrence of nonrecurring charges such as equipment usage, material purchases, discounts, special charges, bonuses, and penalties for late projects. The project accounting system tracks these nonrecurring charges for cost and revenue reporting purposes.

Taxes

Various taxes may have to be taken into consideration—state sales taxes and value-added taxes (VAT in Europe and GST/PST in Canada) to mention a few. For example, services are taxed in Canada and many countries in Europe. Expenses and charges can also be marked as taxable or nontaxable.

Negative Entries

Negative time and expense entries, as well as charges to clients, occur when discounts are granted, penalties imposed, and adjustments are made to past entries. Negative entries must be supported and accounted for in the billing and chargeback processes. For example, a negative time adjustment on a nonexempt employee's timesheet from four weeks ago may have an impact on overtime calculations and pay.

Tracking On-Call Time

Employees and consultants who are on call (i.e., carry pagers during off hours) may be compensated in some form. For example, a helpdesk employee may be allowed to enter an hour of extra time per week just for agreeing to carry a pager. Employees' on-call time must be tracked and approved, and limits may also be imposed on how much time they can report.

Multiple Currencies

A company that has offices or customers in more than one country must deal with multiple currencies. Here are some important currency considerations:

- The system's default currency can be overridden for each site in larger organizations with offices in various geographic locations.
- Employees and consultants may have their own preferred currency for payroll processing and reimbursing expense reports.
- Customers may have their own preferred currency; invoices issued to a customer default to the customer's preferred currency.
- Every billing rule may have its own currency, depending on the consultant, the customer, or the project.
- Expenses may be incurred in various currencies.

The system automatically converts all of these different currencies to the system currency for financial reporting, billing, and payment processing.

Billing Methods

Some of the frequently used billing methods and techniques are explained in this section. Since the same rate engine is used for cost accounting and billing, all of the billing methods defined here can also be used to define pay rules for full-time, part-time, and contract employees or consultants working on various projects.

HOURLY. Hourly rates can be specified for a group, resource, customer, project, task, or work type. Rates are effective for a defined date interval. As described in the earlier Rate Precedence section, the same resources may have different hourly billing rates for different customers and projects.

DAILY. Daily rates can be specified for resources working on a client, project, activity, or task. These rates are effective for a defined date interval. Daily charges apply for each day of work completed, no matter how many hours of work are actually performed.

FIXED. Fixed rates can be specified for projects, activities, groups, and resources. Fixed rates are effective for a defined date interval. Fixed billing can be a dollar amount or a number of hours at a specified hourly rate. Flat charging and prorating are two commonly used fixed billing arrangements.

FLAT CHARGING. With this billing method, the customer is charged X number of hours at a specific hourly rate. As soon as even one hour of work is completed, the full amount can be invoiced. Content providers that manage video and multimedia productions often use flat charging. For example, a translation service can cost $5,000 for 50 hours of work. The customer is invoiced $5,000 when the work begins. A flat charge fixed rate adjusts the hourly rate as more work is done so that the total of the work done adds up to the fixed amount. In other words, a flat charge rule adjusts the hourly rate while always maintaining the total fixed amount.

PRORATING. A prorating rule adjusts the rate amount while maintaining a fixed hourly rate up to the total fixed amount. Unlike a flat charge, the customer is only billed for work done up to the maximum number of billable hours. In a prorated rule, the number of hours of work done exceeding the number of hours specified by the rule is rated at $0.

The following example highlights the differences between flat charging and prorating. Assume a fixed billing of $10,000 for 100 hours of work from January 1 to January 9:

- If someone works 5 hours on January 1:
    - —*Flat charge:* The total rate from January 1 to January 9 is 10,000/5 = $2,000 per hour; the total billing is $2,000 × 5 = $10,000.
    - —*Prorate:* The hourly rate from January 1 to January 9 is $10,000/100 = $100; the total billing is 100 × 5 = $500.
- If total hours of work total 200 hours on January 9:
    - —*Flat charge:* The hourly rate from January 1 to January 9 is 10,000/200 = $50 per hour; the total rate is $50 × 200 = $10,000.
    - —*Prorate:* The hourly rate from January 1 to January 9 is $10,000/100 = $100; the rate for the first 100 hours of work is $100, and the rate for the remaining hours is $0. The total rate is $100 × 100 = $10,000.

Work and Organization Breakdown Structure Billing Rules

Cost and billing information can be associated with the company's hierarchical work breakdown structure (WBS) or organization breakdown structure (OBS) items (see Chapter 6, "Organization and Work Breakdown Structures"). For example, a billing rule of $100 per hour can be associated with Stability Test Projects in Table 14.2. Since the rule is defined at the higher level, all subprojects under this item will automatically be rated using this billing rule, unless a more specific rule is associated to any of the lower level items such as testing done for Drug A3.

VARIANCE BILLING.   Consultants, lawyers, accountants, and other service professionals often have minimum time billing rules. Minimum charges can

STABILITY TEST PROJECTS			$100 PER HOUR
	Pharma Company A		–
		Drug A1	–
		Drug A2	–
	Pharma Company B		–
		Drug A3	$120 per hour

Table 14.2   Stability Test Projects Rate Rules

ACTIVITY	TIME (MINUTES)	BILLABLE TIME (MINUTES)	PAYABLE TIME (MINUTES)
Client ABC phone consulting	5	15	5

Table 14.3   Actual versus Billable Time

vary depending on the type of service provided. For example, a consultant may speak to a customer ABC on the telephone for five minutes, but the agreement is that every phone conversation will be billable for a minimum of 15 minutes. Agreements may vary by customer, type of service, or even the resource being billed.

To support variance time entry, users enter information of actual and billable time as shown in Table 14.3.

Up-To Billing.   Up-to billing defines a maximum billable amount for a project or engagement. When an invoice is created for that project the total amount to be invoiced is compared to the specified maximum billing. If the total billable amount exceeds the maximum, the user who is generating the invoice has to review the time entries and decide which entries should be invoiced at a lower billing rate (in certain cases some entries may have to be billed at zero).

Consider the following example: Project XYZ should be billed for $10,000, assuming project is charged at $100 per hour. When generating an invoice, the total billable charges are $12,000. However, because the maximum billing cannot exceed $10,000, there is a variance between the total agreed upon by the customer and the billing total. Therefore, the user must select which activities and what amounts to invoice (Table 14.4).

The billable time for XYZ support is reduced from 40 to 20 hours. A second less commonly used alternative is to bill 40 hours of billable time at the lower billing rate of $50 per hour. Note that prorating and flat charging are both a form of the up-to billing rule.

Milestone or Progressive Billing.   Invoices are often created for a given period based on work or milestones completed. For example, Customer ABC is invoiced for services and expenses on a monthly basis. The billing engine computes the invoice amount based on the completed milestones.

With milestone billing, the customer can be charged when predefined date-based milestones or specific agreed-upon project deliverables are reached. The milestones are defined and tracked as dates or deliverables against the billable project. The billing amount is associated to the project milestone.

After a specific milestone is reached (whether it is date based or deliverable based), the system automatically creates billable entries and may optionally notify those responsible to ensure that the customer is billed in a timely manner.

TASK	TIME (HOURS)	CHARGE ($)
XYZ: Analysis	30	3,000
XYZ: Support	40	4,000
XYZ: Consulting	50	5,000
Total Billing		12,000

TASK	TIME (HOURS)	BILLABLE TIME (HOURS)	CHARGE ($)
XYZ: Analysis	30	30	3,000
XYZ: Support	40	20	2,000
XYZ: Consulting	50	50	5,000
Total Billing			10,000

Table 14.4   XYZ Up-To Billing Example

Table 14.5 shows an example of date-based progressive billing and Table 14.6 shows an example of milestone billing with fixed charges.

Recurring Rates.   A recurring rate rule allows the company to quickly create a recurring fixed billing rule that applies for a specified date interval. Such a rule would be useful to track salaried employees, support contracts, and other recurring fixed cost and billing scenarios. Recurring rates are defined using the following parameters:

- Fixed amount per cycle
- Number of hours per cycle

PHASE	DATE INTERVAL	BILLING METHOD
Analysis	5/1/2007 to 9/3/2007	Flat fee: $10,000 on end date
Prototyping	10/1/2007 to 10/31/2007	All billable time and expenses for this date interval on end date
Development	11/1/2007 to 5/1/2008	Flat fee: $100,000 on end date
Final delivery	5/2/2007 to 6/1/2008	All billable time and expense for this date interval on end date

Table 14.5   Date-Based Progressive Billing Example

MILESTONE	DATE INTERVAL	BILLING METHOD
Specification	5/1/2007 to TBD	Flat fee: $10,000 upon reaching milestone
Completion of phase 1	TBD (user provides estimated start and end dates)	All billable time and expenses for this date interval upon reaching milestone
Completion of phase 2	TBD (user provides estimated start and end dates)	Flat fee: $100,000 upon reaching milestone
Final delivery	TBD (user provides estimated start and end dates)	All billable time and expenses for this date interval upon reaching milestone

Note: TBD = To be defined; date is determined when project manager indicates that milestone has been reached.

Table 14.6   Milestone Billing With Fixed Charges Example

- Recurring cycle
- Start and end date
- Flat charge (see Flat Charge and Prorating sections of this chapter)

The following examples demonstrate two common recurring rate application scenarios:

- A customer is to be billed $10,000 per month for up to 100 hours of billable work. Customer is only charged for work actually performed (no flat charging is desired). This agreement is in effect on a monthly basis for the next 12 months. Using a recurring rate, the company can define this rule as follows:

  —Fixed amount per cycle: $10,000

  —Number of hours per cycle: 100

  —Recurring cycle: Monthly

  —No flat charge

  The system generates 12 prorated fixed billing rule entries of $10,000, with 100 hours per entry. Customer is charged $100 per hour for any work done up to $10,000 on a monthly basis.

- A consultant is paid a fixed amount of $1,000 per week for the calendar year. Consultant gets paid the same amount regardless of the number of hours worked (flat charging is in effect). Using a recurring rate, the rule can be defined as follows:

—Fixed amount per cycle: $1,000

—Number of hours per cycle: 40

—Recurring cycle: Weekly

The system generates 52 flat-charge fixed billing rule entries of $1,000, with 40 hours per entry.

COST-PLUS BILLING. In some scenarios, the billing rule depends on the cost of the service delivered, plus a markup. The cost-plus method is most often used in government or public works contracts. A cost-plus billing rule uses the following parameters:

- A cost rule
- A multiplication factor that is applied to in the cost rate
- A markup that is added to the cost rate

The following examples show two possible applications of cost-plus billing:

- A tax preparation firm hires an accountant to prepare year-end tax filings. The accountant charges $50 per hour. The firm has a rule to mark up every hour of work performed by 25 percent. The cost-plus billing rule would be defined as follows:

  —*Cost rule:* $50 per hour accountant cost rule

  —*Multiple:* 1.25—Markup: $0
- Work is subcontracted to a consulting company that has agreed to charge $10,000 for 100 hours of work. The customer is to be billed with an hourly markup rate of 30 percent and a project overhead of $5,000 for work performed. The cost-plus billing rule would be defined as follows:

  —*Cost rule:* $10,000/100 hours sub prorated contract cost rule

  —*Multiple:* 1.30—Markup: $5,000

SPLIT BILLING. Split billing occurs when the same project is charged to multiple customers. Total charges may exceed 100 percent (there are no restrictions on the split). Split billing can occur in the following two instances:

1. Each customer is charged a percentage of the project's billing based on the split.
2. Every customer has a specific billing rate. The project is billed based on each customer's own hourly billing rate, whereby the appropriate percentage of the time entry is billed at that customer's billing rate. In other words, projects can be split by hours or by a dollar amount.

SPLITTING BY HOUR. A project that is split by the hour is billed to each client at its own billing rate. For example, 10 hours of work is done on Project A. Project A has been split by hour to Client 1 at 50 percent and Client 2 at 80 percent. Project A has a billing rate defined as $100 per hour. Client 1 has no billing rate. Client 2 has a billing rate of $200 per hour. For this scenario:

> 10 hours × $100 × 0.50 = $500 billable to Client 1 (gets project's split hours and standard project rate)
>
> 10 hours × $200 × 0.80 = $1,600 billable to Client 2 (get project's split hours at its own rate)

SPLITTING BY DOLLAR AMOUNT. A project is split by amount and billed to each client at the project's billing rate: 10 hours of work on Project A. Project A has been split by amount to Client 1 at 50 percent and Client 2 at 80 percent. Project A has a billing rate of $100 per hour. Client 1 has a billing rate of $150 per hour. Client 2 has a billing rate of $200 per hour. For this scenario:

> 10 × $100 × 0.50 = $500 billable to Client 1 (since the project's billing amount is being split, client's billing rate is ignored)
>
> 10 × $100 × 0.80 = $800 billable to Client 2 (since the project's billing amount is being split, client's billing rate is ignored)

Chargeback

For chargeback reports, companies use time and expense reports and charts to allocate costs to various revenue generating business units. The chargeback reports can be automatically created and sent to the line of business managers based on an agreed upon chargeback reporting cycle or included in an executive dashboard.

Invoicing

An *invoice* is defined as a detailed or summary list of goods shipped, material and equipment used, expenses incurred, and services rendered. Organizations depend heavily on their invoicing processes. Any deficiencies, oversights, and delays can result in significant losses. Naturally, the accuracy and efficiency of invoicing is very much dependent on the systems implemented to streamline the process and to make it error-free. An invoicing system can reduce the invoicing collection and processing dramatically:

- The expected gain in productivity and reduction in administrative tasks is approximately one hour per invoice.
- An automated solution can reduce the total invoicing imprecision caused by human error by 1 percent to 3 percent.

Typically, organizations rely on an extensive and error-prone paper, e-mail and spreadsheet trail to collect and issue invoices, and to manually enter the data into its accounting systems. The root of the problem is that the invoicing process is too disconnected from the actual project management system. It is simpler and more effective to create and manage invoices using the same system that is used to track the project workforce. Next, we describe how the invoicing process can be streamlined.

Prevent Double Charges

Invoicing, payroll, and accounts payable support the concept of issuing an invoice or an invoice batch (a collection of invoices). Once an invoice is issued, all entries (time, expenses, and other charges) that are included in the invoice are automatically marked as billed. Similarly, after a payroll or accounts payable batch is issued, all entries included are automatically marked as posted. This prevents double charging and double payment for the same work and expenses.

Invoice Line Items

Invoice line items consist of the billable services rendered, expenses incurred, products delivered to, and materials used by a customer. A line item can present summary information such as billable work performed for project ABC for the month of April, or detail information such as a billable time entry entered for project ABC.

Billable Time and Expenses

During the invoice-generation process, the person who creates invoices performs the following tasks:

- Decides what range of billable entries to include or exclude
- Specifies which projects are being invoiced
- Selects all or some of the users that have worked on the selected projects
- Selects line items to include or exclude
- Adjusts the billable amounts as necessary

Charges

An invoice may include billable charges, including time and money charges that are entered against billable projects. These charges may be positive (e.g., bonuses for early project delivery) or negative (penalties for late delivery or special discounts). These charges may be automatically added by the system when certain milestones are reached, or management may add them after discussions with a customer or project contributors.

Invoicing/Chargeback Workflow

A sample invoicing/chargeback workflow is shown in Figure 14.1. A company may have one or more invoicing workflows for various departments and customer types.

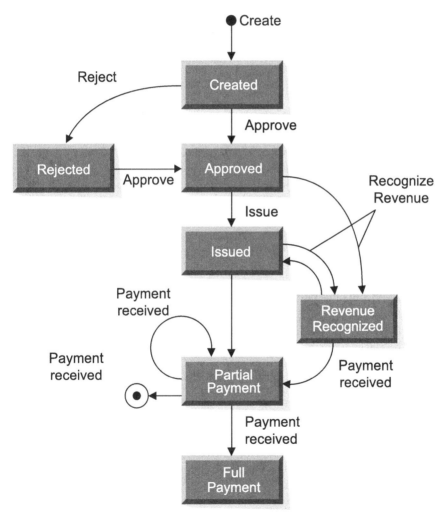

Figure 14.1   Sample Invoicing Workflow

Invoice Generation

Data Collection

The first challenge of preparing invoices is the timely and reliable collection of data (see Chapter 11, "Enterprise Timesheet Management," and Chapter 12, "Travel and Entertainment Expense Management"). The data that feeds the invoice includes time entries, expense entries, charges, markups and markdowns, equipment, and additional billing related information. For example, a time or expense entry must be associated to:

- Customer to be invoiced
- Invoice number and date interval (for future reference and reporting, to prevent double charging and auditing purposes)
- Note (if any)
- Documents attached (if any)

Approval and Submission

The first stage in the approval process is the review of the initial billing data that is collected. A billing manager or project manager can review, approve, or reject timesheets, expense reports, and charges. Invoice approval can be an internal process, or include pre-approval by the customer using an online time and expense approval tool.

INVOICE PREPARATION STEPS. After invoice data is approved, the following steps should be considered:

1. Apply discount rate (if any) based on the negotiated customer terms.
2. Choose how to display work details and notes to describe the work performed. Show billable time in hours or days. Average rates per user can be calculated and shown by dividing the billable amount by the number of hours entered.
3. Sort entries on the invoice by user, project, or task.
4. Decide whether the invoice shows high level summary of the work done, drills down to the task level, or includes the detailed time and expense entries.
5. Add billing information, including details such as company and invoice payment contact(s), associated purchase order number (if any), and billing address.
6. Use the appropriate currency to show taxable amounts; include the tax jurisdiction (country, state, and method) and tax rates.

7. Include potential interest and finance charges.
8. Include terms and conditions, such as payment terms, return policies, and warranties.
9. Use an invoice template that presents the information based on customer preferences.

Return on Investment

Table 14.7 shows the savings that can be realized by automating the invoicing process. Figure 14.2 graphs the return on investment of automated invoicing using the above assumptions.

Number of invoices processed annually	20	50	100	200	1,000	10,000
Savings from impre-cision caused by human error	$4,000	$10,000	$20,000	$40,000	$200,000	$2,000,000
Number of resources involved in the invoicing process	1	1	1	1	3	10
Savings from gained productivity and administrative tasks reduction	$2,500	$2,500	$2,500	$2,500	$7,500	$25,000
Total actual cost savings annually	$6,500	$12,500	$22,500	$42,500	$207,500	$2,025,000

[a] Based on savings from improvements in human error imprecision (1 percent) in the invoicing cycle and an average amount of $20,000 per invoice.
[b] The productivity gain per invoice is one hour, which represents a savings per invoice of $25, assuming an average salary of $25/hour.

Table 14.7   Savings from Automated Invoicing

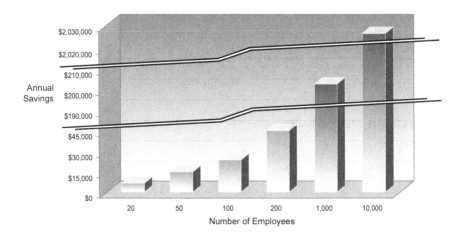

Figure 14.2   Invoice Automation Savings

15

Work in Progress and Forecasting

Clearly directors and management have not accepted their responsibility for the company's inadequate risk, forecasting and financial controls.

—John Curry

While tracking past performance is a necessary function, an organization's competence is mostly measured by its ability to prepare for and execute future projects as well as to accurately forecast revenue and demand. The previous chapters explained the controls, processes, and tools that are necessary for effective project initiation, execution, cost accounting, and billing. In this chapter, we describe how companies can account for work in progress in financial reports and in their revenue estimates, recognize revenue in a manner consistent with generally accepted accounting principles (GAAP), and more accurately forecast project revenue.

Work in Progress

Work in progress (WIP) is defined as projects (or work) that has not been completed but has already incurred a capital investment such as employee salaries, material, and equipment used to execute the project. Work in progress is usually recorded as an asset on the balance sheet to account for projects that are not yet delivered but still have an inherent value. Here, we discuss WIP as it relates to a project or service-driven organization, which is somewhat different from the work in progress definition commonly used in manufacturing.

For a project or service-oriented organization, WIP is the difference between the work that has been performed and the work that has been invoiced or charged back. For example, if a $100,000 service project is 70 percent completed, but only $20,000 has been invoiced, then the work in progress is $50,000.

A WIP report provides a quick snapshot of the current work in progress. The WIP report can be generated for a specific customer, project, or for the company's entire project portfolio. The following cost and revenue reports help assess the WIP and billing efficiency in a given date interval:

- Total billable revenue by project, broken down into billable services and expenses.
- Total nonbillable time by project.
- Total billed by project for services, expenses, and charges.
- WIP report includes the total unbilled by project for services, expenses, and charges (work done and expenses incurred that have not yet been invoiced).

Work in progress is an important input into the financial reporting process. With a manual system, the accounting department has to analyze the individual projects to calculate and manually record WIP. With WIP and project financial reports, the required information is available in real time and this lengthy and tedious process is eliminated.

Unearned Revenue for Professional Services

Unearned revenue is money received for a service that has yet to be delivered. The amount is treated as a liability in the company's financial reporting until it has been earned. For example, if a customer prepays support fees for 12 months, the company can recognize $\frac{1}{12}$ of that amount as revenue on a monthly basis and the balance is reported as unearned revenue in the company's balance sheet.

Revenue Recognition Policy

For as long as companies have had to report revenue and earnings, revenue recognition principles have been at the center of debates and discussions. This is true not only for public companies that use aggressive revenue recognition methods, but also for private, profitable companies that try to understate revenue to reduce or defer tax liabilities.

Historically, revenue recognition has not been a major topic of discussion. In recent years, however, several high profile companies were plagued with controversy regarding their deceptive revenue recognition policies. In an effort to meet expectations, a number of companies resorted to dishonest accounting and fabricated schemes to create false revenue so that their executive team would earn substantial bonuses for meeting revenue targets. As a result, the regulating bodies found it necessary to address the problem by issuing special communiqués with regard to revenue recognition as is evidenced by position papers such as the AICPA Statement of Position 97-2, "Software Revenue Recognition," or Statement of Position 98-1, "Accounting for the Costs of Computer Software Developed or Obtained for Internal Use" (see Chapter 5, "Complying with Labor Laws and Accounting Regulations").

There is a constant demand from financial stakeholders for prompt and accurate revenue reporting. It is essential that a Project Workforce Management system enable the organization to define its revenue recognition policy and then report project revenue accurately and in real time.

For example, Company A may define its revenue recognition policy to state that all billable time, expenses, and charges are immediately recognized as project revenue, because it has signed contracts (such as government contracts with cost-plus billing arrangements) where the customer is highly likely to pay for all billable work and expenses. However, Company B may define its revenue recognition policy so that project revenue is recognized only when the customer is invoiced.

Revenue recognition policy may also vary from one type of customer to another and from one size of project to another. For example, a company that has $100 million in revenue may immediately recognize 30-day money-back sales of $5,000 or less, since the money is paid up front, and based on past experience that 90 percent of such customers are unlikely to ask for a refund. Therefore project revenue can be recognized:

- For all billable time and expense entries that are approved internally
- For projects and services delivered and accepted by the customer, but for which no invoice has been issued (proof of delivery or milestone acceptance)
- When an invoice is issued for the project

The company can define a global revenue recognition policy and override the policy on a customer-by-customer or deal-by-deal basis. Revenue recognition and WIP reports provide management with excellent project revenue visibility and financial reporting tools.

GENERALLY ACCEPTED ACCOUNTING PRINCIPLES FOR REVENUE RECOGNITION. There are two main methods used in the industry to recognize revenue: the critical event approach and the accretion approach.

Critical Event Approach. Most popular of the two methods, this approach allows recognition of revenue when the significant risks and rewards of ownership have been passed on to the purchaser. In the context of project or service delivery, there has to be overwhelming evidence that the project has reached an agreed-on milestone by which all or a portion of the project revenue can be recognized. Some companies may decide to recognize revenue at the signing of a contract or even at completion of production (applies mostly in the production of commodities). Two examples shed more light on this method. In the first example an item is purchased in a traditional store. In the second, two software license purchase scenarios are explored:

> *Example 1:* An example of a critical event is an individual's purchase of an item in a store. The risks and rewards of ownership have been passed on to the purchaser at the point of sale, and the revenue has been recognized by the store.

> *Example 2:* For licensed software products, the terms and conditions of the license agreement define when the transfer of ownership occurs; for example terms, and conditions can state:

>> *Delivery:* Licensed Product will be presumed delivered once Company has provided Client with the instructions permitting Client to proceed with downloading the Licensed Product. Pursuant to the download of the Licensed Product, Client is obligated to request a license activation key corresponding to the quantity of licenses it has purchased.

The software vendor's obligation is to complete the transfer of ownership (or grant and transfer of license rights) of the product by delivering the product to the customer and/or giving the customer access to use the goods. This is accomplished by:

- *For online software sales:* Transfer files and deliver license keys:
  - —Send the customer an e-mail giving them access to the FTP site where they can download the software and instructions.
  - —Send the customer an e-mail with clear instructions on how to install and how to request license key.
  - —Follow up a few days after instructions are sent with a telephone call to make sure customer has successfully installed the software.
- *For software delivered on a physical media:*
  - —Send a CD to the customer with clear instructions on how to install and how to request license key.
  - —Send the customer an e-mail informing them of the same instructions.
  - —Follow up a few days after the instructions are sent, with a telephone call to make sure customer has successfully installed the software.

Accretion Approach. In the services industry, this approach is commonly adopted on long-term contracts. It is most commonly referred to as the percentage-of-completion method. The contract's performance is measured, and revenue is recorded, based on that performance. Under this method, it is critical to keep track of costs in a given project, including time and expenses. The company can compare actual time and expenses to its budget (agreed on with the customer) to determine the percentage of project completion. In this case, invoicing has little to do with the revenue recognized for the project (a more accurate method is earned value analysis, see Chapter 10, "Project Planning").

AUTOMATING REVENUE RECOGNITION. The benefit of automating revenue recognition is that the recognition rules can be set up at the onset of the project using a company-wide or a project-specific policy. The accounting department does not need to refer to the actual terms of the contract to determine at which point revenue should be recognized, which can be a time-consuming process for even small professional services companies or departments.

For fixed-price contracts, periodic evaluations of the percentage of completion must be performed to determine the total project value, as well as any unbillable amounts that must be written off if unexpected costs have occurred. Flat charging is one way this type of fixed price project can be handled (see Chapter 14, "Billing, Chargeback, and Invoicing"). The revenue recognition challenge is only compounded for larger companies who have a more diverse customer base and a larger number of ongoing projects.

Specifying the revenue recognition policy for every project during the initiation phase enables the Project Workforce Management system to automatically calculate the revenue that can be recognized for a given project at any point in time. The system uses the project's billable time and expense entries, billing rules, milestones reached, and invoices issued combined with the specified revenue recognition policy to instantly report project revenue to management.

Forecasting

Project managers and executives need several types of forecasts to get their jobs done. A few of the typical forecasting questions they ask include:

- What is our forecasted resource utilization for the next 12 months?
- What is our anticipated cost (or billing) for currently planned projects?
- How much project revenue can we book in the next quarter?
- What percentage of this project is truly complete?

Project Workforce Management helps answer these questions.

Resource Utilization Forecast

A resource utilization report provides a forecast of the anticipated utilization rates in the requested date interval (see Figure 15.1). This report is used by executives and resource managers to determine the appropriate staffing levels for various

Resource Utilization by Type

	Jan					Feb				Mar	
	W1	W2	W3	W4	W5	W6	W7	W8	W9	W10	W11
Business Analyst											
Usage (FTE)	2.7	2.7	3.1	3.2	3.2	4	4.2	4.2	3.9	1	1
Utilization	68%	68%	78%	107%	107%	133%	140%	105%	98%	50%	50%
DBA											
Usage (FTE)	6	6	5.5	5.5	6.5	6.5	6	4	4	4	4
Utilization	83%	83%	91%	118%	118%	108%	50%	75%	75%	75%	75%
Junior .Net Developers											
Usage (FTE)	15.5	15.5	15.3	10	10	11	12.5	12.5	15.5	15	17
Utilization	71%	81%	99%	153%	110%	100%	80%	80%	65%	88%	88%
Senior .Net Developers											
Usage (FTE)	6	6	5.5	5.5	5.5	0	3	5	5	3	3
Utilization	83%	83%	100%	118%	0%	0%	50%	125%	125%	75%	75%

Legend: 0 - 90% | 91 - 110% | > 110%

Utilization by Department

January - 2007 / February - 2007 / March - 2007

IT	69%
R&D	73%
Sales	76%
Professional Services	95%
Marketing	54%
Administration	72%

(Hours axis: 100 | 200 | 300 | 400 | 500 | 600 Hours)

Project / Resource Utilization

Projects	Status	JAN	FEB	MAR	APR	MAY	JUN	JUL	AUG	SEP	OCT
☑ Help Desk Update	◄										
☑ CRM Implementation	◄										
☐ KB Development	■										
☑ CMM Compliancy	◄										
☑ Client Portal	■										
☑ ERP Integration	►										
☐ BPM Platform	►										

Resource Types	JAN	FEB	MAR	APR	MAY	JUN	JUL	AUG	SEP	OCT
All	70%	57%	65%	62%	58%	92%	70%	85%	65%	0%
DBA	60%	45%	62%	80%	55%	65%	45%	65%	62%	0%
Senior .Net Dev	20%	30%	45%	83%	96%	165%	115%	110%	45%	0%
Junior .Net Dev	130%	95%	96%	23%	45%	45%	50%	80%	96%	0%

Figure 15.1 Resource Utilization Forecast

194

skill sets and competencies. For example, the utilization report may show that solution consultants are in extremely high demand for the next 12 months and are overloaded with multiple projects. Alternatively, business analysts may have only 25 percent average utilization rate in the same time period. From this information, the company can make hiring, reorganization, and staff redeployment decisions (see Chapter 9, "Workforce Planning").

Anticipated Cost of Planned Projects

Anticipated hourly cost and billing rates can be associated with actual or *generic resources* (defined in Chapter 9) so that costs and billing for upcoming projects can be forecasted.

An information technology or internal shared service department will use the forecasted cost of planned projects as part of its budget planning process. Similarly, a service firm would use the forecasted revenue and utilization rates to measure bench time (billable resources that are not doing billable work), make plans for its workforce (such as hiring, training, reorganization), or make financial decisions (such as budgeting, investment, and strategy reviews).

Project Revenue Forecast

Project revenue, from both services rendered and services to be rendered, can be forecasted as follows (see Figure 15.2):

Current work in progress + Forecasted billing of planned projects
= Project revenue forecast

Forecasted Billing of Planned Projects is an estimate of the billable amount of work that will be performed and delivered in the next quarter. The WIP of the current quarter, for example, can be assumed to become revenue in the next quarter when it will be invoiced. Adding the two numbers usually provides an accurate revenue forecast. The forecast can be further improved by subtracting the anticipated new WIP based on the past average quarterly WIP that is carried forward.

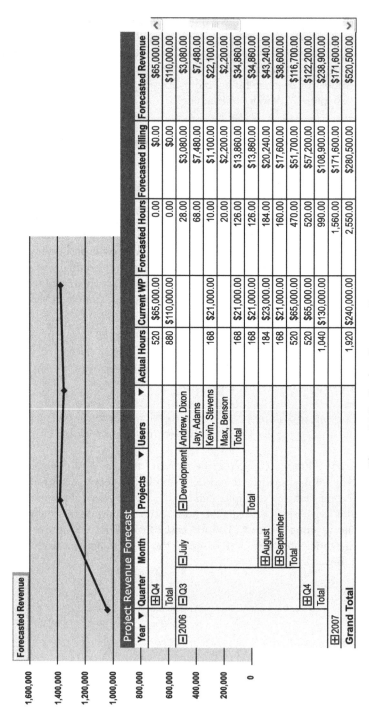

Figure 15.2 Project Revenue Forecast

16

Risk, Scope, and Issue Tracking

Even though you are on the right track—you will get run over if you just sit there.

—Will Rogers

Projects rarely repeat, yet business processes must be repeatable. Repeatable processes bring stability to the project and service-delivery processes, and minimize the risks that projects will fail.

Three of the most common challenges of project execution—risk management, scope management, and issue tracking—can be greatly enhanced by enforcing formal, repeatable policies, procedures, rules, and checklists. Risks, issues, and scope change have much in common:

- Project managers mostly take a reactive approach to managing them.
- They occur in any project.
- Best practices to manage them are generally not shared across the enterprise and multiple projects.
- Management often overlooks their connection to effective internal controls because traditional project management systems do not address labor compliance, governance, and the financial implications of project execution.

Project initiation, risk/scope/issue tracking, and other processes designed specifically for project management and control are collectively referred to as *Project Process Management.* It focuses on controlling, tracking, and auditing repeatable project processes. It enforces policies and best practices on project processes by monitoring and analyzing their execution to gain efficiencies as well as to achieve and maintain compliance.

197

This chapter highlights the perils of poor risk assessment, scope management, and issue tracking, and recommends ways that companies can implement effective project process controls.

Project Risk Management

Project risk management is the process of assessing potential threats to a project and making decisions on how to handle them. Actions may include:

- Deciding that the risk is a non-issue
- Accepting or ignoring a risk if it has a low probability of occurrence
- Containing the risk
- Changing the project scope to avoid or manage the risk
- Transferring the risk to another party

Table 16.1 shows some of the risks that can impact a project.

Risk management is a wide-ranging and often complex field in its own right. Financial institutions, for example, use sophisticated risk analysis software to assess the risks associated with their customers and portfolios for financial offerings such as loans, mortgages, insurance, annuities, and other investments. Project Workforce Management is not an extensive risk analysis solution; it

RISK TYPE	DESCRIPTION
Complexity	The risk relates to an unanticipated increase in the level of complexity of the project or of a specific part of the project.
Financial	The risk relates to a needed additional financial investment.
Technology	A new technology risk has been identified that needs to be assessed.
Resources	The talent required to continue or complete the project cannot be found, or abandons the project.
Strategic	Market conditions have changed, making this project either more or less strategic for the company.
Sponsorship	Management's sponsorship of the project has weakened due to changes in personnel or focus on other initiatives.
Customer	Customer's priorities for the project have changed; the customer may have either a more or less urgent need for the project.
Schedule	Project is likely to finish late, negatively impacting other initiatives and strategic objectives.

Table 16.1   Types of Risks That Can Impact an Organization

does not define algorithms that determine which projects carry more risk, or which risks deserve a more careful analysis. Rather, Project Workforce Management provides a workflow-driven framework for consistent and transparent risk reporting, assessment, analysis, and management.

Risk tracking is a first and necessary step toward more mature risk management. Once risks are systematically tracked, managers can then decide whether to develop algorithms and incorporate a more scientific approach to risk management.

Risk Assessment Workflow

Risks are managed using a risk assessment workflow. Figure 16.1 illustrates a sample risk reporting process in Project Workforce Management. In this example, project stakeholders and team members use a company-wide or project-specific risk entry form to report risks discovered at any point in the project life cycle. Based on the predefined assignments in the risk workflow, designated individuals receive automatic notifications as soon as a risk has been reported. The risk assessment committee then uses the risk report and any accompanying

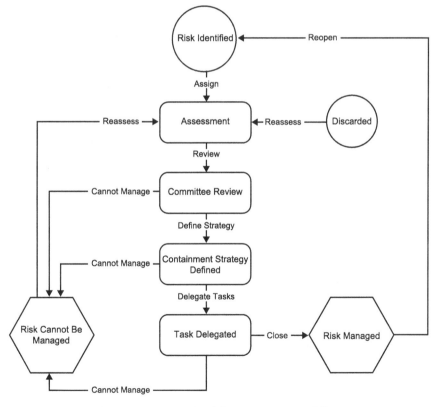

Figure 16.1   Sample Risk Assessment Workflow

Owner	Risk owner.
Type	Risk type; defined in the previous table.
Severity	The risk's impact on the project: Severe Impact, High Impact, Moderate Impact, or Low Impact.
Likelihood of occurrence	Highly Likely, Somewhat Likely, Likely, Somewhat Unlikely, Unlikely.
Occurrence frequency	How many times has the risk occurred in the past and how often will it occur in the future?
Urgency	How quickly the risk needs attention: Immediately, Soon, Later.
Risk relevance (date interval)	The period during which the risk is relevant; outside of this time period it is assumed that the risk is invalid and can be discarded.

Table 16.2 Attributes of a Risk Report

documentation to decide what needs be done. Risks may be ignored if nothing can be done or they are unlikely to occur, or the assessment committee may decide to propose a project scope change to preempt the risk. All risk, scope changes, and action items are tracked, audited, and reported by the system for future analysis, enterprise-wide access, management decision making, reporting, and accountability.

Risks can be reported by anyone involved in the project by completing a risk report form. Table 16.2 lists the major attributes of a risk report.

Project Scope Management

The most commonly cited issues for challenged projects are:

- Lack of executive support
- Lack of stakeholder input
- Incomplete or changing requirements, specifications, and objectives
- Unrealistic expectations[1]

A project's scope is the clear identification of the work required to successfully complete or deliver a given project. One of the project manager's responsibilities is to ensure that *only* the required work (the *scope*) will be performed and that each of the deliverables can be completed in the allotted time and within budget.

Project scope control and management is often overlooked in the management ranks. However, the impact of lax scope control on the organization, its customers, and its employees' careers can be devastating. Scope management is not someone else's problem; executives have to recognize this threat and establish effective internal controls that deal with this often invisible and consistently underestimated risk.

Scope management helps avoid challenged projects. Scope defines what is or is not included in the project, and controls what gets added or removed as the project proceeds. Scope management establishes control processes to address factors that may result in project change during the project life cycle. Project changes that impact scope include:

- *Requirements:* The ultimate objectives of the project
- *Constraints:* Limitations such as time, budget, resource dependency, business, legal, organizational, technological, and management constraints
- *Assumptions:* Statements that are considered facts for planning purposes but require verification; for example, a software project may assume a new system will not require a full-time database administrator after implementation is complete
- *Risks:* Any business or technical factor that has reasonable potential to impact the project (or its assumptions); key risk characteristics include probability of occurrence, impact, mitigating action, and contingent action

Cost of Scope Change

Poor scope control has tremendous impact on project costs and is one of the main factors that can lead to project budget overruns and delays. As Figure 16.2 shows, scope changes in the later stages of a project can cost as much as 200 times more than changes that occur in the requirements gathering phase.

There is nothing wrong with scope change; it is how scope change requests are managed that can have a detrimental impact on the project. In the early stages of a project, the customer often cannot identify or clearly describe all requirements and objectives. Furthermore, business and market changes may force requirement, specification, and scope changes.

If not addressed carefully, the following scope management issues can have a detrimental impact on a project:

- *Scope creep:* Seemingly small and incremental scope changes lead to substantial cost, budget, and schedule overruns (the proverbial death by a thousand wounds).
- *Unapproved changes:* Without discipline and clear scope management processes, team members can too easily deviate from the original project definition and requirements.

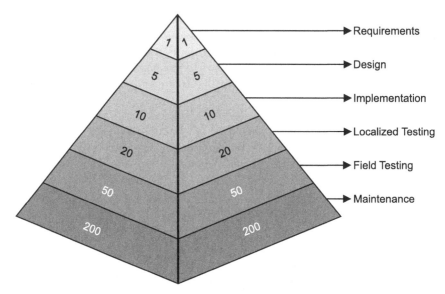

Relative cost of repairing defects at different phases of a project.

Figure 16.2   Cost of Scope Change

- *Inconsistent scope management processes:* Projects that are dependent on multiple teams and external resources often lack consistent and centralized scope management processes, which can lead to scope creep.
- *E-mail, conversation, project team member solo initiatives:* If not controlled, well-intentioned team members sometimes act on their own initiative, based on e-mails and conversations, to change project scope.

Project scope management is commonly broken down into four separate processes after project initiation: scope planning, scope definition, scope verification, and scope change control (see Table 16.3). Each of these processes is briefly described in the following list and illustrated in Figure 16.3:

PROCESS	DESCRIPTION
Project initiation	Approve business case, feasibility, budget
Scope planning	Gather requirements
Scope definition	Create scope components, subdivide work
Scope verification	Get approval from all stakeholders
Scope change control	Manage scope change requests

Table 16.3   Project Scope Management

| Project Initiation | Requirements Gathering (Scope Planning) | Project Scope Statement (Scope Definition) | Project Committment (Scope Verification) | Scope Change Control |

Figure 16.3   Scope Management Processes

- *Scope planning:* Developing a written scope statement is the key element of the scope planning process. The written statement of the project's scope ensures that the deliverables are defined exactly as intended in the project's scope plan. Scope statements can be created by the members of the team in collaboration with the entity commissioning the project.
- *Scope definition:* The major deliverables of a project must be broken down into easily manageable phases or subprojects. This process ensures that resources can be clearly assigned to their areas of expertise and responsibility, and that resource needs, time and cost budgets can be more accurately estimated and detailed.
- *Scope verification:* Scope verification is the acceptance by the entity commissioning the project of the project's scope of work. During this process, the results of the work already completed, as well as all related documentation, must be ready for review so that the project can be launched.
- *Scope change control:* It is an undeniable fact that most projects experience scope changes during their life cycle. When a change occurs, the primary concern of the project manager is to ensure that the changes are in line with the project's objectives, and are factored into the scheduling, allocation of resources, the budgeted time, and cost estimates.

Scope Maturity and Project Scope Management Tools

A scope management test introduced in a later section can help you quickly assess your team's scope maturity. The management of scope processes and their related data can be accomplished in a number of different ways, such as centralizing documents in a version control or change management system. Tools adopted must allow team members to easily share and review documents and to associate any documents containing scope changes to the appropriate project activities.

A Work Process

Unlike projects, which are almost never alike, a *process* has a predictable—in fact a predetermined—sequence. A work process is a unit of work that is tracked based on expected (or implied) completion date, service level agreement (how fast a task must be completed), aging, and escalation rules and policies. It follows a predefined flow and is routed based on the roles people play in the organization. There are also automatic notifications and assignments as a work process goes through its defined flow.

Scope Management Processes

For each process, stakeholders agree on states, roles, assignments, and responsibilities—who is responsible for what, and who has approval authority. A workflow system controls the process flow and provides auditing, reporting, and analytics so that project managers and executives can measure performance and capture best practices. Figure 16.4 illustrates a sample scope change process.

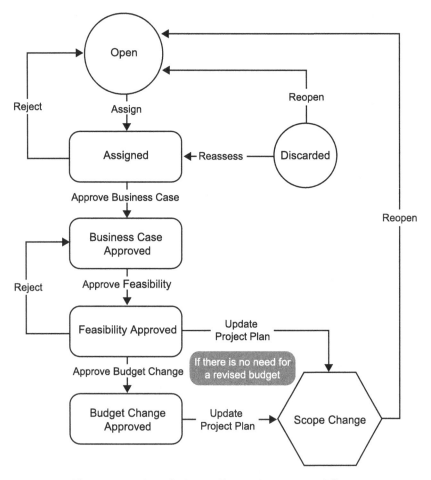

Figure 16.4　Sample Scope Change Request Workflow

SCOPING BEST PRACTICES.   Scope can be controlled and managed by applying the following best practices:

- A workflow system enforces scope control policies, and it monitors, institutionalizes, and audits scope and risk management processes. Workflows make work activity real-time traceable: You can report on the status of any work that is in progress, who did what, and who moved the process through its various steps.
- Establish control and approval processes for work breakdown structure (WBS) changes so that project scope change is not initiated through unapproved WBS changes and task assignments.
- Group small scope changes into one change request.
- Incorporate a contingency buffer for each approved scope to account for uncertainty; add contingency buffers for key milestones at the project level, not at the task level.

AVOIDING SCOPE CREEP.   Regardless of your best efforts, and even after implementing a consistent system to manage change, scope creep remains a potential threat. The following are some of the steps you can take to prevent or reduce scope creep:

- Establish a scope baseline through a scope statement sign-off before the project begins. New scope baselines can be defined and requirements may evolve naturally, but at least there is a reference point to compare to.
- Client may say: "that is not what I wanted" or "that is not what I meant." Make incremental adjustments and clarifications as the project moves from concept to reality.
- Establish official project milestones and make sure all stakeholders agree (even sign off) when a milestone is reached.

There will be resistance to scope freeze; if it is too early, you may have an unhappy customer, too late and the project will be over budget or late. Striking the right balance between the customer's needs and your ability to deliver on time and on budget is a judgment call; timing varies from project to project, but the scope should always be frozen before a financial commitment is made.

What if a scope baseline cannot be agreed to? One of the following approaches might be helpful:

- Work more with the customer until scope freeze is achieved.
- Agree to the work in phases: proceed with partial project execution, clarify and agree to the rest of the scope during the course of the

project. Pilot, prototype, or fit-to-business-analysis mini-projects are very effective.

- Structure the project with many predetermined milestones and phases of short duration; such a project is far more likely to remain aligned with its ultimate objectives.

Self-Assessment Test

Here is a quick scope management test that can help you assess your team's scope management maturity (see Table 16.4).

Project Issue Tracking

Project issue tracking consists of the process, tools, and techniques that are used to log and track the problems, questions, or requests reported during the project execution phase. The benefits of using an issue tracking system, as an integral part of a Project Workforce Management system, are as follows:

- One workflow system, with the same concepts and functions, is used to track all work processes.
- The issue tracking system is integrated with a timesheet system to track time spent on the issues for cost allocation and billing purposes.
- Managers and users have access to project dashboards that provide a 360-degree view of the current project status, including:
  - The project's financial standing, including total cost, budget, and earned value;
  - A report on the project's schedule, forecast, and estimates versus actuals;
  - A report of all time and expense entries against the project; and
  - A list of the project's risks, scope change requests, and issues with their current status.
- Project issues across the enterprise are tracked in a central location and in one database, facilitating analysis, sharing of best practices, and reporting.
- All issues are logged, and any issue activity (such as a state change, addition of a comment, or issue assignment) is audited; it is therefore much easier to find out the current project status, and any areas of the project that may require additional investments or further scrutiny.
- Overdue issues that are not resolved within a predefined time period are automatically escalated to a manager who can decide what action to take.

Table 16.5 shows some of the important attributes of an issue.

FUNDAMENTALS (1 POINT EACH)	RESPONSE	SCORE
Which is better, more or fewer milestones?	○ More ○ Less	
Do you believe in enforcing processes?	○ Always ○ Never	
Does your project team operate using an agreed on SLA (Service Level Agreement)?	○ Yes ○ No	
Are roles and processes clearly defined, written and agreed to?	○ Yes ○ No	
Are project managers and stakeholders instructed to document their roles, their work, and best practices?	○ Yes ○ No	
Do you have templates for various types of projects?	○ Yes ○ No	
Do you have emergency procedures and change management guidelines?	○ Yes ○ No	
Alignment (10 Points)		
Are promotions, bonuses, and rewards tied to enforcing, reviewing, and updating roles, processes, best practices, and checklists?	○ Yes ○ No	
Roles (1 Point Each)		
Is someone officially designated to be the project scope change request manager?	○ Yes ○ No	
Are project stakeholders clearly defined (e.g., internal departments, C executives, specific customers or target market)?	○ Yes ○ No	
Do you have a risk assessment committee?	○ Yes ○ No	
Processes (1 Point Each)		
Do you have a formal requirements gathering process?	○ Yes ○ No	
Do you have a formal scope definition process?	○ Yes ○ No	
Do you have a formal risk assessment process?	○ Yes ○ No	

Table 16.4   Scope Management Maturity Self-Assessment Test (Continued)

FUNDAMENTALS (1 POINT EACH)	RESPONSE	SCORE
Do you have a formal scope change process?	○ Yes ○ No	
Do you have a formal stakeholder review and approval process?	○ Yes ○ No	
Do you have a verifiable change management process?	○ Yes ○ No	
Do you have a formal project close process?	○ Yes ○ No ,	
Checklists (1 Point Each)		
Do stakeholders sign-off on scope definitions, milestones, and review sessions?	○ Yes ○ No	
Do you have a checklist for implementing a scope change (e.g., impact analysis, regression testing, stakeholder review)?	○ Yes ○ No	
Are checklists reviewed and improved on a quarterly basis?	○ Yes ○ No	
Total		
Score Interpretation (any response that includes more, always or yes is correct): 1 to 10: Scope management by prayer 10 to 24: Inconsistent project scope management 25 to 30: Mature and consistent scope management system		

Table 16.4   (Continued)

DETAILED DESCRIPTION	A DETAILED EXPLANATION OF THE ISSUE
Tracking ID	Use a trouble ticket or unique identification number in e-mails and inquiries.
Summary	A one line summary of the Issue.
Detailed description	A detailed explanation of the Issue.
Priority	Priority of the issue such as Blocking, High, Medium, Low.
Project	The Project the Issue belongs to.
Date of entry	Date the issue is reported.
User defined fields	The company's own specific data.

Table 16.5   Attributes of an Issue

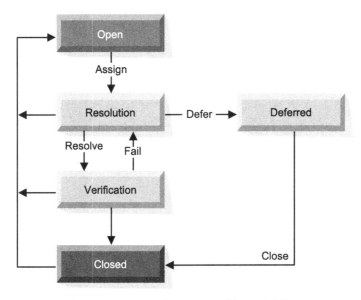

Figure 16.5   Sample Issue Tracking Workflow

Issue Tracking Workflow

Issues are submitted using an issue entry form. The workflow can automatically assign the issue to someone, or a manager may review and assign it to the person most qualified to work on it. The same benefits and capabilities offered by the core workflow engine of a Project Workforce Management system are available for issue tracking (see Figure 16.5). (See Chapter 7, "The Workflow Foundation.")

NOTE

1. *CIO Magazine,* The Secret to Software Success, http://www.cio.com/archive/070101 /secret.html.

Purchasing Workflows

There is a dollar amount above which you cannot make purchases without bidding, and you can't split purchases in order to avoid reaching that dollar amount.

—John Norris

Today, we take it for granted that when a package is given to a courier, the sender can inquire as to its exact location at every stage of the delivery process. For organizations to apply a similar standard to their purchasing process, an automated purchasing system is required—a system that can report on the status of the purchase request throughout the entire process from start to finish. Benefits include reduction in administrative costs, self-service purchase request tracking, purchase order processing, shortened fulfillment cycles, and a streamlined and audited approval process.

Purchasing, as a workflow, has much in common with timesheet and expense reporting workflows. Therefore, the company reaps remarkable synergetic benefits when the same workflow foundation is used to automate, track, and audit all of these processes in one system.

This chapter describes the benefits of automating the purchase request process, using Project Workforce Management's workflow foundation. We describe the benefits of purchase request automation and define the purchasing cycle, the information needed in a purchase request, purchasing workflows, and integration with accounting and project management systems.

Automating Purchasing

Purchasing workflow streamlines the internal processes related to material, equipment, training, and service requests. Whether it is for a trivial item such as pens, or a large expense such as suppliers, equipment, services, or software, an efficient purchasing process has to follow a set of predefined step-by-step actions. However, many purchasing processes are not efficient. The steps in the process, if they are defined at all, are usually poorly documented, misunderstood, and inconsistently followed. There can be numerous problems, for example:

- Requester forgets to provide some key information in the purchase request.
- Purchaser does not use the preferred supplier since requester did not know or forgot to mention.
- Purchaser did not seek proper approval for the request which has put the project over budget.

One of the first steps involved in making a purchase request is to determine the initial contact to receive the request. Without a formal process, the employee is obligated to make a verbal (or e-mail) request to his or her manager, who in turn refers the employee to the appropriate individual to handle the request. The request may be sent back and forth and rerouted until the appropriate approvals are obtained. This unproductive communication slows down project execution and takes away valuable time and focus from project contributors.

Another issue is the authority level of the person approving purchases. Often, depending on the cost of an item, its type, or both, different people must authorize different purchases. Therefore, with a manual procedure, many requests end up in the hands of the wrong people, who must then reroute the requests they receive—often resulting in a virtual blizzard of e-mail follow-ups.

Once the purchase request has been submitted through the right channel, the requester has no way of determining the status of the request. That person must initiate another chain of queries (such as, "Has it been approved?" "Did it get ordered?" "Has it arrived yet?") that propagate through the same channels.

This chapter describes the benefits of purchase request automation, the purchasing cycle, what information is captured by a purchase request entry, purchasing workflows and integration with account and project management systems.

Automation Benefits

Although the time wasted on a single purchase may not seem to impact the productivity of employees, when repeated many times throughout the year (as is typical in most organizations), it adds up to a significant amount of unproductive time and unnecessary cost to the organization (see Figure 17.1). Table 17.1 illustrates the cost savings of streamlining purchasing for various numbers of purchases made in one year.

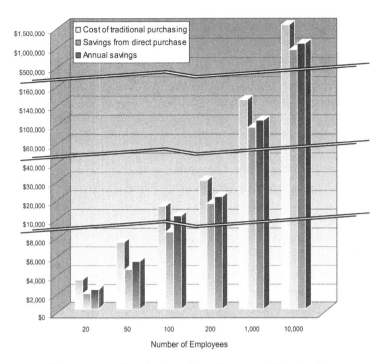

Figure 17.1 Cost Savings from Automated Purchasing

Number of purchase orders processed	20	50	100	200	1,000	10,000
Cost of traditional purchasing process[a]	$2,800	$7,000	$14,000	$28,000	$140,000	$1,400,000
Maverick buying savings[b]	$350	$878	$1,755	$3,510	$17,550	$ 175,500
Savings from direct purchases[c]	$1,600	$4,000	$8,000	$16,000	$80,000	$800,000
Total annual savings	$1,950	$4,878	$9,755	$19,510	$97,550	$975,500

[a]VISA U.S.A. estimates that transaction costs associated with traditional purchasing processes range from $130 to $150 (mandtbank.com/commercial/card.html).

[b]33% of spending for indirect goods and services takes place outside authorized buying agreements in most organizations (computingsa.co.za/2001/06/18/News/new04.htm.); ; and 38% reduction can be achieved in such purchases when a streamlined and online system is available to users in the organization; and 38% reduction can be achieved in such purchases when a streamlined and on-line system is available to users in the organization (McKinsey & Company, purchasesoft.com/eprocurementinfo.html).

[c]85% cost savings can be achieved by making direct purchases online. In this table, this saving is applied after the reduction in number of purchases because of reducing maverick purchasing (McKinsey & Company, purchasesoft.com/eprocurementinfo.html).

Table 17.1 Cost Savings over a Year

Purchasing Cycle

Purchase management automates the internal purchasing cycle (see Figure 17.2) into the following steps:

1. Users create and submit purchase request using a purchase request form.
2. Managers approve or reject requests.
3. Purchasing manager converts purchase requests into purchase orders.
4. Purchases are verified against the project budget; any notifications and limit alerts are triggered as necessary.
5. Purchases related to billable projects are sent to a billing manager for invoicing.
6. Purchase orders that have to be paid are sent to the accounting system's accounts payable (A/P), or are referenced on vendor invoices.

Purchase Request Form

The purchase request form includes the requester's name, date of the request, the project that the purchase will be allocated to (which may be overridden per purchase entry), a list of purchase entries, estimated prices and quantities per line item, and any user-defined fields. The form must be configurable based on

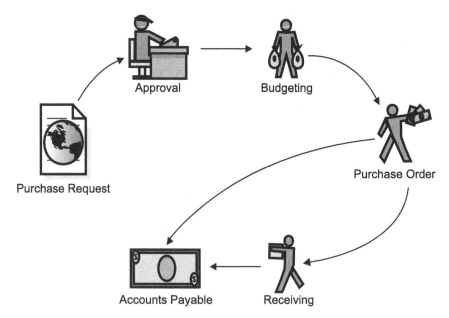

Figure 17.2 The Purchase Request Process

the company's requirements and policies. For example, a company may add a user-defined field labeled "Why is this purchase required?" or the form may take into account the company's approved or preferred supplier list for certain types of purchases.

The Purchase Entry

Figure 17.3 shows the many different attributes and information that are linked to a purchase entry. Behind the scenes, an enterprise purchasing system is tracking this information so that the accounts payable processing, cost allocation, project tracking and reporting can occur in real time.

Typically, requesters omit key information that would expedite the process. For example, one may request "Replacement battery for my laptop computer" without specifying model number or the requested battery size. Two scenarios can occur:

1. The purchasing agent notices the unspecified parameters and sends the request back to the requester.
2. The purchasing agent does not notice the unspecified information and orders the wrong item.

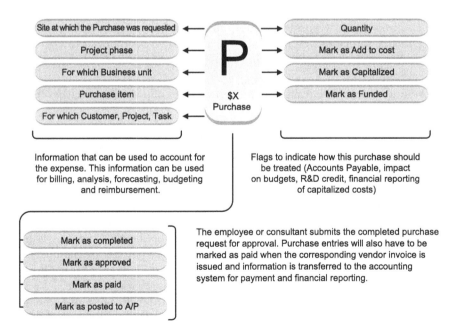

Figure 17.3   A Purchase Entry

However, with a purchasing workflow, the purchase request follows a set of predefined rules that are enforced at the point of entry. The rules and required fields ensure that the user specifies the necessary information, even if that requires the requester to attach images, drawings, or brochures. Additional documents can be attached to purchase requests or to specific purchase entries.

Purchase Workflows

Purchasing processes are considered to be financial workflows. Purchasing workflows have a lot of the same requirements as the workflows described in Chapter 7, "The Workflow Foundation" and in Chapters 11 and 12 that discuss time and expense workflows. Because of these similarities, a company can reap tremendous benefits when the same workflow foundation is used to automate, track, and audit all of these related processes. Not only does a common workflow engine unify the tracking and auditing processes, it also allows the company to assess project and resource group performance in real time and throughout the enterprise.

Approval Workflow

The following characteristics are typical of approval workflows:

- Multiple levels of approval for purchase requests depending on the resource group, type of purchase, and limits. For example, for storage media purchases, the first-level manager may be authorized to approve amounts under $1,000, but for larger amounts, a second level of approval is required.
- Automatic line item approval for certain types of purchases, such as office supplies under $50.

Figure 17.4 illustrates a typical approval workflow. The purchasing workflow can be configured to accommodate these scenarios. In fact, different approval workflows can be created to accommodate the specialized needs of various business units. For example, the professional services unit would have a more elaborate purchasing approval process (since it may involve billable purchases) than the purchasing workflow used by internal nonbillable resources.

Approval workflows support various forms of notification such as dashboards, e-mail, and cell phone. A notification is sent if a purchase request needs to be approved, or has been escalated because the original request has not been processed.

The approval workflow defines the approval process. It also allows the administrator to define and enforce enterprise purchasing policies, rules, and thresholds. Every workflow has its own states and its own set of user-defined fields.

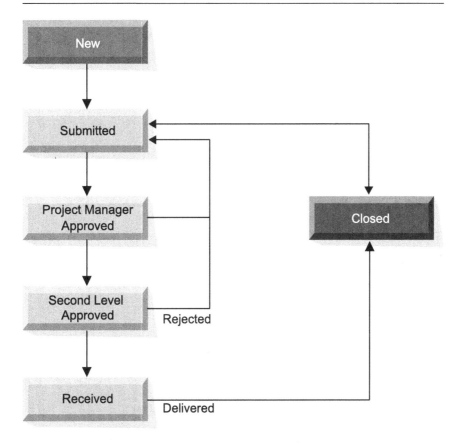

Figure 17.4   Approval Workflow

LINE ITEM APPROVAL.   A purchase request may include purchases for multiple projects. Each manager approves or rejects purchase entries for his or her project—also known as line item approval—but managers can only approve the line items that belong to their respective projects.

Training Request Workflow

Figure 17.5 illustrates a training request workflow. Project and service-driven organizations must invest in training their project workforce on a continuous basis. The training request workflow is a specialized purchasing workflow that is tailored to training requests. In many organizations, it is more efficient to handle and track training requests separately, since the training request form requires the requester to provide specialized information, such as the reason the training is needed, the location, estimated travel costs, and what skills are being obtained or upgraded.

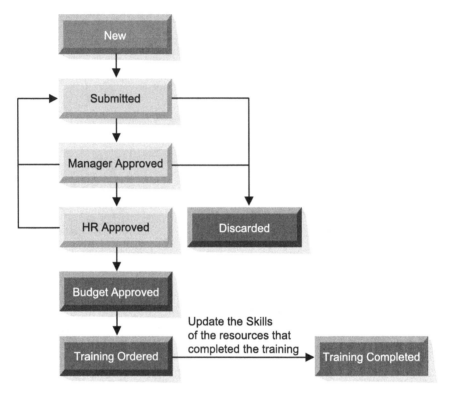

Figure 17.5   Training Request Workflow

Furthermore, a training request workflow is the source of information that is useful in workforce planning. Once the training is completed, the workflow should automatically update the skills of the resources that completed the training.

User Roles

More often than not, several individuals are involved in the purchasing cycle. The larger the organization the more individuals are involved in the process. In the workflow, every user role should have designated security privileges for accessing various functions. The concept of *role* makes the association between a group of users and the rights they have to accessing various functions. The common purchasing-related roles include:

- *Requester:* This type of user has the right to make a purchase request only. Requesters typically cannot approve purchase requests.
- *Manager:* The manager can approve purchase requests. Usually, there are limits on the dollar amounts that a manager can approve. When any pur-

chase request exceeds the manager's approval authority, the request is automatically routed to the next level of management. (In addition, there is the possibility of auto-approval for preapproved and budgeting items. This allows basic recurring purchase requests to proceed without managerial intervention.)

- *Chief financial officer:* A senior executive approves purchase requests that are above certain predefined limits. After the purchase requests are created and approved by lower level management, they will be automatically routed for second level approval, if it is needed.
- *Purchasing manager:* This individual converts purchase requests into purchase orders, combines purchases to save costs, deals with vendors, and orders goods.
- *Receiving agent:* In some cases, the receiving agent may be different from the purchasing manager. The responsibility of the receiving agent is to ensure that the goods received match the orders, and to deliver them to the requester.

Integration

Purchase orders provide several integration points with other enterprise systems. Here are a few common scenarios:

- An approved purchase order is required before any vendor is paid. This control ensures that only legitimate vendor invoices are paid and prevents double payment.
- Purchase orders made against billable projects result in billable expenses that are invoiced to customers.
- Purchase order entries are exported to the accounting system as accounts payable transactions.

Trend Analysis

Over time, valuable information is accumulated by the purchasing system that allows managers to analyze patterns in purchasing, spending, ordering, and approval. This information can be used to optimize operations. For instance, consider a large consulting organization in which many independent groups work on customer projects, and where members of each group routinely order similar equipment, training, and services. Analysis from a global perspective may determine that certain purchases can be shared or combined across various groups to reduce costs, or that some items could be ordered in larger quantities for better pricing and lower shipping fees.

Part of the cost of a project is the equipment, material, consulting, training, and other items that are purchased in the execution phase. By adding purchasing data to the tools used for tracking projects, a manager can report on such costs. Here are some useful applications of project purchase tracking as part of Project Workforce Management:

- Report on purchases made for research and development or funded activities.
- Measure project, team, and resource group profitability (by accounting for all costs including pay, overhead, expenses, and purchases).
- Analyze purchasing patterns and trends for various services, projects, business units, and resource groups.

18

Project Prioritization and Selection

Pick battles big enough to matter, small enough to win.

—Jonathan Kozol

Project Workforce Management optimizes financial, team, and overall project performance with better information and collaboration for stakeholders. However, individual project success does not imply business success. What if the attention and resources allocated to a successful project starve another more critical project? Lack of facts and unbiased analysis lead executives to make poor decisions when selecting new projects or assigning resources to existing ones. These decisions lead to unmet goals and cost the business lost opportunities. In addition to the misuse of funds, an environment is created where strategic projects take back seat while "pet" projects are promoted to higher priority. Managers have no way to know what percentage of their projects are high risk and they end up spending significantly more on operations ("keeping the lights on") instead of value creating projects.

A *project portfolio* is a collection of projects (investments) that is usually owned by one business unit or by the corporation. It is a series of projects that share a combination of common objectives, cost centers, resources, risks, or other associations, and allow management to making funding decisions, and to report on and analyze a collection of projects as one entity. For example, an Information Technology (IT) portfolio would consist of all IT projects funded for the next two years; a software portfolio would consist of all software development projects currently in progress. The company can look at its portfolios and decide which ones are strategic, require additional funding, and which ones are not reaching the expected end results.

Successful executives have to make the right decisions not only at the project level but also at the business level, where there can be tens and, possibly hundreds of projects to evaluate at any given time. These projects rely on the same

221

enterprise resource pool and obtain funding from the same global budget. *Project prioritization and selection* is a methodology that organizes and manages projects as a group or a *portfolio* at a business or departmental level. It elevates decision making from project management to a more strategic viewpoint by aligning and assigning projects with business priorities, and helps optimize resource allocation. This methodology also provides guidance for new projects so that they can be validated and prioritized against assumptions and risks while creating value for the business and its customers. Risks at the portfolio level are assessed from a global perspective on their overall impact, and not just their project impact. If projects are prioritized and selected properly (referred to as a *managed portfolio*), risk is greatly reduced and the business operates at an optimal capacity with a higher number of successful projects (see Figure 18.1).

Good project prioritization and selection depend on two key factors—a well thought-out structure and reliable information. Project teams should have an understanding of their business needs. They should also embrace a culture where structured project execution and following processes are the foundation of their collective teamwork. In order for this culture to thrive, it must be supplemented with the availability of timely and correct information, such as project plans and resource allocation across the enterprise. Fact-based decisions regarding project priorities and new project selection align projects and resource utilization with the company's ultimate goals and improve the odds of creating tremendous value.

Most of these organizations have adopted some level of project prioritization and selection where the strategic objectives and priorities are constantly evaluated at the portfolio level. It is critical for any organization to implement a

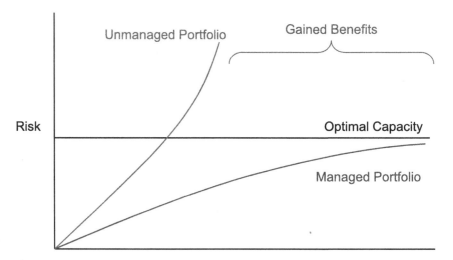

Figure 18.1   Project Prioritization and Selection Reduces Risk and Improves Overall Performance

methodology and a system to optimize projects' portfolio and resource allocation. If projects are not prioritized systematically, then the company runs the increased risk of:

- Misallocating critical resources to poorly performing projects
- Not funding important projects in a timely manner
- Shifting focus away from the needs of key customers

Using a sample scenario, this chapter:

- Outlines the steps for project prioritization and selection
- Introduces simple selection techniques
- Describes how a new project is selected and added to a portfolio
- Presents an approach to implementing a system
- Provides guidance to proactively managing a project portfolio

As an example, we will use the IT department of ABC Corporation. This is a midsize bank facing increased competitive pressure. Its aim is to reduce cost and innovate in order to increase its market share and stay competitive. The IT department has a large resource pool primarily trained on legacy platforms. There are scores of projects at any given time and the managers are constantly short of budget and resources. At the same time, the bank's executives are constantly increasing the demands for innovation and cost reduction. This challenge is further compounded by the fact that the bank is trying to adopt new technologies while some compliance and quality initiatives are also underway.

Steps in Project Prioritization and Selection

Balancing and managing project portfolios can be accomplished using simple spreadsheets or more sophisticated project management and resource planning tools. In either case, the timely availability of accurate data is more important than the sophistication of the tools. The following steps explain the process and walk you through a typical project prioritization exercise. The Implementation section later in the chapter explains when some steps can be skipped. Some steps have to be performed iteratively to refine the prioritization.

Step 1: Select Project Ranking Criteria

The company first identifies which criteria will be used to prioritize or rank your projects. It is also important to assign weights or level of importance with

Ranking Criteria	Weights
Increase Market Share	10
Improve Customer Service	9
Reduce Costs	15
Supports Innovation	11
Organizational Impact	5
Project Uncertainty	8
Resource Capability Level	10
Project Size	15
Resource/Skill Availability	11
Project Complexity	6
Ranking Criteria	100

Figure 18.2   Ranking Criteria Balanced with Business Goals

each selected criterion. This process starts with an understanding of the key business drivers and objectives.

Any criteria can be selected as long as it aligns with business objectives and priorities. Figure 18.2 shows the criteria selected for ABC Bank—each criterion is given a weight as a percentage of the total weight. Cost reduction has more weight since it is important for the bank to reduce costs. ABC is also facing challenges finding and retaining highly specialized IT staff particularly in new technologies like .NET. Therefore, it must select this criterion to assess its internal capability to deliver the project and its impact on the organization or the business unit. Since specialized skills are required to deliver the project, Resource/skills availability criterion is also ranked high at 11 percent of the total weight. Organizations often make the mistake of ranking criteria that are not aligned with business priorities or they use criteria that are not agreed to or understood by all stakeholders. It is good practice, particularly for small and midsize organizations, to use fewer ranking criteria that are easily understood and communicated. Mid- to large-size companies often deploy more advanced criteria such as net present value (NPV) or return on investments (ROI) and combine them with sophisticated measuring tools such as balanced score cards. These concepts are not covered here because this chapter serves as an introduction to project prioritization with a simple and quickly executable strategy.

Step 2: Rank Projects

The top 20 percent of projects will deliver 80 percent of the value to the business. The challenge is knowing how to identify that top 20 percent. Similarly, it is important for managers and executives to know the percentage of their project portfolio that is geared toward improving operations versus creating value

Ranking Criteria	Increase Market Share	Improve Customer Service	Reduce Costs	Supports Innovation	Organizational Impact	Project Uncertainty	Resource Capability Level	Project Size	Resource/Skills Availability	Project Complexity	Total
Weights	10	9	15	11	5	8	10	15	11	6	100
Projects											
Help Desk Update	3	5	5	1	2	2	3	2	3	3	344
CRM Implementation	3	5	3	3	4	4	4	2	3	3	340
Reachout Project	1	3	3	5	3	2	5	3	3	3	330
KB Development	3	4	4	4	4	2	3	5	3	4	324
CMM Compliancy	3	3	3	1	3	3	2	2	3	2	277
HR Portal	2	3	3	2	1	2	2	2	2	4	277
ERP Integration	2	4	2	2	5	3	2	4	4	4	275
Vista Update	1	2	3	3	1	1	2	3	2	3	256
BPM Platform	4	4	3	4	2	5	1	4	1	2	246

Figure 18.3   Project Ranking Helps with Project and Resources Decisions

(or innovation), a prerequisite for long-term success. We rank both existing and new projects against each of the selected criteria. As shown in Figure 18.3, the HelpDesk Update is the most critical project for the bank since it contributes the most toward cost reduction (an identified high priority), while it has low ratings of project uncertainty and project size (a relatively safe project). The weight of each criterion is then used to calculate the overall weight of the project. This weight is used to obtain a meaningful ranking of the projects which helps guide managers in their decision making. For example, every project or any new project request can be ranked on a scale of 1 to 5. The ranking is used to compare projects and to make decisions on timelines, prioritization, funding, and resource allocation.

Step 3: Balance the Portfolio

Portfolio Balancing provides the organization with the right mix of projects. This process helps increase the priority of those projects that offer high reward for low risk against those that offer significant business transformation

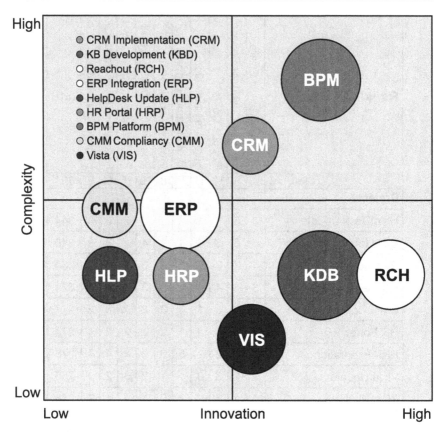

Figure 18.4   Portfolio Balancing Helps the Company Invest in the Right Mix of Projects

for low effort. While project ranking helps identify high priority projects, the portfolio balancing tools help balance projects with respect to risk, value, complexity or any other criteria key to the success of the business. Development of a project's view for balancing, such as a bubble chart shown in Figure 18.4, requires plotting of any two or three criteria (one depicted as the bubble size). These can include:

- Project size (length of project in time)
- Project size (size of budget)
- Level of risk
- Resource utilization
- Type of product
- Level of innovation
- Impact on areas of operation

In the case of ABC bank, the Helpdesk project was clearly ranked at the top due to cost reduction. When evaluating projects for their innovative capacities (see example in Figure 18.4), three projects look more attractive—see third quadrant where innovation is high and complexity is low. Here, Reachout (RCH) and KB Development projects (KBD) both look more attractive, although Reachout appears to be more so due to the smaller investment required (bubble size). This project Web-enables the internal systems and allows the bank's customers to do online banking, pay bills, manage credit cards, and receive personalized service 24 hours a day. This level of analysis helps screen new projects as well as balances your existing portfolio. Similar analysis reveals that the Vista (VIS) Implementation project, despite being low on the ranking, is also a good candidate for the active project list since it offers more innovation while being the least complex.

Step 4: Balance Capacity/Resources

A key element of portfolio level planning is to ensure there is adequate resource availability to execute the projects in the pipeline. It is equally important to understand the organization's capacity to deliver and its ability to develop internal capabilities. To assess resource availability, skill pool assessment, and capacity planning, resource balancing is performed after the project ranking and balancing steps have been completed. As demonstrated in Figure 18.5, a rolled up view of resource availability by resource type helps in balancing the project portfolio. In this example, .NET developers are either over allocated or are close to capacity. Here, the prioritization or selection of that project will largely depend on the availability of .NET resources regardless of the ranking or balancing of the project. As part of resource balancing, resources are allocated to

Projects	JAN	FEB	MAR	APR	MAY
☑ HelpDesk Update					
☑ CRM Implementation					
☐ Reachout Project					
☑ KB Development					
☑ CMM Compliancy					
☑ HR Portal					
☐ ERP Integration					
☐ Vista Update					
☐ BPM Platform					
Resource Types	**JAN**	**FEB**	**MAR**	**APR**	**MAY**
Overall	70%	90%	77%	65%	
Business Analysts	60%	45%	62%	80%	
Architects	20%	30%		83%	
.Net Developers	130%	95%	96%	23%	

Figure 18.5   Resource Balancing Requires Accurate and Timely Data

Status	Projects	Score	Rank
Active	HelpDesk Update	344	1
OnHold	CRM Implementation	340	2
Active	Reachout Project	330	3
Active	KB Development	324	4
Active	CMM Compliancy	277	5
OnHold	HR Portal	277	6
OnHold	ERP Integration	275	7
Active	Vista Update	256	8
OnHold	BPM Platform	246	9

Figure 18.6   Project Score and Ranking Example

high-priority projects and this process is repeated until the resources are exhausted. In the case of ABC bank, the following technique revealed the best option—reallocation of .NET resources from customer relationship management (CRM) project to Reachout, which is a more strategic, higher priority project. Once all resources are allocated or reassigned, the remaining projects are put on hold or additional resources are added to the resource pool. Some project work may be outsourced if no resources are available and if they are a high priority.

Step 5: Prioritize Overall Portfolio

Once the projects are ranked and balanced, the portfolio is prioritized by marking lower ranked projects or those that cannot be funded immediately (due to insufficient resources) as inactive (or on hold). In the case of ABC bank (see Figure 18.6), several projects are put on hold including a high-ranked project like the CRM implementation project because resources are redeployed to the Reachout project, which is a higher ranked and a more strategic project. Similarly, low-ranked projects like Vista Update are made active due to less complexity and higher innovation ranking (see Step 3). One of the big pitfalls is not prioritizing active projects. Successful project prioritization and selection implementation requires that all projects be prioritized, including new or approved projects in the pipeline.

New Project Selection

Project prioritization and selection provides a framework to evaluate new project requests or opportunities in a systematic manner (see Figure 18.7). Each opportunity is considered against the current priorities and resource availability. New opportunities resulting from business or customer needs are formally

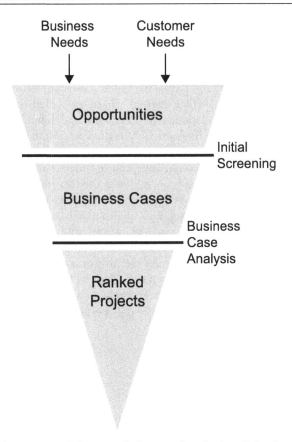

Figure 18.7   A Systematic Approach to Project Selection

submitted to project sponsors as *Opportunity Concepts.* Business analysts typically get involved to analyze the request and provide high level project information. The information submitted in the *Project Proposal* document may include
information such as:

- Alignment with business objectives (increase market share, improve cus-
  tomer service, cost reduction)
- Scope, duration, and timeframes
- High-level estimates for costs
- Types of resources required

The information included in the Opportunity Concept is used by the project
sponsors to do initial screening of the project by checking for alignment with
business and internal priorities. Priorities include cost reduction, time to market, and customer service improvement. It may also include internal priorities,

such as delivering projects on time and on budget, improving internal capabilities, or developing critical skills. If the opportunity does not pass this initial screening, it is rejected. Some are totally discarded and others may be archived for possible future consideration.

If the Opportunity Concept passes the initial screening, it is sent back to the business analyst team for further analysis where a detailed *Business Case* or *Project Charter* is developed along with detailed scope definition, budget, and resource requirements. The Business Case is then submitted for a comprehensive review and detailed ranking based on the new information. This step also involves rebalancing against the portfolio and resource availability. If the Business Case fails to justify the project selection in the current portfolio, it may be rejected or deferred. If the project is selected, it is presented to the executive team for formal approval, funding, and final ranking. After this approval, the project stays in the pipeline with an inactive status until it is reviewed as part of the periodic review process—conducted monthly or quarterly—at which point it may become an active project. Once the project is made active, the project team begins the planning and requirements phase of the project. The following steps are performed when adding a new project (project selection), however, the entire portfolio is prioritized (Step 5) only periodically:

Step 2: Rank Projects

Step 3: Balance Portfolio

Step 4: Balance Capacity/Resources

Implementation

The project prioritization and selection implementation methodology outlined in this section consists of two sets of activities (see Figure 18.8). One set is performed as part of launching project prioritization and selection, and the other

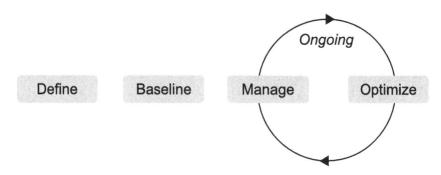

Figure 18.8   Implementing Project Prioritization and Selection

set is performed as part of regular project prioritization and selection management. These activities use similar tools and techniques and, in most cases, can be performed by the same teams or individuals at agreed on time intervals. The implementation starts by creating or defining the framework and then using it to baseline the existing portfolio as a one-time activity. From there on, the ongoing activities are carried out as described in this section.

Define (Readiness Phase)

The most critical factor in the implementation of project prioritization and selection is to have executive level commitment—both financial and resource commitment—without which the efforts are meaningless and the goals highly unattainable. Once this commitment has been secured, the implementation process truly begins. It starts with understanding the business needs—both short term and long term. This is usually done with the help of all key individuals including executives and project sponsors. A clear understanding of organization's needs must be agreed on and communicated. This includes business goals and objectives as well as any constraints such as lack of resources or impending compliance deadlines. This information helps in the development of the project ranking criteria as explained in the earlier section.

> 95% of the workforce does not understand their organization's strategy.
> —David Norton, "Project Balanced Scorecards:
> a Tool for Alignment, Teamwork and Results"

As part of the readiness phase, an assessment of the current landscape and a gap analysis is performed to assess the level of capability maturity and the culture of the organization with respect to project and portfolio management practices. This helps identify areas to improve in support of these practices. The organization must support this initiative at all levels, especially at the executive level. Identification of formal or informal teams that will perform the project prioritization and selection functions must be clearly defined. One of the most effective and simple tools organizations should develop and share with project stakeholders is the RASCI model (Figure 18.9). RASCI is a simple management tool used for identifying roles and responsibilities that helps bring about any significant change in the organization such as the implementation of a project prioritization and selection process. RASCI stands for:

R Responsible—identifies the problem or project owner

A Accountable person—who must sign off (approve) work before it is effective

S Supporting individual or role—provides resources or participates in implementation

	CEO	Executive Team	EPO Management Team	Project Sponsors	EPM Project Office	Program Managers	Project Managers	Business Analysts	System Analysts	Finance	Functional Managers	Risk and Compliance	Training
Opportunity Evaluation													
Activity	A, R	R	S	S	S	I	I	I	I	I	I	I	I
Activity	S	A, R	S	S	S	S	S	C	C	S	S	S	S
Activity	A	R	R	R	R	R	S	S	S	S	C	C	C
Business Case Review	I	S	S	S	A, R	S	S	S	I	S	C	I	C
Activity	I	S	S	S	A, R	S	S	I	C	S	C	I	C
Activity	S	S	S	S	A, R	S	S	I	I	S	C	I	C
Monthly PPS Review	A	R	R	R	R	R	S	S	S	S	C	C	C
Activity	A	R	R	R	R	R	S	I	I	S	C	C	C
Activity	I	R	A	R	R	S	S	S	S	S	C		
Activity	A, R	R	R	R	R	R	C	S	C	S	C	C	C

R: Responsible, A: Accountable, S: Supports, C: Consults, I: Informed

Figure 18.9 Sample RASCI Chart—A Simple Management Tool for Identifying Roles and Responsibilities

C Consulting support—person(s) with information and/or capability necessary to complete the work

I Informed—individuals who must be notified of results, but need not be consulted

This model provides clear guidance to those involved in this change and maximizes the likelihood of success by maintaining interest and momentum among the diverse set of stakeholders.

Project prioritization and selection requires involvement at all levels of the organization, such as executives, the project management office, project managers, and other stakeholders. The information is collected, shared, and presented for analysis in a systematic and easy-to-use manner. For example, there should be a quick and easy way to distribute and collect ranking information using surveys or questionnaires. Since these are ongoing but critical activities, some level of automation greatly assists in the adoption of the methodology at all levels—particularly for time-constrained managers and executives. Technology can play a great role in streamlining and automating these tasks. For example, workflows can automate and enforce the task of collecting and processing information from different stakeholders in a timely manner. Workflows bring discipline and enforce governance for processes such as portfolio ranking, new project selection, or decommissioning/deactivating projects.

If a formal PMO has not been established, then this is the time to create an Enterprise Portfolio Management (EPM) team consisting of senior managers and a rotating pool of cross-functional project managers. The biggest barrier to project prioritization and selection adoption is the organizational politics and culture—this demands change, which inherently encounters resistance at many levels; a resistance that has to be dealt with if the initiative is to succeed.

Baseline Existing Project Portfolio

The first step in implementing project prioritization and selection is to take inventory of all current projects and proposals. This list is then reviewed, ranked, and balanced to create the initial ranked project portfolio. This initial exercise must involve all project stakeholders and is lead by the EPM team. Each opportunity is evaluated against project selection criteria, prioritized within the existing project portfolio and ranked (active or on hold) based on window of opportunity and resource availability. As part of the ranking process, some high priority projects may get lower priorities while some active projects may be put on hold. The data collection and prioritization is a time-consuming process which may bring to surface personnel or departmental issues. As such, this effort will be the most challenging part of the project prioritization and selection implementation and may require an external facilitator. It is important to get an alignment around common business goals as opposed to individual or departmental priorities. Once an agreement is reached and the baseline portfolio is created, it is important to reprioritize this list at least once a quarter. Piloting with a smaller set of projects can ensure success and help validate the approach. Regardless of the level of success, this portfolio must be constantly reviewed and adjusted for alignment and prioritization. The following steps are performed to establish a baseline. Some of the steps will be performed iteratively. For example, after ranking and balancing portfolio (Steps 2 and 4), the resource balancing (Step 4) may show resource unavailability, which can lead to iterations until the portfolio is prioritized to meet the business needs and optimized based on resource availability:

Step 1: Select Project Ranking Criteria

Step 2: Rank Projects

Step 3: Balance Portfolio

Step 4: Balance Capacity/Resources

Step 5: Prioritize overall Portfolio

Managing Prioritization and Selection

Management of prioritization and selection involves evaluating and periodically reviewing new projects by the EPM team, as well as reporting to the executives. The management of project portfolio is an ongoing exercise performed with the help of project managers and, in some cases, project sponsors and executives. It is important not to upset the portfolio too frequently by constant prioritization and resource balancing. It is recommended to have a minor review each month and a major portfolio review once every quarter.

MONTHLY REVIEWS. The EPM team reviews the status of each project with respect to any significant variances in its schedule, budget, and/or resource utilization. As a result of the review, resources may be moved from low to high priority projects:

Step 4: Balance Capacity/Resources

Step 5: Prioritize Overall Portfolio (if a scope changes or new projects have been added)

QUARTERLY REVIEWS. The entire portfolio is ranked, prioritized, and balanced. Underperforming or nonstrategic projects are placed on hold or canceled, and promotion is given to more important projects by reallocating resources. Most new projects in the pipeline are activated after quarterly reviews:

Step 2: Rank Projects

Step 3: Balance Portfolio

Step 4: Balance Capacity/Resources

Step 5: Prioritize overall Portfolio

ANNUAL REVIEW. It is not recommended to change the project ranking criteria too frequently—though they must be reviewed at least once a year or as the business priorities and objectives change. The project selection and prioritization information provided in the form of dashboards or portfolio reporting helps executives and managers make better fact-based business decisions when setting new goals and reviewing the current situation:

Step 1: Select Project Ranking Criteria

Optimize

For the executives to see the overall picture of the portfolio and make key decisions, it is essential that the organization collect all the relevant information from multiple sources and present it in a summarized or dashboard view. This is where portfolio reporting or dashboard techniques are used to consolidate and summarize key project information. For all active projects, it is important to include information related to project health such as variances in costs and schedule as well as some indication of risks and issues. When combined with the project ranking and resource data, this information facilitates what-if analysis, decision making, and the portfolio rebalancing.

Some projects do not deliver the promised value despite their success related to on-time and on-budget project delivery. Such projects can be identified with the help of surveys and feedback from the customers and other stakeholders. This information, combined with the wealth of knowledge in the portfolio repository of both current and archived projects creates a *project memory*. Managers can analyze past decisions with respect to project prioritization and selection and use this knowledge to improve their decision-making and forecasting abilities. A framework for continued process improvement must be established so that lessons learned and metrics obtained are used to improve future project selection, estimation, and ranking decisions.

19

Reporting and Dashboards

Instead of telling us who is doing what and how, we got a few spreadsheets.

—David Obey

Organizations are generally data rich but information poor. However, those that employ Project Workforce Management compile data on their customers, projects, and talent that is easier to harvest into useful information. Dashboards and real-time analytics built on Project Workforce Management close the fact gap, lower costs, improve productivity, and increase satisfaction for both employees and customers.

Harvesting information from Project Workforce Management also results in the discovery of new revenue opportunities. Decisions that were previously based on incomplete information, intuition, memory, and experience can now be made based on reliable real-time data, leading to faster and better decision making supported by facts.

This chapter describes the problem with disconnected information islands, the dangers of decision making based on incomplete or inaccurate data, and the benefits of using reporting and dashboard technology to provide real-time project and resource performance, as well as status information to empower the project workforce.

Real-Time Analysis

Project Workforce Management workflows, approval processes, point-of-entry validation, and auditing generate valuable data that can be used to monitor project execution, assess resource group performance, and report on project status, cost, revenue, and profitability. Information can be reported in a variety of report formats, such as project cost and billing, resource utilization, and workflow activity—all in two-dimensional tables, bar charts, pie charts, gauges, or other graphic forms.

The same information can also be added easily to *Executive Dashboards*, which are summary reports, usually displayed on a single page and built on information assembled from various business systems such as Project Workforce Management, customer relationship management (CRM), and accounting applications. Dashboards are designed to report on project and resource-group metrics, also known as key performance indicators (KPIs). Key performance indicators are both financial and nonfinancial metrics that quantify objectives and report on the performance of a project, resource, or business unit benchmarked against its strategic goals.

Dashboards and reports let decision makers view the status of current projects and engagements visually and concisely. They provide managers with the ability to drill through live data to identify trouble spots and discover new best practices, and share this knowledge with the project workforce, customers, partners, and suppliers. Real-time reporting and dashboard technologies significantly enhance decision making because managers and executives are no longer forced to make decisions based on insufficient results, incomplete information, or purely on their gut feeling, memory, or experience.

Data Warehousing

Many organizations use diverse applications and information systems, each having their own database. The data from disparate systems can be merged into a single database (centralized data) in a process known as *data warehousing.* For example, a company could use a CRM solution from Vendor A, a project management system from Vendor B, and an enterprise resource planning (ERP) or accounting system from Vendor C; data warehousing would be used to aggregate the data from these three sources. Business intelligence and reporting tools are then used to perform detailed analysis on all of the data. Data warehouse reports are usually not real time, since the data aggregation takes time to complete and is typically scheduled for once per week, month, or even quarter.

Data warehousing has been rendered obsolete for managing projects and talent with the advent of Web Services (see Chapter 20, "Integration"), which connects disparate information systems to each other and by Project Workforce Management, which combines the customer, the project, and the talent into a global system of record. Dashboards and reports based on the Project Workforce Management data provide real-time project visibility and eliminate the need for expensive and time-consuming data warehousing.

Decision Making

What is a good decision? One that is made quickly and decisively helping the organization move closer to its goal. What helps a manager make a good decision? Timely and easily accessible problem-related facts and background information.

Hundreds of decisions are made daily, such as:

- Assign this project to the same team as last time.
- Delay this project because the expertise is unavailable.
- Accept this engagement because we can allocate or hire the resources we need.
- Business unit A is our most capable operating unit, so assign this strategic project to that unit.

How are decisions made in most organizations today? Often, these decisions are based more on experience, gut feeling, and rule of thumb than on facts. How can managers improve the quality of their decisions? The most effective approach is to empower information workers by giving them the means to make better decisions. Access to real-time quantitative project and service execution information and the ability to analyze it leads to better decisions. For example, a project manager plans the project, creates schedules, assigns tasks, and follows up to ensure the project is progressing as planned. Real-time online analytical information on the entire project allows the manager to instantly assess whether the project is meeting its cost, schedule, and milestone objectives. Actionable information is a powerful motivator and empowers project managers and executives to get their job done effectively and efficiently.

The Information Problem

The problem with the decision-making process is the "fact gap" (see Figure 19.1). Organizations often maintain vast and growing quantities of dispersed

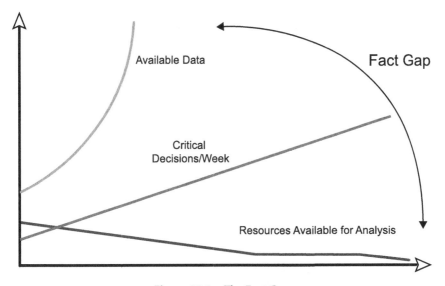

Figure 19.1   The Fact Gap

data, while increasingly most decisions require the real-time access to all of this data collectively. The management team is unable to absorb the flood of data in the form of spreadsheets, e-mails, conversations, and meetings, and is forced to make judgment calls based on instinct, experience, and memory—a tendency that leads to the fact gap.

Vast quantities of data are stored in legacy systems, diverse and disconnected databases, ERPs, data warehouses, spreadsheets, web sites, hard disks of personal computers, and a large number of dispersed documents. This data must be transformed into knowledge.

Data in context = Information
Information in context = Knowledge

Organizations are in a data jailhouse:

- It takes hours, days, and sometimes longer to get answers to questions.
- Data is scattered:
  —Project details are maintained in the project management system.
  —Customer details, orders, purchase history, and support information is in the CRM, a separate helpdesk application, and accounting system.
  —Customer invoices and payment history is in the accounting system.
- Employee costs are not allocated to projects and are tracked only in the payroll system.
- Budgets, risks, issues, and scope changes are tracked using spreadsheets, management by e-mail and document exchange (see Figure 19.2).

The Solution: Unlocking the Information

The combination of Project Workforce Management, Web Services, reporting, and dashboard technologies are the key to unlocking the accumulated knowledge of the project workforce. Project Workforce Management reports and dashboards close the fact gap by providing users with a single point of access to reliable, real-time information that enables them to analyze and share information across the enterprise without extra overhead or additional effort. Analysis based on reliable information enables the company to increase revenue, avoid or reduce costs, and improve customer satisfaction (see Figure 19.3 on p. 242).

Here are some of the questions that can be instantly answered using this powerful combination:

Project Management
- Which projects are late?
- Which projects and activities were over budget?

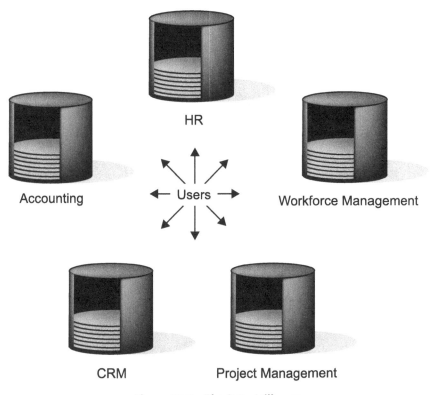

Figure 19.2   The Data Jailhouse

- Which projects have too many problems?
- Which projects have a lot of risk?
- Which team delivered the most projects in the last quarter?
- Which projects were the most profitable?

Capacity Planning
- What types of skills are in shortage?
- Which resources are underutilized?
- Which departments are overloaded?

Finance
- Which department has the highest travel costs per resource?
- Which activities have delivered the highest profit margins?
- What is our work in progress (see Chapter 15, "Work in Progress and Forecasting")?

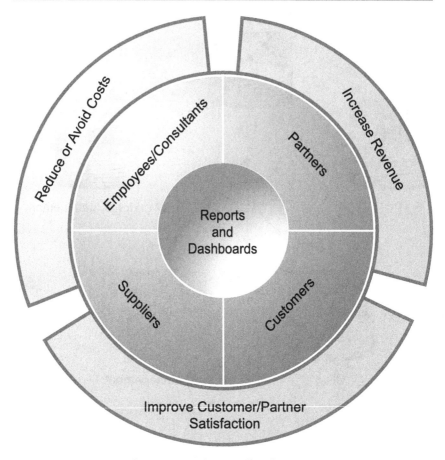

Figure 19.3 The Benefits of Analysis

Sales and Marketing
- What is the status of this customer's project?
- How much of the project has been invoiced to the customer? How much has the customer paid?
- Where is the greatest sales opportunity?
- Which type of service generates the most revenue?

REAL-TIME REPORTS AND DASHBOARDS. Real-time reports and dashboards can help answer these questions. Here is why:

- Projects and services are delivered on time, on budget, and profitably. If they are not, management gets ample advanced warnings with alerts, reports, and yellow or red flags appearing on their dashboards.

- Poor performing business units are held accountable for missing their targets.
- Unnecessary costs are identified and eliminated quickly.
- The company avoids backlog and project execution delays.
- Resources are utilized more effectively.
- Management is able to forecast better and plan better for future demand.
- Management can make course corrections and revise strategy as needed with access to better analysis tools.
- The salesforce gains more insight into its customers, can monitor project execution, and is able to discover new opportunities in the process.

Sample Reports

The following examples will help you design your own graphs and reports. Where applicable, tables with the raw data are included.

WBS/OBS Cost/Revenue Analytics

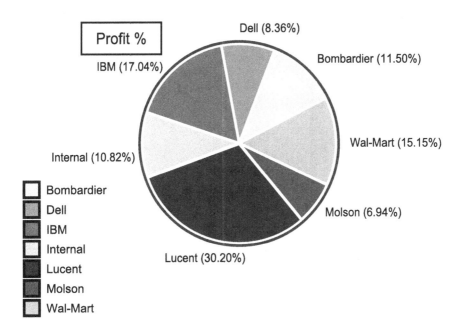

Sample Profit Chart Report

CLIENT	PROJECT	COST AMOUNT	REVENUE AMOUNT
Bombardier	Bombardier Project 1	20,111,800.00	60,398,000
Bombardier	Bombardier Project 2	10,062,400.00	28,624,000
Dell	Dell Project 1	1,492,250.00	−2,037,500
IBM	IBM Project 1	2,265,000.00	12,730,000
Internal	General	2,900.00	−11,000
Lucent	Lucent Project 1	367,500.00	1,680,000
Lucent	Lucent Project 2	1,880,000.00	5,280,000
Molson	Molson Promotion	817,600.00	5,406,000
Wal-Mart	Wal-Mart Project 1	129,075.00	390,750
Wal-Mart	Wal-Mart Project 2	62,300.00	193,000

Client Table

WBS/OBS Time/Expense Analytics

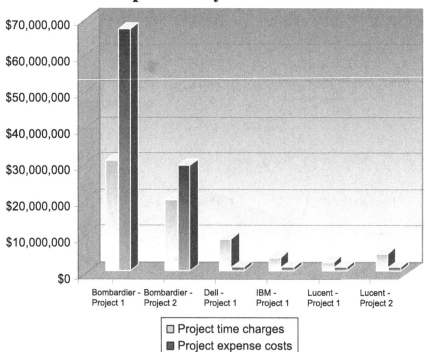

Sample Time and Expense Bar Chart

244

WBS/OBS Workflow Analytics

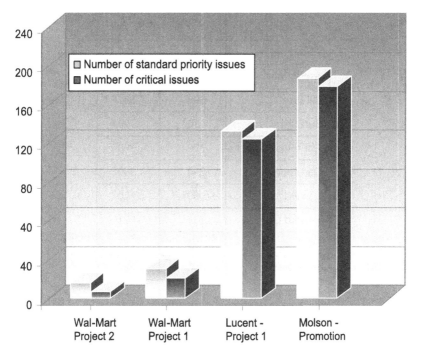

Sample Issue Report

	PROJECT ISSUES	
RESOURCES	OPEN	CLOSED
Adam West	88	78
Andy Bogart	390	380
Ashley Moore	390	380
Bill Turin	390	380
Burt Bixby	30	20
Chris Redmond	390	380
Dan Loomis	390	380
Edward Asner	30	20
Edward Gierrek	131	121
Eric Diaz	95	85
Frank Ramsey	390	380
Gail Ranford	390	380
Glenda Gates	390	380
Horace Yates	390	380

Issue Report Data Table

Project Status

(i)	Projects/Task	Planned				Actual				% Complete
		Schedule		Work		Schedule		Effort		
		Start	End	Planned	Allocated	Start	End	Work	ETC	
	▼ Module A Dev	5-Jan	20-Apr	925 hrs	445 hrs	5-Jan		160 hrs	115 hrs	17%
	▼ Specifications	5-Jan	25-Jan	220 hrs	220 hrs	5-Jan		150 hrs	70 hrs	68%
	Daniel Berlin			-	110 hrs			110 hrs	0 hrs	100%
	James Willington							40 hrs	70 hrs	36%
	▼ Spec Review	5-Jan	30-Jan	80 hrs	55 hrs	10-Jan	-	10 hrs	45 hrs	18%
	George Filmon			-	55 hrs	10-Jan		10 hrs	45 hrs	18%
	▲ Task C			125 hrs	85 hrs					0%
	▲ Task E	30-Jan	20-Feb	75 hrs	30 hrs	-				0%
	▲ Task F	25-Jan	1-Apr	100 hrs	55 hrs	-				0%
	▲ Task G	1-Apr	20-Apr	100 hrs	55 hrs	-				0%
	▲ SAP Integration	10-Jan	4-Aug	1500 hrs	545 hrs	10-Jan	-	230 hrs	315 hrs	15%
	▲ Module B Dev	10-Feb	12-Dec	2100 hrs	1000 hrs	-	-	-		0%

Project Issues

Issue #	Project	Priority	Severity	State	Summary
10033	Module A Dev	High	Blocking	Open	Report ID: 126 does not show resource utilization correct
11445	SAP Integration	Med	Critical	In resolution	
11700	Module A Dev	Low	High	Closed	UI Error
10117	Module B Dev	High	High	Escalated	Rule ID 221 formula needs update
11190	SAP Integration	High	Low	In resolution	

Upcoming Milestones

▼ 15-Jan - Module A Dev - Design Doc

State Overdue

% Complete 89%

Budget Status 100% Consumed

▼ 15-Jan - CRM Dev Project - SRS Doc

State In Progress

% Complete 54%

Budget Status 45%

▲ 05-Mar - SAP Integration - Testing Doc

▲ 22-Mar - Module B Dev - Phase 1

▲ 01-Jul - SAP Integration - Testing Phase 1

Alerts

- (4) Timesheets pending approval
- (3) Unread Messages
- (2) Critical Issues
- (2) Expense Reports pending approval
- (6) New Assignment Requests

Sample Project Manager's Dashboard

247

Department / Resource Utilization

Dept / Resource	January 2007			February 2007			March 2007		
	Available	Reserved	Usage	Available	Reserved	Usage	Available	Reserved	Usage
▼ **Development**	460 hrs	673 hrs	59%	440 hrs	832 hrs	65%	492 hrs	655 hrs	57%
▼ Nancy Gilmour	100 hrs	220 hrs	68%	50 hrs	190 hrs	79%	190 hrs	40 hrs	17%
Module A Dev	-	110 hrs	34%	-	150 hrs	83%	-	0 hrs	0%
Module B Dev	-	110 hrs	34%	-	40 hrs	16%	-	40 hrs	17%
▼ Harry Hunts	80 hrs	75 hrs	48%	0 hrs	55 hrs	100%	80 hrs	55 hrs	41%
SAP Integration	-	75 hrs	48%	-	55 hrs	100%	-	55 hrs	41%
▲ Jeffery Moore	5 hrs	240 hrs	98%	125 hrs	85 hrs	40%	125 hrs	85 hrs	40%
▲ Sarah Peterson	75 hrs	30 hrs	29%	-25 hrs	250 hrs	111%	-15 hrs	190 hrs	109%
▲ Judy Smith	100 hrs	55 hrs	35%	45 hrs	197 hrs	81%	12 hrs	230 hrs	95%
▲ Philip Williams	100 hrs	23 hrs	19%	200 hrs	55 hrs	22%	100 hrs	55 hrs	35%
▲ **IT**	280 hrs	980 hrs	78%	-20 hrs	1250 hrs	102%	500 hrs	545 hrs	52%
▲ **Quality Assurance**	180 hrs	1545 hrs	90%	440 hrs	1266 hrs	74%	809 hrs	677 hrs	46%

0 - 90%	91 - 110%	> 110%

Skill Updates

Request #	Resource	Skill	State	Summary
221	Sandra Ryan	Project Management	Open	Obtained PMP Certification
102	Nancy Gilmore	.Net Development	In Evaluation	Completed training course
389	Drew Smith	Oracle DBA	Closed	Finished 1 year class
167	Joseph Kaplan	Finance	In Evaluation	Completed Level 3 CFA
322	Laura Right	Payroll	In Evaluation	Training in new payroll system

Project / Department Utilization

Department: Development

Project Utilization of the Development Department

345.10%
600.18%
200.60%
400.12%
230.70%
850.25%
750.22%

- Dev Module A
- SAP Integration
- HR Integration
- Dev Module D
- Dev Module B
- ERP Implementation
- Dev Module C

Alerts

- (4) Resource Assignment Requests
- (6) Unread Messages
- (2) Skill Update Requests
- (2) Critical Resource Reservation Requests

Sample Resource Manager's Dashboard

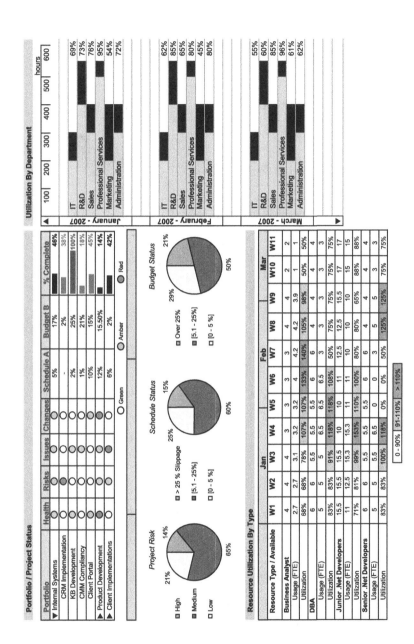

Sample Project Workforce Management Executive Dashboard

249

Category	Portfolio Names	Projects	Progress
Application	Workforce Management	6	65%
Development Projects	Application Release 10	5	35%
Portfolio by Region	Westcoast Projects	2	75%
Strategic Initiatives	IT Projects	4	25%
Organizational Improvements	Process Enhancements	5	90%

By Region	Status	Overall Health	Budgeted Cost	Project Schedule	Planned Effort	Primary Objective	Org Impact	Priority	Objective	Weighting
Westcoast Project 1	Active	○	○	○	○	Client Project	High	High	Contract	25%
Westcoast Project 2	Delayed	●	●	●	●	Internal Improvements	Medium	Low	Increase Revenue	15%
Westcoast Project 3	Completed	✓	○	●	○	Client Project	High	Medium	Upgrade	20%
Westcoast Project 4	Active	●	●	●	●	Client Project	High	High	Customization	20%
Westcoast Project 5	Active	○	●	●	●	Network Enhancement	Low	Low	Improve Quality	5%

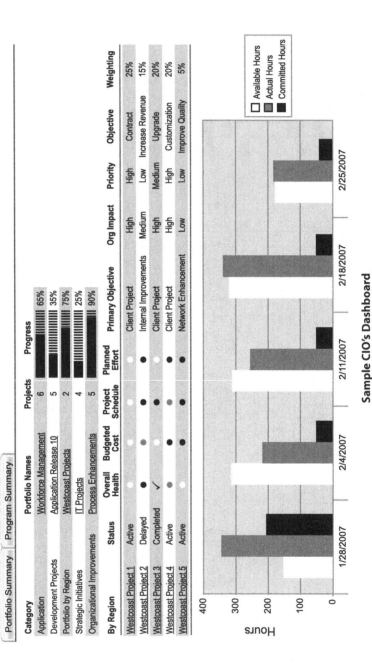

Sample CIO's Dashboard

Legend: Available Hours, Actual Hours, Committed Hours

Hours

1/28/2007 2/4/2007 2/11/2007 2/18/2007 2/25/2007

Year ▼	Quarter ▼	Month	Portfolio ▼	Forcated Cost	Forcated Billable	Forcated Revenue
2006	Q1	January		$2,244,506.29	$1,373,415.41	($871,090.88)
		February		$2,195,625.99	$1,530,520.55	($665,106.44)
		March		$0.00	$1,715,031.35	$1,715,031.35
		Total		$4,440,132.28	$4,618,967.31	$178,835.03
	Q2			$0.00	$4,271,429.80	$4,271,429.80
	Q3			$0.00	$2,979,532.73	$2,979,532.73
	Q4			$0.00	$3,347,436.63	$3,347,436.63
	Total			$4,440,132.28	$15,217,366.47	$10,777,234.19
2007				$0.00	$13,330,638.49	$13,330,638.49
2008				$0.00	$9,198.48	$9,198.48
Grand Total				$4,440,132.28	$28,567,203.44	$24,117,071.16

Chart legend: Actual Cost, Budgeted Cost, Estimated Cost
Categories: Development, Professional Services, Quality Assurance, Technical Support
Y-axis: 0, 2,500,000, 5,000,000, 7,500,000, 10,000,000

Work in Progress / Revenue Information

Region ▼	Customer ▼	Engagement Type	Year ▼	Month	Time Amount	Time Hours	Fixed Fees	Invoiced Amount	Invoices	Adjustment	Balance
West	Westcoast Acme	Hourly	2007	Jan	$33,000.00	300	-	($33,000.00)	Inv0002121	$0.00	($33,000.00)
	Client X	-	2007	Jan	-	-	-	-	Inv0004341	$5,400.00	$5,400.00
	ABC Inc.	Fixed	2007	Feb	$0.00	0	$30,000.00	($30,000.00)	Inv0004343	$0.00	($30,000.00)
	XYZ	Hourly	2007	Feb	$24,420.00	222	-	($15,000.00)	Inv0005454	$0.00	($15,000.00)
	Total Engagement				$57,420.00	522	$30,000.00	-$78,000.00		$5,400.00	-$72,600.00
East	Eastcoast Inc.	Hourly	2007	Jan	$13,750.00	125	-	($13,750.00)	Inv0006532	$0.00	($13,750.00)
	Company.com	Fixed	2007	Feb	$0.00	-	$27,000.00	($27,000.00)	Inv0007574	$0.00	($27,000.00)
	Total Engagement				$13,750.00	125	$27,000.00	-$40,750.00		$0.00	-$40,750.00

Sample CFO's Dashboard

Revenue by Region by Quarter

Demand vs Capacity

Profitability by Line of Business

KPI

Sample CEO's Dashboard

PART III

Implementation

20

Integration

Once everyone's applications started to connect to everyone else's applications . . . work could not only flow like never before, but it could be chopped up and disaggregated like never before and sent to the four corners of the world.

—Thomas L. Friedman[1]

Most project managers, IT professionals, executives, and line of business managers share a common yet seemingly unattainable goal when it comes to enterprise software. Many express their preference to work with multiple software providers, each being the best-of-breed leader and innovator in its own category. Yet, they do not want to deal with the software integration issues and costs that a best-of-breed strategy entails.

The analyst firm Gartner asserts that integration is "the job of making new software work with existing systems at a cost equal to 40 percent to 60 percent the price of the software itself."[2] Clearly, integrating best-of-breed systems to create a true enterprise system has costs and complexities that are prohibitive for many companies, making integration the Achilles heel of many enterprise software implementations.

To avoid integration issues, some companies opt for a single vendor strategy, wherein they select one major software suite to automate the company's entire operations, including project management and workforce management. The single vendor option has the advantage of consolidated, centralized reporting. However, it typically requires a large investment in a broad (but not deep) feature set that has a high switching cost, intense resistance to upgrades, is not innovative, and cannot be used to build an enterprise software advantage. Furthermore, when trying to reduce the number of enterprise software applications that are in use, the company is likely to spend substantial amounts of money and resources on customizations and consulting fees to fill the gaps in the solution, and to make the "reduced vendor" approach work; which only leads to the company getting stuck with legacy custom software,

255

built by external consultants or inhouse developers, requiring continued investment and ongoing maintenance costs.

However, with the emergence of Web Services and Service Oriented Architecture (SOA) as a viable and mature new integration technology, companies have a third option. Web Services technologies provide a common business language for integrating best-of-breed applications. This new integration paradigm allows companies to choose the best solutions in every functional area, and leverage their enterprise software investments to become more innovative, and differentiate themselves in the marketplace. Furthermore, SOA and Web Services help extend the life of existing software applications and provide significantly higher return on investment than replacing existing software investments and best-of-breed solutions with a single vendor offering.

The benefits and potential pitfalls of Web Service based integration are described in this chapter. We also outline the key integration points between Project Workforce Management and several other enterprise applications.

Why Integrate?

In a highly competitive environment the ability to differentiate and innovate is the key to survival. Companies have to constantly refine their business strategy and delivery models by redesigning or improving their business processes. Exploiting the information assets that are contained in a mish-mash of disconnected custom, packaged, and legacy applications can be a great source of new perspectives and insights. By unlocking this knowledge through automation and integration, companies have the essential facts and tools they need to innovate and differentiate.

Enterprise Software Strategies

Traditional Single Vendor Solutions

With this strategy, the organization selects and deploys the software of an enterprise resource planning (ERP) vendor such as SAP or Oracle. The key benefit is integrated reporting and an effective holistic view of the organization's operations. The software is usually massive in size and complexity, very expensive, and takes years to fully install, configure, and deploy. Such implementations lead to the customer being locked in to a single vendor and platform for a very long period of time with very high switching costs. There is also tremendous resistance to any upgrade due to cost, complexity, and the number of organizational areas affected. Single vendor applications offer few real competitive advantages since the feature set and strategy of the ERP targets a large homogenized and standardized customer base.

Traditional Best-of-Breed Solutions

Companies may also opt to select best-of-breed applications from multiple vendors, including the best-of-breed modules of ERP vendors, and then undertake the arduous and expensive task of integrating these disconnected applications. Best-of-breed applications are usually less expensive to purchase, and can lead to significant competitive advantages in a given functional area. They are also faster to roll out and upgrade when necessary. The points of failure in this strategy are almost always the lack of a single-source reporting system, the integration costs and complexities, and the need to rely on multiple vendors to support the enterprise solution.

The Web Services Solution

With a Web Services strategy, software vendors, on their own initiative, partition their applications into a set of distinct and highly independent business processes. These business processes interact with external entities using Web Services. Users of this technology no longer have to manage and maintain custom-built integration software. The data is always synchronized in real-time and without ever having to manually import or export it between two systems.

Web Services integration leverages Enterprise Application Integration (EAI) that is now an integral part of Business Process Management (see Chapter 7, "The Workflow Foundation"). This universal and standard-based architecture provides automatic integration of data with a common object model. Integration processes are defined independently of the underlying applications and automatically support the exchange of data as required by the process. This new application integration approach offers a rich library of pre-packaged, industry-specific integration applications and a powerful architecture based on XML and Web Services standards.

The Universal Adapter Network (UAN), a standards-based technology, has already defined common objects for enterprise applications and transformations to leading business applications from vendors such as IBM, SAP, and Oracle. Therefore, processes can be defined independently of the underlying applications and will automatically support the exchange of data as required by the process. This level of integration reduces implementation risk considerably and removes much of the inefficiencies related to integrating best-of-breed applications. Web Services eliminates the best-of-breed versus single vendor application discussions. Instead, the focus shifts to selecting the best Web services, regardless of whether they are from a single vendor or multiple vendors, to get the job done.

BENEFITS FOR THE COMPANY

- Significantly lowers costs, due to increased competition between software vendors, and more innovation as opposed to expensive locked-in single vendor offerings.

- Phase in or quickly deploy new best-of-breed applications.
- Upgrade any module without upgrading the entire system.

BENEFITS FOR SYSTEM ADMINISTRATORS

- The vendors deal with integration challenges using their own resources and standards-based Web Services connectors.
- Companies can focus on innovation and maximizing enterprise software investments instead of maintaining multiple disconnected or custom connected systems.

BENEFITS FOR END USERS

- Access to the latest best-of-breed solutions.
- Users no longer have to accept washed down features of a single vendor offering.

Some notes of caution on the state of Web Services integrations today:

- Web Services integration is the best EAI approach but very few companies (except large global 2000 type companies) are truly investing in this technology. Most software developers limit themselves to point-to-point integration or worse file based import/exports.
- Enterprise software vendors have limited support for Web Services especially in the mid-market.
- Integration costs incurred by the vendor is somewhat higher due to high-level of skill set required.

In these times of globalization, rapid technological change, and extreme competition, companies are looking for solutions that will leverage their current software investments yet reduce costs, improve access to information, promote sharing/collaboration, lead to significant competitive advantages, and quickly result in intangible benefits along with a measurable return on investment. With the advent of Web Services and real-time integration, the trend is toward this new integration paradigm.

Link between Project and Workforce Management

By focusing on a workflow driven approach and what they have in common, Project Workforce Management combines project management and workforce management to provide a unified solution, which eliminates the gaps between human resources, finance, sales, and project/service delivery teams with a unified solution (see Figure 20.1):

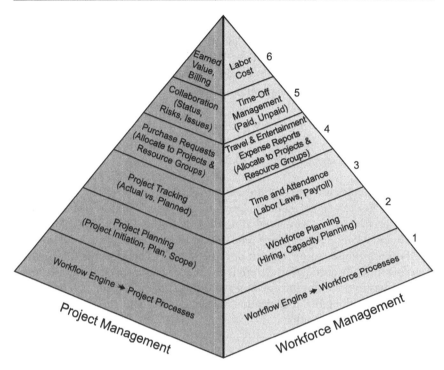

Figure 20.1 Project Management and Workforce Management

- A common workflow engine drives all project and workforce management processes.
- Projects and work are planned and resources are booked.
- Projects, budgets, and resources are tracked.
- Purchases are made, expenses are incurred.
- Project processes (such as scope, risks, and issues) and workforce processes (such as leave time) are managed.
- Work is completed and delivered, projects are billed, and the true value created is determined and employees are paid.

Integrating with an Accounting System

The main components of an accounting system are:

- *System manager:* Defines general ledger account structure, system currency, and other global setup
- *General ledger (GL):* The company's chart of accounts used to produce financial reports

- *Accounts receivable (AR):* The money the company expects to receive
- *Accounts payable (AP):* Vendor information, bill payment, managing the amounts owed to other companies and individuals
- *Billing:* The module used to create customer invoices and credit notes
- *Payroll:* Employee information, salary and benefits management, and payment system
- *Purchase order:* Order entry system
- *Inventory:* Inventory management system for manufacturing/product based businesses (see Figure 20.2)

These modules are named differently by various vendors. There are essentially two choices when it comes to integrating Project Workforce Management with an accounting system: integrating directly to the GL, or integrating with the AR and AP modules. In most scenarios, it is more effective to send invoices to AR and expenses to AP instead of directly to GL, because the information transferred to the accounting system is customer/vendor specific, and the organization has to track this information accordingly. If the information is sent directly to GL, then the organization would not be able to track its AR by customer and AP by vendor.

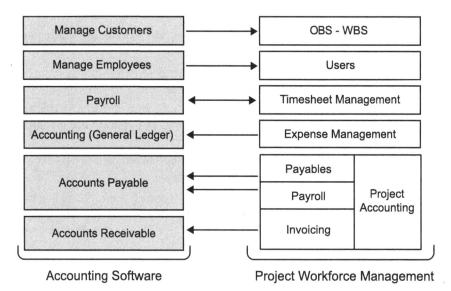

Figure 20.2   Project Workforce Management and Accounting

What Can Be Imported from the Accounting System?

- Employees (maps to users)
- Accounts Receivable Items (maps to tasks, billable expenses, billable charges)
- Chart of accounts
- Pay codes and earning codes
- Customers (maps to clients)
- Vendors (maps to suppliers)

What Can Be Exported to the Accounting System?

- Clients (maps to customers)
- Users (maps to employees and AP vendors)
- Tasks/expenses/charges (map to AR Items)
- Timesheets exported into payroll timecards
- Invoices exported into AR invoices
- Payable batches exported to AP invoices

Exporting Time to the Accounting System. Employee work (including any overtime) and leave time data can be exported to an accounting system's payroll module for payroll processing. The following steps outline the process to export time data to the accounting system:

1. Define users, tasks, projects.
2. Work tracked in the Project Workforce Management system.
3. Create a payroll batch in the Project Workforce Management system.
4. Export and issue the payroll batch.
5. Timesheets exported to the accounting system with associated pay and billing codes.
6. Payroll administrator processes payroll.
7. Payroll batches marked as submitted to prevent duplications.

Exporting Invoices to the Accounting System. Project Workforce Management systems can be used to generate invoices since billable work and expense can be tracked with the system. Invoices created in the Project Workforce Management system can be exported to the accounting application for accounts receivable (AR) processing:

1. Define users, tasks, or projects; expenses and charges.
2. Billable work tracked (timesheets, expense reports, and charges) in the Project Workforce Management system.

3. Define billing rules in the Project Workforce Management system.
4. Create and approve invoices in the Project Workforce Management system.
5. Export invoices to the accounting system's AR module.
6. All associated expenses and charges marked as submitted in order to prevent duplications.

EXPORTING PAYABLES TO THE ACCOUNTING SYSTEM. Project Workforce Management systems can be used to generate payable reports since project costs and reimbursable expenses are being tracked with the system. Payable reports created in the Project Workforce Management system can be exported to the accounting application for accounts payable (AP) processing:

1. Define users, expenses, and charges.
2. Track expense reports to be reimbursed and enter payable money charges.
3. Create payable batches.
4. Export payable batch to the accounting system.
5. All associated expenses and charges marked as submitted in order to prevent duplications.

Integrating with a Payroll System

Project Workforce Management can integrate with a payroll system in two ways: by exporting timesheet data, or by exporting cost information (see Figure 20.3).

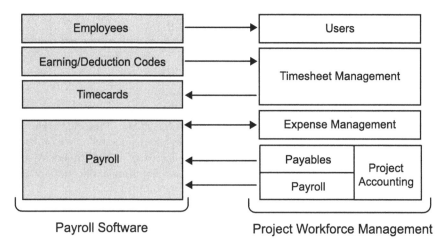

Figure 20.3 Project Workforce Management and Payroll

In the first scenario, the system's validated and approved time and expense data is exported to the payroll system. Timesheet data includes regular time, overtime, time charges (to accounts for on-call time and standby time), and paid leave time. Every entry is associated to pay and earning codes so that the payroll system can determine the amount to pay the employee.

Alternatively, since the Project Workforce Management system has all the cost rates, overtime rules, leave time policy, and shift and premium data, it can calculate the employee's pay before payroll taxes and deductions, also referred to as gross pay. The system can export the gross pay amounts to the payroll system instead of the raw timesheet data. This is the preferred method of integration because most payroll systems do not have the capability to process the pay rules, overtime calculations, and labor laws that the Project Workforce Management can manage, validate, and enforce. The same integration points apply to an accounting system's payroll module, or when using an outsourced payroll service.

WHAT CAN BE IMPORTED FROM THE PAYROLL SYSTEM?
- Employees map to Project Workforce Management users
- Service items map to Project Workforce Management tasks
- Pay codes map to Project Workforce Management pay codes
- Expenses map to Project Workforce Management expense items

WHAT CAN BE EXPORTED TO THE PAYROLL SYSTEM?
- Users map to employees
- Tasks map to service items
- Expenses/charges map to expense transactions
- Timesheets are exported using pay and earning codes as payroll transactions
- Payable Batches exported as reimbursable expenses

EXPORTING TIME AND EXPENSE TO THE PAYROLL SYSTEM. Payable time and expense information can be exported directly to a payroll management system. Here is an overview of the process:

1. Define users, tasks, projects, expenses, and charges.
2. Work is tracked (timesheets, expense reports, and charges) in the Project Workforce Management system.
3. Create a payroll batch to select which timesheets and expense reports to export, based on date interval and other parameters.
4. Export time and expense data to the payroll system.
5. All associated time, expense, and charges marked as submitted in order to prevent duplications.

EXPORTING GROSS PAY TO THE PAYROLL SYSTEM. Gross pay and expense information can be exported directly to a payroll system. In this case the Project Workforce Management system is calculating gross pay based on the employee's timesheets, salary or hourly rate, and any overtime rules. Here is an overview of the process:

1. Define users, tasks, projects, expenses, and charges.
2. Define cost rules in the Project Workforce Management system.
3. Work done and tracked (timesheets, expense reports, and charges) in the Project Workforce Management system.
4. Create a payroll batch to select which timesheets and expense reports to export based on date interval and other parameters.
5. Export gross pay data and expenses to the payroll system.
6. All associated time, expenses, and charges marked as submitted in order to prevent duplications.

Integrating with Project Management

Project Workforce Management integrates with Enterprise Project Management (also referred to as EPM or PM) systems for project planning and collaboration (see Figure 20.4). While Project Workforce Management includes some of the functions offered by an EPM system, there are some differences and factors to consider that make this integration highly desirable in certain scenarios. These factors are as follows:

- Project Workforce Management is intended to accommodate all sorts of projects, including short or routine projects that have a simple plan or no

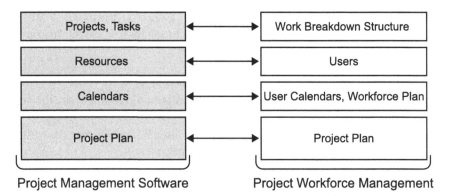

Project Management Software   Project Workforce Management

Figure 20.4   Project Workforce Management and PM Applications

formal plan at all. Projects that can be managed by a Project Workforce Management include billable projects, fixed bid customer projects, product development projects, and information technology (IT) and other internal projects with varying planning needs. Enterprise Project Management is used mostly by IT and engineering to manage large projects with complex plans. Therefore, it makes sense to integrate the two systems and leverage each system's best-of-breed capabilities.

- Project Workforce Management and EPM plans, resource assignments, and project progress tracking are easily interchangeable. Therefore they can coexist and cooperate quite effectively. By providing both options, users who have no project plans or have simple project planning needs can use the Project Workforce Management's project planning and tracking modules. Users who need more complex project planning capabilities can use the EPM tool.

- Project Workforce Management's workforce planning component books resources against projects, not detailed tasks, because most companies do not have detailed project plans until the project is launched. However, they still need to tentatively estimate and book resources for these projects far in advance of any formal planning. More specifically, EPM is designed to manage resources at the task level, which is desirable for large or complex projects that have reached the detailed planning stage.

WHAT CAN BE IMPORTED FROM THE EPM APPLICATION?

- Resources map to Project Workforce Management users
- Tasks map to Project Workforce Management tasks
- Plans map to Project Workforce Management project plans
- Assignments map to Project Workforce Management assignments

WHAT CAN BE EXPORTED TO THE EPM APPLICATION?

- Users map to EPM resources
- Tasks map to EPM tasks
- Project plans map to EPM plans

EXPORTING PLANS TO THE EPM APPLICATION. There are several usage and integration patterns. Here are some of the more common scenarios.

Steps to Take without Workforce Planning Workflow. In this scenario, the project manager builds a detailed project plan first. The project manager then assigns the resources that will be working on the project. The project manager has the ability to assign resources to the project by finding the right resources and verifying their availability without the need to go through a request workflow. The project plan is updated when required as the project is being worked on. Here is an overview of the process:

1. Create a project plan in the EPM application.
2. Build the project team by importing users from the Project Workforce Management system.
3. Assign resources to the plan.
4. Export the plan to the Project Workforce Management system for tracking, compliance, and approval management.
5. Update the plan at any time to review the plan's current status.
6. View earned value reports at any time to assess progress.
7. Update the Project Workforce Management system with any plan changes.

Steps to Take with Workforce Planning Workflow. In this scenario, the project manager builds a project plan first. The project manager then proposes and gets approval for the resources that will be working on the project. The project plan is updated when required as the project is being worked on. Here is an overview of the process:

1. Create a project plan in the EPM application; the initial plan can be very simple—only for the purpose of estimating resource needs.
2. Build the project team by importing users from the Project Workforce Management system; use generic resources instead of named resources if no preferences (for example, use System Analyst instead of John Smith).
3. Update the Project Workforce Management system by creating and submitting a resource request.
4. The resource request is approved and the resources are booked for the project in the Project Workforce Management system.
5. When the project is ready to launch, review the plan, make any necessary changes, and drill the plan down to the detailed task levels.
6. Make any resource booking changes in the Project Workforce Management system as necessary.
7. Assign resources to the plan.
8. Export the plan to the Project Workforce Management system for tracking, compliance, and approval management.
9. Update the plan at any time to review the plan's current status.
10. View earned value reports at any time to assess progress.
11. Update the Project Workforce Management system with any plan changes.

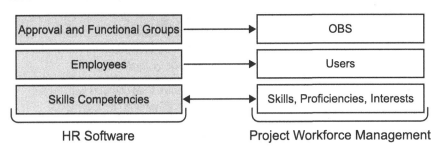

Figure 20.5   HR Software and Project Workforce Management

Integrating with Human Resources

The human resource (HR) application is the system of record for detailed employee information, including employee name, address, role, compensation (pay, benefits, etc.), skills, competencies, and interests. This information can be imported into the Project Workforce Management system usually using a scheduled integration process (see Figure 20.5).

Integrating with Customer Relationship Management

CRM and Project Workforce Management combine to provide a fully consolidated customer and project view that is always available to all authorized users during the entire customer and project life cycle, from the initial discussion stages to contract signing, project initiation, planning, implementation, and support (see Figure 20.6). The sales team gains access to up-to-the-minute information on

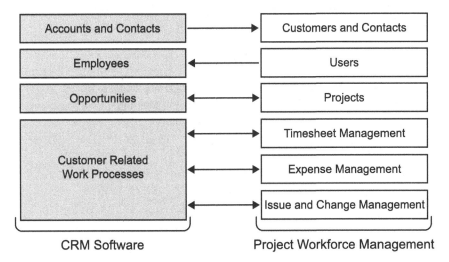

Figure 20.6   CRM Software and Project Workforce Management

INTEGRATION POINTS	DESCRIPTION
Accounts → Clients	Synchronize CRM accounts with Project Workforce System's client list.
Contacts → Contacts	Synchronize CRM contacts with Project Workforce System's client contacts.
Opportunities → Projects or project initiation requests	Synchronize CRM opportunities to create Project Workforce System's projects or project initiation requests for launching new projects, managing those projects, and forecasting/scheduling resources.
Opportunities → Scope change requests	Project manager can trigger new opportunities in the CRM based on project scope changes entered in the Project Workforce System.
Opportunities/Reporting → Project Workforce KPIs	CRM users have access to up-to-the-minute project status and billing information for all account opportunities.

Table 20.1   CRM Integration Points

customer projects, including key milestones, billing and invoicing information, projects and service contracts that are nearing completion, and issues or scope change requests that could trigger new opportunities (see Table 20.1). The project teams get more visibility into upcoming project and service demands and can do a better job of project and capacity planning.

NOTES

1. *The World Is Flat* (New York: Farrar, Straus and Giroux, 2006), p. 76.
2. "Software's Next Stage?" *BusinessWeek,* December 4, 2002, http://www.businessweek.com/technology/content/dec2002/tc2002124_2624.htm.

21

Deployment Roadmap

There is nothing so useless as doing efficiently that which should not be done at all.

—Peter F. Drucker

Most companies spend a great deal of resources and energy on planning, reporting, and analytics using report design and business intelligence technologies. However, not enough attention is paid to the quality of the data they use to actually build these plans and reports. Good planning, forecasting, and analytics start with capturing project data that is accurate, compliant, and reliable. This chapter presents a best-practice implementation roadmap for Project Workforce Management by placing a stronger emphasis on the implementation of the tracking modules first.

Most companies cannot and generally should not undertake massive and sudden changes to their project and workforce management structures, tools, and processes. Enterprise software implementations (such as multiyear enterprise resource planning or ERP implementations and platform-type investments) are famous for huge costs, highly questionable return on investment (ROI), and impose an unacceptable level of risk on the organization. After completing and deploying a large software project, companies often become risk averse, change resistant, and comfortable with the status quo. Their exhausted leadership and information technology (IT) organization has lost the energy and desire to innovate or to invest in new tools and technologies. Multiyear projects with no measurable returns often bolster "We do it all" claims. However, over a long period of time, they almost always end with extensive customizations, reduced scope, downsizing, or a substantial change of mission.

It is therefore hardly a surprise how successful salesforce.com has been with both large and small companies. Salesforce.com's focus on providing immediate benefits to its customers has been its "not so secret" advantage over much larger competitors such as traditional "all-in-one" ERPs and broad ERP-like on-demand solutions. While many enterprise software companies offer massive suites of software, salesforce.com chose to focus on one thing: to provide an on-demand customer relationship management (CRM) solution that is very easy to use and could be implemented quickly. The end-user adoption of salesforce.com has been phenomenal, and the ROI has been faster than most other enterprise software implemented by companies. All of which creates a large internal advocacy group for the continued investment in on-demand CRM.

Similarly, a phased and focused approach to Project Workforce Management provides companies with immediate benefits and ROI. It also enables organizations to establish a long-term vision for their enterprise-software strategy, allowing companies to then take gradual steps toward achieving this vision, with clearly defined milestones, objectives, and ROI measures.

Phased Deployment

Figure 21.1 shows a recommended roadmap to Project Workforce Management. The roadmap shown here is a general-ease, best-practice recommendation. For some companies, depending on their process maturity and competitive standing, some of the steps may have to be skipped or may be executed simultaneously. A step-by-step discussion of this best-practices roadmap follows.

Step One: Time and Expense Tracking

- "Anecdotal evidence suggests that 20% to 40% of spreadsheets have errors, but recent audits of 54 spreadsheets found that 49 (or 91%) had errors," according to research by Raymond R. Panko, a professor at the University of Hawaii.
- The *Journal of Property Management* stated, "30% to 90% of all spreadsheets suffer from at least one major user error. The range in error rates

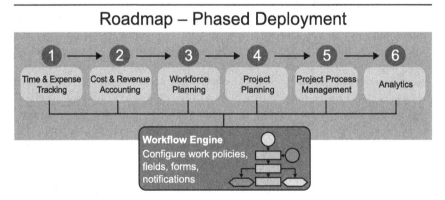

Figure 21.1   Roadmap to Project Workforce Management

depends on the complexity of the spreadsheet being tested. None of the tests included spreadsheets with more than 200 line items where the probability of error approaches 100 percent."

- Perform an online search for spreadsheet errors or spreadsheet audit, and you will find a number of major failures attributed to spreadsheet inaccuracies that hit the press in the past year alone.[1]

Statistics abound that show the dangers of using spreadsheets and any other such custom-built programs. Therefore, it is imperative for companies to start eliminating spreadsheets, manual processes, and multiple redundant systems related to time and expense tracking (having one system for project time, another for time and billing, and another for payroll time, etc.). This first step enables companies to track and audit true project costs and billing in real-time based on enforced and audited time-and-expense reporting policies in a single system. Tracking true effort and costs provides the foundation for reliable data companies can trust. Without accurate and dependable tracking, any plans, analysis and decisions are based on faulty inconsistent data. The company will not be able to learn from its past experiences, improve, adapt, or find new best practices based on market changes. Additional automation can occur once a company has made this first move toward eliminating manual and disconnected systems.

By automating time and expense tracking, companies are able to account for and analyze "differentiated time" by project, by resource group, or any other breakdown as needed (see Chapter 1, "The Rise of the Project Workforce"). With a real-time view of all the people and resource groups working on various projects at different times worldwide, the company's management is empowered to make decisions quickly, not after the fact.

Recommended integrations in this step: Timesheet data (including work time, overtime, and shift premiums where applicable) can be exported into payroll and accounting systems for payroll, billing and expense reimbursement (see Chapter 20, "Integration").

Step Two: Cost and Revenue Accounting

Eliminate more spreadsheets by automating budgeting, billing calculations, and cost accounting. Whether companies are concerned with billable projects, chargebacks, or budgets, every activity detail is accounted for and allocated to the various elements of the organization and work-breakdown structures. With pay and billing rules calculating cost and revenue, companies can automatically generate invoices for approved time, expenses and charges, as well as view up-to-the-minute cost-and-revenue status updates in both "live" dashboards and reports.

Recommended integrations in this step: Cost and billing rules associated to customers, projects, and resources provide the foundation for project financials. Summary of detailed billable information can be exported into an accounting system's accounts receivable module. Similarly, cost information can be exported into an accounting system's accounts payable module. Other workflow-driven integrations include:

- *Billing → Chargeback approval:* An IT or shared-service business unit manager uses a chargeback-approval workflow to chargeback other business units for services rendered. Once approved, chargebacks are automatically allocated to their respective cost-center accounts in the accounting system for financial reporting and line of business performance and profit analysis.
- *Billing → Invoice approval:* A billing manager uses the invoice-approval process to authorize invoices before they get sent to customers. Once approved, invoices are automatically posted to the accounting system's accounts-receivable module.
- *Cost accounting → Work in progress:* Managers calculate billable work and expenses that has not yet been billed (also known as work in progress) by customer, project, or resource group. They can also update the accounting system with this information for financial reporting purposes.

Step Three: Workforce Planning

Most companies invest a great deal of time and effort on project planning which enables a manager to prepare a detailed project plan. Workforce planning allows companies to allocate resources to projects without having to create a detailed project plan. A workforce planning system manages the talent within an organization, tracks the skills and experience of talent pools, and helps forecast resource allocation into the future so companies can optimize resource utilization and minimize bench time or resource shortages. Workforce planning is of particular importance to high-tech and professional-service environments where a diverse set of skills and resource types, possibly located in multiple remote sites, are required to plan and execute projects (see Chapter 9, "Workforce Planning").

Recommended integrations in this step: Timesheet assignments are automatically populated based on the projects for which the resource is booked to work. Workforce planning data can also be used to set baseline resource-and-time budgets for detailed project planning and earned-value analysis. Other workflow-driven integrations include:

- Once a travel or leave request is approved, the system automatically updates the user's availability so projects are not assigned during out-of-office or nonworking days.
- Users are responsible for updating the system when they upgrade their skills. A skill update request workflow is used to report a skill update. Once approved, the skill is added to the user's skill set for future matching. For example, users are rewarded for reporting when they have com-

pleted a training course or earned a new certification that upgrades their skills. This is the best way to make sure the workforce-planning module has updated and accurate skill information.

Step Four: Project Planning

With a good tracking-and-project accounting system in place and resources booked for projects based on skills, cost, and experience, project managers can start planning projects in detail. Project planning is the function of dividing an initiative into a work breakdown structure (to the level of task details) and assigning resources to those tasks (see Chapter 10, "Project Planning").

Recommended integrations in this step: Detailed task assignments can automatically update users' timesheet assignments. The task information can also be used to set baseline time and cost budgets for earned-value analysis.

Step Five: Project Process Management

Following a successful implementation of the core project and resource tracking, as well as planning processes, the next step involves the institutionalization of project management methodologies and best practices, also known as project process management. Project process management enables companies to find, standardize, and establish the most efficient project-and-service delivery models throughout the enterprise.

Key project processes to manage include project selection and prioritization (see Chapter 18, "Project Prioritization and Selection"), project initiation (see Chapter 8, "Initiating Projects"), scope management, and risk-and-issue tracking (see Chapter 16, "Risk, Scope, and Issue Tracking"). At this point of the implementation roadmap, the organization has the experience and process maturity level necessary to complete the deployment and achieve Project Workforce Management excellence.

Recommended integrations in this step: There is a wide array of integration opportunities around project processes. Some of those integration points (see Chapter 20, "Integration") are as follows:

- *CRM—Opportunities to projects:* Projects can be initiated when an opportunity is closed in the sales force automation (SFA) software. A project-initiation workflow is the official mechanism for sales to inform project-and-service delivery teams that a deal has been signed and a new project needs to be planned and executed.
- *Project management—Scope change request to budgeting:* Scope-change request workflows can trigger new budget approvals.
- *Budget approval:* A budget-approval workflow is used to secure any project-related budget requests. The same workflow can update the accounting system or other enterprise systems as necessary.

Step Six: Analytics

Companies can incrementally implement role-based dashboards and analytics after any one of the steps mentioned previously. Considerable analytics and internal-team collaboration on project status and change control can occur after the cost-and-revenue accounting step. By adding analytics, executives will have live, role-based, self-service dashboards that display operational and compliance information such as:

- Budgeted versus actual time and expense by project or resource group
- Project and resource group cost, revenue (or chargebacks), and margins
- Project health indicators, issues, risks, and scope changes
- Resource utilization, resource gaps, skill pool, and availability
- Project and workforce financials

Recommended integrations in this step: With standards-based enterprise applications, Web Services, and portal technology, companies can combine Project Workforce Management, accounting systems, payroll, human resources, and CRM dashboard parts to build enterprise-wide portals and real-time Executive Dashboards that combine the information from all of these systems.

Collaboration with Your Customers and Partners

A compelling byproduct of implementing Project Workforce Management will be the ability to collaborate with customers—whether they are other business units within the company or external parties—like never before. Project Workforce Management software, role-based security, and dashboard technology can be used to quickly configure portals to help a company collaborate with its customers in ways that were previously impossible to perform in a cost-effective manner. The following are examples of the types of the information that can be exchanged with customers:

- Online bill presentment and approval for professional service organizations
- Project-status review
- Scope-change requests approvals, as well as issue tracking and reporting
- Resource booking

NOTE

1. "The Use of Spreadsheets: Considerations for Section 404 of the Sarbanes-Oxley Act," *Computer World,* May 24, 2004, article based on a PricewaterhouseCoopers study.

22

Implementation and Operations

When you have completed 95 percent of your journey, you are only halfway there.

—Japanese Proverb

Many organizations think the job is done once they build a business case, document requirements and business processes, select a Project Workforce Management solution, and install and deploy the new software. However, the time has now come to start the real work—the implementation, operations, and system administration phase of the project. Although many enterprise software projects fail in the implementation phase, many more are negatively impacted in the operational and administration phase due to neglect and especially due to a poor initial implementation. The administration of a Project Workforce Management system requires careful planning, management, training, and continued investments.

This chapter explains the importance of defining a project team, designating a system administrator, and carefully planning the implementation phase with the long-term view in mind. It also presents a typical Project Workforce Management implementation roadmap for a small to medium-sized organization that is automating a limited number of workflows.

The system administrators' roles and responsibilities have to be clearly delineated, and the administrator must remain active with the Project Workforce Management system to monitor performance, automate new processes, and continuously improve existing operations. The key role and extensive responsibilities of the administrator should not be underestimated. Project Workforce Management is not a destination, but rather it is a never-ending process improvement journey that requires constant work, long-term executive-supported commitment, and dedicated resources.

However, the implementation of Project Workforce Management results in significant tangible and intangible benefits, producing the potential for tremendous savings; improvements in efficiency; and a more process-mature, streamlined, agile, and competitive organization.

Specifically, this chapter:

- Examines the administrative and operational aspects of a Project Workforce Management system
- Describes an effective operational structure and recommends actions to ensure the system is used and managed optimally and consistently
- Lists administrative resource responsibilities, qualifications, and expected time commitment level
- Provides recommendations that will lead to a fundamentally sound and operationally efficient implementation

Implementation and Operation Team

There is a substantial amount of readily available information regarding the benefits, tools, technologies, and implementation guidelines for project-management and workforce-management solutions. However, a vital topic that often gets overlooked is the day-to-day operation and administration of such systems. Even careful prepurchase analysis and a comprehensive selection process do not guarantee operational success. It is the effective daily running of routine administrative procedures and processes that makes the difference between a failed or poorly executed project and one that reaps recurring short- and long-term benefits.

Improving and optimizing project workforce processes should be treated as an ongoing continuous improvement journey and one of the operation team's responsibilities. All processes have to be reviewed on a regular basis and Project Workforce Management concepts and tools revisited to determine whether the methodologies and technology are being leveraged to their maximum potential, best practices are being applied, and any productivity enhancement opportunities that were overlooked or not implemented previously are being discovered.

Personnel

Regardless of the size of the company and the budget allocated for enterprise software solutions, a Project Workforce Management project has a significant impact on an organization and its day-to-day processes. The operations and administration team in charge of the enterprise software project has a tremendous impact on the success of the project as well as user adoption rates (see Chapter 23, "User Adoption"). The resources dedicated to these tasks have to be qualified, enthusiastic, and supportive as the company transitions itself into a workflow-driven enterprise.

TURNOVER. While workflows and audited processes help capture and enforce the company's policies and business methods, there are still many nuances and important contributions by the operations team that systems cannot replace. Today's highly mobile workforce changes jobs more frequently than ever before. Therefore, it is important to document all project workforce processes and to cross train resources in case key personnel leave. This ensures a smooth transition and an efficient knowledge transfer.

Consulting Team

The solution provider's domain experts play a key role in starting the project off on the right foot. The following professionals are required in the implementation and predeployment phases.

PROJECT WORKFORCE MANAGEMENT SOLUTION—PROJECT MANAGER. The project manager is a domain expert assigned to the project who is responsible for ensuring that the implementation and initial operational phases of the project are a total success. The project manager works with the company's project team to analyze, plan, and deploy the software. Regularly scheduled conference calls or meetings throughout the implementation and operational phases provide great insight into business modeling, training, workflow design, reporting, integrations, and optimal application access by Web and offline users, as well as the server(s)/database setup in case of an on-premise installation.

PROJECT WORKFORCE MANAGEMENT TRAINER(S). Understanding how to manage and operate the system is not just about learning the functions of each and every module. Concepts such as workflows, project management, timesheet management, expense reporting, billing, and project financials and analytics involve a considerable amount of domain knowledge. Trainers have the difficult task of conveying this information in a limited time to the organization's project team and executives. Highly focused training, as opposed to general sessions and e-learning tools, are the most effective forms of education.

IMPLEMENTATION CONSULTANTS. Implementation consultants, managed by the Project Workforce Management Solution—Project Manager, can quickly and efficiently provide services such as:

On-Demand Implementation
- Work with the company's project team to plan launch, model processes, configure the data instance, train administrators, plan and configure integrations, and conduct other predeployment activities.

- Respond to system usage questions.
- Diagnose integration problems and challenges.
- For business-critical installations (in connection with payroll or billing), create a development sandbox for testing fixes, upgrades, new reports, and integrations outside of the production system (see Development Sandbox section that follows on p. 287).

On-Premise Implementation

- Oversee system launch, upgrades, and new integrations onsite.
- Conduct server farming or performance optimization depending on user counts.

Customer Project Team

The consultants, who have expertise in Project Workforce Management solutions and best practices, partner with the Customer Project Team to gain intimate knowledge of company and business requirements. The success of the project depends on the investment and dedication of these resources and their active collaboration with the consulting team. Table 22.1 outlines the different internal resource roles recommended for the execution of such an implementation. Keep in mind, one resource can play multiple roles.

The Project Workforce System Administrator's responsibilities include:

- *System:* Set and manage system currency, terminology, regional settings, user defined fields, role-base security, auditing options, and system defaults.
- *Organization:* Create and manage business units, users, and groups.
- *Work:* Create and manage customers, portfolios, projects, and tasks; define project and resource group budgets, limits, and notifications.
- *Workforce planning:* Create and manage skills, resource types, and calendars; set up workforce planning options and defaults.
- *Expenses:* Create and manage expense items, categories, defaults, and limits.
- *Business rules and policies:*
  —Define work time, time-off and expense reporting policies, timesheet and expense reporting views, approval workflows, and notifications.
  —Create and manage cost rules, billing rules, invoicing templates, and options.
  —Set up project initiation, scope change, risk-and-issue tracking, user-defined fields, views, workflows, and notifications.
- *Financials:* Import chart of accounts, taxes, and currencies; create and manage money charge types.

RESOURCE ROLE	DESCRIPTION
Executive sponsor	A contact that can make key decisions on process changes, scope changes, and other matters required as part of this implementation.
Project Workforce System Management administrator	The individual who will administer the system once implemented and will also be intimately involved during the implementation.
Database and network administrator	For on-premise implementation: Contact(s) with administrative rights to the internal database and network environment.
Accounting/finance	Individual with knowledge of the existing accounting, payroll, billing, and invoicing systems.
Business process owner(s)	A contact with extensive knowledge of current project management, workforce management, and billing business policies and procedures.

Table 22.1   Customer Project Team

- *Reports and analytics:* Create and manage new reports, templates, and report access rights.
- *Integration:* Set up integration with accounting, project planning, customer relationship management (CRM), human resources, and other applications (see Figure 22.1).

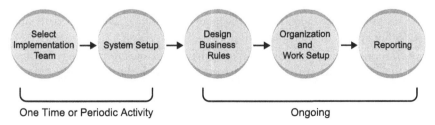

Figure 22.1   Project Workforce Management Setup and Administration

Depending on the organization's size and the implementation's complexity, these responsibilities can represent a part-time assignment for a single staff member or a full-time assignment for one or two individuals. The organization has to determine and define this function based on an assessment of the amount of work involved. The role may also include some analysis, reports, and dashboard-creation responsibilities to accompany the administrative tasks.

Project Workforce Management Administrator

This is a make it or break it role for a Project Workforce Management implementation. A highly competent, strong-minded, and positive administrator will be able to overcome all of the user adoption, management, and technology challenges that may occur during the implementation and administration phases of such a system. A carefully selected administrator will take every step necessary to maximize the company's investment in the new enterprise software. The following sections describe the administrator's role and responsibilities in more detail.

SYSTEM SETUP. Every organization defines a set of standards and guidelines to establish the manner in which its teams and projects are managed, work is performed, and processes are tracked. This information is defined at the global level and is established as the company's standard policy. Depending on a variety of parameters, some of the global settings can be overridden on a case-by-case basis. For example, a base currency for the organization can be overridden by local-site currency for a company with customers and employees in several countries.

An administrator's responsibility for system setup includes configuring:

- *Regional settings and formats:* The organization adopts a uniform format for dates (for example, two-digit month/two-digit day/four-digit year); decimal/thousand separators; accounting figures (for example, 1,000.00); telephone numbers; a uniform login ID length and naming convention; a password policy or an operating system-based user authentication scheme; and other related formatting, reporting, display standards, and conventions.
- *System parameters:* System-wide parameters include base currency, base tax group, base calendar, the company's accounting fiscal start date, and other system defaults.
- *Terminology:* Since most companies have their own terminology for how the business is structured and work is tracked, the Project Workforce Management system's terminology has to be adjusted to follow the organization's terms, for example, *line of business* (business unit), *group* (department), *client* (customer or account), *project* (contract or job), *employee* (resource or consultant), and *task* (activity).

- *User-defined fields:* Enterprise-software systems cannot provide a perfect match to an organization's requirements. User-defined fields offer a simple and efficient way for the administrator to add any required, specialized fields. User-defined fields can be created and shared across the various modules.

- *Role-based security:* An administrator defines what modules a user has access to, specifying, for example, setup, entry, reporting, and access to the various system modules. Standard roles include administrator, manager, project manager, engineer, account executive, helpdesk user, project contributor, and standard user.

- *Auditing:* The administrator sets up system auditing, decides what actions should be audited—the more actions are audited, the larger the storage requirements.

Organization Breakdown Structure

Organization breakdown structure (OBS) management refers to the setup and administration of the hierarchy of sites, business units, groups, users, and other organization elements (see Chapter 6, "Organization and Work Breakdown Structure"). The administrator creates, modifies, merges, or deletes OBS items such as business units, groups, and users based on requests as well as the company's reporting and approval hierarchy.

Work Breakdown Structure

Work breakdown structure (WBS) management refers to the setup and administration of the hierarchy of customers, projects, tasks, and other work types (see Chapter 6, "Organization and Work Breakdown Structure"). The administrator creates, modifies, merges, or deletes WBS items such as customers and projects based on requests and the company's work structure.

Workforce Planning

The administrator creates and manages skills, skill sets, user roles and calendars; sets up workforce planning options such as base calendars and defaults like working days and overload thresholds; and overrides group or user-specific calendars as necessary.

Expense

The administrator creates and manages expense categories such as travel, lodging, transportation, and entertainment; and expense items such as office supplies, mileage, meals, and equipment.

Business Rules

Once the initial business structure modeling, terminology, and global setup have been completed, it is time to collaborate on incorporating the company's business rules into the system. The administrator drives the following activities:

- *Reporting cycle:* Sets up timesheet period, expense reporting, payroll, and billing cycles.
- *Compliance to government regulations:* Configures the timesheet module to be in compliance with labor laws (for exempt, nonexempt employees, and shift workers) and cost-accounting regulations (see Chapter 5, "Complying with Labor Laws and Accounting Regulations").
- *Policies:* In addition to government regulations, an organization has its own set of policies and procedures, such as overtime policy (for example, a maximum overtime of four hours per week), expense reporting policy (for example, all expense entries must be accompanied by a note and a receipt), and timesheet policy (for example, timesheets must be completed on Friday by 5 p.m.). Companies may also decide to impose very strict policies for unauthorized overtime or expense reports that cannot exceed $5,000. The thresholds can be defined as hard limits, which cannot be exceeded, or soft limits, which treat the exceeded limits as exceptions and color code or highlight them for managers to see or trigger e-mail notification for verification and follow-up.
- *Service level agreement (SLA):* Internal departments or companies who provide services and execute projects for other business units or external customers have to collaborate with their customer based on an agreed-on process including response times for different types of inquiries and general turnaround times for a variety of project/service related-issues and activities. The administrator can use the workflow system to define automatic escalation rules, notifications and alerts to ensure that any eminent violation of the SLA response times and limits is brought to the manager's attention for immediate corrective action.
- *Notifications:* These alerts are valuable warning and reporting tools used to ensure projects are on track and everyone is in compliance with defined policies and parameters. For example, repeated policy violations, exceeding defined thresholds, late submissions, too many invalid access attempts, budget overruns, and late projects can prompt a notification to the management team so they can quickly take proper action.
- *Background scheduled processing:* Background processing is used to monitor the occurrence of various events such as upcoming project-related reminders, leave-time accrual, SLA validations, a scheduled im-

port of the master user list from the human resource system, and other background processes. If needed, appropriate database updates are performed and notifications sent. The background process does not interact with the user. It simply triggers notifications and states changes in workflow entries and event-triggered data updates.

Financial

Financial setup consists of importing the chart of accounts from the accounting system, editing the system's default tax tables or importing them from the accounting system, and establishing currencies including automatic online currency-exchange-rate updates. In this instance, the administrator's role involves:

- *Creating and managing money charge types:* Money charges track bonuses, discounts, premiums, and other special charges. Money charges can be billable amounts, for example, fixed-price overhead of $10,000 for a project as agreed with the customer or payable amounts when John Smith gets a bonus of $3,000 for his contribution to Project ABC.

Analysis

The system administrator reviews the standard reports and analytics that are available as part of the system and determines if any modifications need to be made. Administrators also establish role-based access to reports and analytics in addition to the responsibility of adding any new reports, charts, and role-based dashboards.

Implementation Roadmap

A sample implementation roadmap (Figure 22.2) describes a typical Project Workforce Management implementation for a small- to medium-sized organization that is automating a limited number of workflows. The roadmap and the steps described next are simplified compared to those for larger implementations that involve many workflows or complex business processes.

An implementation consultant starts the deployment with a project kick-off meeting covering the following topics:

- Understanding the goals and objectives of the project
- Defining the implementation teams, roles, and contact information
- Establishing implementation milestones, project schedule, and tasks

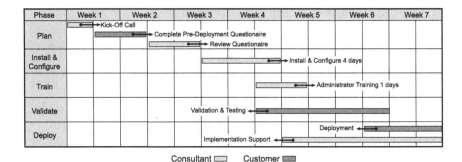

Figure 22.2   A Sample Implementation Roadmap

- Reviewing the implementation predeployment checklists and data-import templates
- Scheduling the Business Requirements and Business Process Review session

Predeployment Questionnaire

The implementation consultant uses a predeployment questionnaire to provide an initial overview of the complexities of the company's business environment, processes, and priorities. The questionnaire covers the following areas:

- Business processes and rules
- Technical system requirements and hardware (specially for an on-premise implementation)

Business Requirements and Business Process Review

The implementation consultant works with the company's project team to complete the following activities:

- Review predeployment checklists and preparations.
- Decide what data will be imported into the system.
- Discuss and review current processes.
- Confirm the implementation team's availability.
- Schedule the install and Configure business modeling and configuration sessions.

INSTALL AND CONFIGURE.   In the case of an on-premise implementation, the implementation consultant installs and configures the Project Workforce

Management solution based on the information gathered during the business requirements and process review session.

In case of an on-demand solution, the implementation consultant configures the Project Workforce Management's hosted instance, based on the information gathered during the business requirements and process review session.

Training

During this phase, the implementation consultant collaborates with the designated system administrator on product maintenance and configuration training. This training provides the system administrator with the required domain knowledge transfer to complete the solution rollout, make any additional configuration changes, and conduct end-user training. By educating the trainer, the administrator can be responsible for providing manager and user training throughout the organization.

Validation

In collaboration with the implementation consultant, the administrator tests the Project Workforce Management system to validate that the configuration meets the company's requirements. Due to the business critical nature of such a system, the validation phase is a crucial one for initial rollout, system upgrades, or any subsequent changes. The change management of a system that reports on the company's project financials and has payroll as well as accounting integrations, has potential Sarbanes-Oxley implications (effective controls); (see Chapter 4, "Why Project Managers Need to Know about Sarbanes-Oxley").

Deployment

The implementation consultant develops a roll-out plan and schedules end-user training sessions.

Implementation Close-Out

The implementation consultant schedules a project close-out call to review the implementation, address any final questions or concerns, and to go over the postdeployment support processes.

Customization

Customization is the process of adapting a product to fit the company's particular requirements using custom programming. Here, we describe best practices as it relates to leveraging customizations in your Project Workforce Management implementation.

Configurable workflows, rule engine, user-defined fields and forms, and vendor-developed integrations that do not require special programming reduce the need to develop customizations. However, there are areas in which customizations may be considered such as:

- Timesheets, expense reports, purchasing, and other work-process, end-user forms.
- Import/export of organization and work breakdown structure items, financials (such as general leader accounts), and historical data to/from unsupported or legacy applications (custom code may need to be written to access the legacy data).
- Extensive out-of-box dashboards and reports, and dashboard/report editing/creation functionality thus largely eliminate the need for report customization. With an ever-changing business reporting needs, the ability to quickly analyze and reshape information is increasingly more important.

As much as possible the company in collaboration with the vendor has to make every effort to avoid customizations or to limit the effort (cost) to no more than 5 percent to 10 percent of the project's total investment. The company should work with consultants to find workarounds and alternative strategies.

Too much customization leads to:

- A solution that is expensive and difficult to upgrade.
- A new source of problems, delays, frustrations, and bugs to fix.
- A dependency for the company on the consultants who developed the customizations.
- A difficult integration. It is much harder to connect a custom program with other modules and applications due to its proprietary "hard-coded" nature.
- A strategy that is forced to be defensive and maintain a new legacy system instead of an innovative approach, to try and differentiate with new enterprise software investments.

In general, a limited and highly focused customization strategy is actually a very good investment. As long as the vendor and the company have made every effort to ensure that there are no reasonable workarounds and alternatives, and that the customization will truly create value for the company.

The best way to manage customizations is to:

- Administer customizations on servers that are quickly accessible by the programmers who develop them. The best option is to maintain a separate

Development Sandbox where customizations can be tested in an environment that mirrors the company's production servers. If this access is not granted, then it becomes much harder to maintain customization and to react quickly if something goes wrong. This is true regardless of an on-demand or on-premise implementation strategy.

- Build them based on Web Services only. As much as possible, avoid any other form of customization that creates code that cannot be quickly upgraded and maintained. Note that developing reports based on a documented data model is acceptable since reporting software works best with direct access to the actual data structures.
- Ask the vendor to develop the customization and commit to adding it to the core product so that future upgrades are completed smoothly.

Development Sandbox

Sandbox and test environments are essential for customized environments but are also a best practice for any enterprise deployment regardless of customization level.

A development sandbox is a test environment offering users the ability to run beta, prerelease, or training copies of the Project Workforce Management application including any custom or third-party applications currently in use. Setting up a development sandbox is necessary for most implementations since Project Workforce Management is a business-critical system that impacts financial reporting, compliance, payroll processing, and billing. The system administrator and other members of the implementation team use the development sandbox to ensure any new reports, integrations, upgrades, or customizations are tested properly before migrating the changes over to the production environment.

.

23

User Adoption

If we're growing, we're always going to be out of our comfort zone.
—John Maxwell

User adoption is a significant challenge for any enterprise-software implementation and process-improvement initiative. This threat can often quickly derail even the most straightforward initiative. Preparation, open communication, and a true long-term commitment and involvement at the executive level help overcome most opposition. The most effective path to user adoption involves choosing the right balance between enforcement (this is the way it has to be for the company to comply) and empowerment (this solution puts employees in charge and provides them with the tools and the visibility to get their jobs done effectively). However, there is no silver bullet that eliminates all of the resistance and concerns.

After implementing a workflow driven enterprise-wide project and workforce management system, it gets much harder to fund projects that do not meet the company's strategic objectives or to continue to fund projects that are not delivering the intended results. The inescapable transparency and real-time reporting make it difficult to hide mistakes and bring an unprecedented level of instant scrutiny and accountability to all management decisions, actions, or inactions. However, as with any other enterprise system, there will be a strong resistance to change where many would prefer the "old way" of getting things done.

This chapter describes the user adoption challenges and provides some recommendations about how to overcome them and move the company's culture toward total transparency and accountability. User adoption challenges can be classified into the following categories: executive sponsorship, financial, internal politics, process maturity, and human nature. For each of these challenges, this chapter also provides recommendations on how to overcome them.

In addition, this chapter demonstrates why Project Workforce Management is far more likely to overcome user adoption challenges and rapidly gain substantial

289

advocacy by key resource groups within the organization than traditional project management initiatives.

Barriers to Project Workforce Management

In November 2006, the Aberdeen Group examined the use of workforce management processes and applications in 243 enterprises.[1] Responding human capital executives and other end-users completed an online survey that included questions in the areas of labor planning, scheduling, timekeeping, and attendance. The study found that the greatest challenge is not the technology, but rather the so-called "softer" issues—the user adoption challenges. In this study, *resistance to changes in work standards* is sighted as the number one implementation problem (see Figure 23.1).

> The biggest issue we see is a lack of willingness for companies to do the proper discovery for requirements and mediocre commitment of resources and management to do the project.
>
> —Vice president, Logistics Solutions Provider

Adoption Challenge 1: Executive Sponsorship

The organization's senior management has to be fully engaged and committed to implementing Project Workforce Management. In most organizations, the implementation and rollout of any new system is quickly delegated to the lower

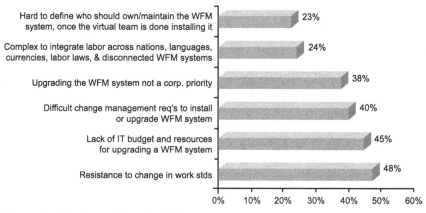

Source: Aberdeen Group, November 2006

Figure 23.1   Soft Barriers to Workforce Management

ranks. Senior management completely removes itself from the process. To encourage user adoption, senior management needs to understand the value and the purpose of the tool and its disciplines, becoming an active system user by accessing the real-time executive dashboards and reports. Mid-level managers and lower ranked employees are far more likely to adopt the solution once they see that their executive team has totally embraced and committed to the tools, policies, and disciplines imposed on project execution and service delivery. Here are some additional suggestions to consider. Executive sponsors should:

- Participate in end-user training as opposed to a one-on-one executive version.
- Be a power user of the system (i.e., learn the system inside out as it relates to reporting and analysis).
- Be vocal; take every opportunity to evangelize the new system and what it means to the employee, not just the organization. Insist that it's the people who will make the initiative successful not the software by itself.

Adoption Challenge 2: Financial Commitment

Depending on the number of modules adopted, an initiative may require a sizable financial investment and resource time commitment. The company's willingness to support such a project in the long run is a major challenge. There are several costs that should be factored into the decision to roll out a Project Workforce Management system, such as:

- *Administration:* Depending on the company's size and sophistication, setting up workflows, creating projects, establishing tasks, and programming cost and billing rules, as well as other administrative tasks, takes time. The company has to ensure sufficient and qualified resources have been allocated to the administration function (see Chapter 22, "Implementation and Operations"). An overwhelmed, part-time administrator is likely to get frustrated, provide poor service, and make mistakes that lead to negative results and lower user adoption rates across the organization.
- *Training:* Project Workforce Management has many benefits that impact the day-to-day responsibilities of many different types of users. The company has to invest in training its internal team so the designated resources learn how to administer the system, train end users, and customize reports and dashboards. Insufficient training can result in a system that is poorly maintained and administered. Users may therefore decide to totally abandon or selectively bypass the system to get their work done. (And, back to manual processes, e-mails, and spreadsheets they go.)

- *Rip and replace or reuse:* The company may have already invested in various enterprise-software tools such as a customer relationship management (CRM) solution that includes a helpdesk system, a bug-tracking system, a project-planning tool, a timesheet application, a custom-built expense reporting program, a reporting or business intelligence module, and other tools. Decisions have to be made about the existing systems and processes. Which ones will be replaced? Why and at what cost? What are the integration costs and challenges if a system is not replaced? Replacing existing systems will also result in additional training costs, and users of those applications may resist the new systems and processes or find it difficult to adapt to them.

- *Integration:* The solution can integrate with the company's accounting, payroll, project management, CRM, and human resources (HR) applications. Decisions have to be made in terms of which solutions to integrate with, and when and who owns the integration deliverables. Lack of integration may result in redundant and inconsistent data in the two disconnected systems. The company may not have the resources and financial means to make it all happen at once.

- *Reports:* Once the system is in operation, an incredible amount of valuable project and workforce data is being collected that can be used to everyone's advantage. Reporting is the gold at the end of the Project Workforce Management rainbow. There is a remarkable amount of diversity when it comes to an organization's reporting needs. The company has to invest in building or customizing the reports that the end users, project managers, line-of-business managers, and various executives need to get their jobs done. If the investment is not made, then many will miss the opportunity to leverage the valuable information that is literally at their fingertips.

- *Customizations:* There are often particular billing rules, point-of-entry validation rules, custom data processing, and integration code or labor law-related overtime pay rule calculations that are required to further automate processes and to fully leverage the new enterprise-software system. These customizations are typically very small but have a high impact on usage, automation, and internal satisfaction levels. The company has to carefully consider customizations and decide which ones, if any, are worth the investment.

Adoption Challenge 3: Internal Politics

Unfortunately, internal politics plays a major role in enterprise-software investments. Project Workforce Management impacts project teams, IT service teams, HR, and finance operations. Therefore, it is quite natural that the executives who lead these teams will push for their own solutions and strategies even if they are silo approaches or a broad ERP-type horizontal enterprise solutions needing heavy customization to meet the challenges of the project workforce. The only way you can fight divisive politics is to present the benefits of the new system, build a business case (see Chapter 25, "Bulding the Business Case"), and thus challenge the status quo or find other alternatives.

Adoption Challenge 4: Process Maturity

Some organizations assume that a workflow system and new software will help them improve their business processes, which of course is not the case. Automating flawed processes gets you the same bad results, only faster. Therefore, the organization has to optimize its work processes first and only then apply technology to them.

The organization's level of maturity in project management, human capital management, business-process automation, and project governance will have a major impact on user adoption. The more mature the organization, the quicker it will adapt and embrace the increased controls and transparencies of the new system. This is especially true for companies realizing that project management, workforce management, accounting, and compliance are not islands managed independently by their own tribe chiefs; that, in fact, a comprehensive, integrated enterprise-wide approach has to be adopted by the executive committee, representing all of these teams, to truly solve these challenges.

Adoption Challenge 5: Human Nature

The new system's champions and promoters are often aware of the dissenters and nonconformists, but do not directly confront them to understand their issues or take any steps to diminish their hostility. It is human nature to resist change. Some will blame the new tool and the new processes to compensate for their own shortcomings that often include lack of knowledge, insufficient training, and an unwillingness to adapt to a new way of getting things done.

The assumption is that all users will eventually come on board when the new system is rolled out. However, it is very important to meet, understand, and document objections from all system users. Then, as the new software and processes are rolled out, the solution champion can clearly demonstrate how the solution is, in fact, addressing the objections that were raised in the predeployment and implementation phases.

One of the best ways to build trust and encourage internal adoption is to promote and share success stories. For example, small unofficial "lunch-and-learn" sessions where one of the company's project contributors or executives explains how the new system helped them get their job done faster and more cost effectively. In particular, the solution champion and executive sponsors must support the new solution by continuous communication with and training of those who feel left behind.

For large implementations it helps to have a user champion from each business unit as a member of the core implementation team. Also, having internal resources designated to conduct the end-user training not only improves the quality of the training but also accelerates user adoption. The training materials can be handed over to the organization's internal training group and/or each department can designate an individual who will be responsible for the ongoing training requirements of their department.

A Corporate Initiative

It is important not to treat Project Workforce Management as a departmental initiative. By positioning it as a corporate initiative to automate project and service delivery the solution is far more likely to gain acceptance and to become a core system. Many project or workforce management initiatives start with a lot of energy then get abandoned with management rank changes; get labeled as something that is only useful for IT, for billing, or another specific resource group; or get pushed aside by executives who have their own agendas.

Traditional project management initiatives, as the name implies, do not focus on the needs of the workforce and are not linked financials, creating even more resistance. That is why so many project management initiatives fail. A common workflow framework, once adopted, drives all project, workforce, and financial-related processes, as well as change requests.

Project Workforce Management ties into payroll, billing, and accounting systems making it a business-critical system everyone has to adopt and work with to get their job done. Its extensive compliance automation capabilities enforce the company's work policies, cost accounting/time, and attendance/expense reporting/billing processes, in addition to other corporate procedures and guidelines that facilitate audits. Since compliance is not an option, this also substantially decreases the user adoption challenge.

NOTE

1. Aberdeen Group Survey, "Beyond Time and Attendance," November 2006.

24

On-Demand or On-Premise

This is a fulfillment of our vision of "The Business Web," enabling companies of any size to manage, organize and share all of their business information on demand.

—Marc Benioff

There are a number of options available for acquiring enterprise software today, and most technology vendors offer several choices. A company can choose to implement a Project Workforce Management system using its own information technology (IT) staff and resources or outsource the entire function to a software vendor or an application service provider (ASP). With such a variety of solutions available today, a company looking to invest in a Project Workforce Management solution should be able to secure an option that meets its own purchasing requirements and preferences.

It is not unusual for any technology decision to be closely tied to the accounting perspective and financial health of a business. This includes whether to select an on-demand or on-premise software solution.

A major determinant in the choice between license purchase and renting the software (also known as *subscription*) will be the number of times the customer will be upgrading the software, as is usually the case with on-premise solutions. Simplistically, if the customer has *absolutely* no plan to upgrade within the renting period and therefore can avoid paying the yearly upgrade fees, it would be less expensive to purchase the software. Conversely, if the customer will be upgrading within the renting period (which may cover a contract of three years, for example), it is usually more cost effective for the customer to rent the software, because often the right to unlimited upgrades is embedded in the rental agreement.

Frequently, the purchased software will be capitalized and written off over the estimated life of the software—say, three years—whereas the renting approach would see the full yearly fees written off as they are incurred.

In turn, companies also have the option of on-demand technology, which requires that the software solution be hosted by an outside entity other than the customer. With this option, the entire solution, including software and hardware, is physically hosted off the customer's premises. However, another hosting option may be for the vendor or a third party to manage the solution on the company's premises. This option provides the customer with all the benefits of remote hosting without the necessity of storing any data offsite, which, in turn, presents another whole set of issues concerning security, bandwidth constraints, and effective control of an off-site business-critical system.

Therefore, in principle, a company has the following software acquisition options:

- *Perpetual license fee:* This fee is paid once, giving the company the right to run the application as long as it chooses. It does not imply a right to upgrades, which are typically sold separately or are included as part of a maintenance program.
- *Subscription:* This cost is paid as a recurring (often annual) fee to continue using the software. The customer does not own the software license but may have installed it on its own internal systems and servers.
- *On-demand:* This option has a similar fee structure to the subscription service. However, the software is hosted by the application service provider.

This chapter highlights the major advantages and disadvantages of on-premise and on-demand software implementation options, differences between subscription and license purchases, the benefits of Statement on Auditing Standards 70 (SAS 70) certification for on-demand software, and presents a decision-making process for an on-demand or on-premise implementation. Ultimately, the implementation approach a company takes depends, in large part, on the enterprise software strategy, the IT department's participation, budget, resources, time-to-project-launch constraints, and the options offered by the Project Workforce Management vendors themselves.

Table 24.1 lists the factors to consider when choosing between an on-demand (hosted) or on-premise software implementation.

SAS 70 Certification

Statement on Auditing Standards 70 (SAS 70)[1] certification has been developed by the American Institute of Certified Public Accountants (AICPA). SAS 70 is an internationally recognized auditing standard to validate that a software hosting and service organization has demonstrated adequate controls and safeguards when hosting or processing data belonging to its customers.

SAS 70 audits are performed by an independent auditing firm in order to assess the on-demand offering's controls, activities, and processes, including its

FACTOR	COMMENTS
One-time costs	Purchasing software will have high startup or initial one-time costs.
Running costs	Running costs of purchased software will be lower than a rented solution; Hosted solution running costs may be higher or lower depending on many factors such as the organization's size, IT capabilities and infrastructure, hosting fees.
IT infrastructure	Organizations that do not have the appropriate IT staff and infrastructure should seriously consider hosting at least initially when implementing such a solution.
IT expertise	IT expertise must include Web/database server and network administration expertise and resources that can implement, operate, and support the system.
User support	Internal user support includes basic training, troubleshooting, and the ability to respond to more advanced requests and issues.
Maintenance	System maintenance includes performance testing, backup, replication, and ensuring scalability and reliability as more users come online or at peak usage.
Upgrades	Software upgrades require server upgrades and possible client workstation upgrades (if any desktop software is involved).
Security	Security depends on many factors. If the organization has an IT team with extensive resources, then it can provide its own security; however, smaller firms with limited IT resources are safer with the security measures and infrastructure provided by a hosted offering.
Performance	Software installed and maintained in an Intranet environment could be faster because Intranets have a private dedicated high bandwidth network. In contrast, the performance of a hosted solution will be limited by the delays and limitations of the Web servers and by the Internet connection between the organization and ASP.

Table 24.1   Choosing On-Demand or On-Premise Software

297

site operations, software applications, internal control processes, and hosting facilities.

With this certification, on-demand customers can be assured that the third-party company has adequate controls and safeguards in place for hosting, delivering, and supporting their business and financial data with effective internal controls, as well as fully audited and compliant security, reliability, and confidentiality. There are two types of SAS 70 reports (Service Auditor's Reports): Type I and Type II.

A Type II report is a rigorous audit and detailed testing of a service organization's control activities and operations over a minimum six-month period. A SAS 70 Type I report, in contrast, only lists the service organization's description of controls as a point in time (e.g., February 9, 2007). Also the auditor's assessment is limited to whether the controls were placed in operation and if they are suitably designed. Receiving an "unqualified" auditor's opinion for a SAS 70 Type II report indicates that all control objectives were achieved without a significant exception or deficiency.

Due to the business-critical nature of Project Workforce Management, look for service providers who offer Type II certified on-demand services.

Subscription and On-Demand Comparison

Subscription has several important advantages:

- *Lower up-front costs:* The cost of the software is spread over a number of years.
- *Upgrades included:* A company automatically receives all the software service release updates and the upgrades are free of charge.
- *No annual support fees:* Usually a standard annual support plan is included.
- A *complete tax write-off:* Subscription fees can be declared as an operating expense, hence, a complete tax write-off.

On-demand offers the following benefits:

- Elimination of hardware and software purchases, integration, support, and maintenance costs
- Lower cost of management and operation
- Shift of IT and software/hardware acquisition costs to the service provider
- Quicker implementation
- Freedom to focus on business issues, not technology
- Automatic and transparent upgrades to the latest technologies and software versions
- Predictability of costs

- State-of-the-art SAS 70 certified security, backup, disaster recovery, and support systems
- Low risk
- Increased performance and scalability

In both cases, the disadvantages are:

- Long-term cost.
- Vendors can raise prices after the initial agreement expires.
- For an on-demand implementation, the vendor may decide to upgrade the customer when the customer, in fact, prefers to remain on the current version of the software.
- For an on-demand implementation, it is harder to make integrations work with other internal systems that are not on-demand, especially when upgrades are involved; although, with Web services and service oriented architecture (SOA) this is less and less of an issue (see Chapter 20, "Integration").

When to Choose On-Demand or On-Premise

See Table 24.2 for a comparison between on-premise and on-demand options.

Figure 24.1 provides a framework for companies to choose between an on-demand/subscription or on-premise/license purchase software implementation. Note that costs have not been mentioned as a factor in the initial decision-making process since it may not be a primary factor. Alignment of the project with the company's strategic goals has a higher priority over a purely cost-based analysis. Once the company has reached a decision on its preferred approach, it can perform a detailed three- to five-year cost analysis between the various options to decide whether the cost advantages confirm the decision or the cost variance can be justified due to the project's strategic fit.

Also, as noted earlier in the chapter, a subscription-based purchase may still be an on-premise solution. The flowchart in Figure 24.1 narrows the decision down to paying for the software including support and upgrades on a recurring basis or an outright license purchase and internal IT management and maintenance of the software.

Other Delivery Models

There are a variety of project management and workforce management software vendors with very different business models. Some are what is referred to as *pure plays*. These are vendors who offer a single-delivery model, for example

ENTERPRISE SOFTWARE	ON-PREMISE	ON-DEMAND
Cost	High up-front cost; must pay for major upgrades and annual support. Company also has to purchase and maintain hardware such as servers.	Monthly cost; over time will cost more than outright purchase because hardware and server operation is managed by an ASP.
Risk	High risk. Company is making a large up-front investment in hardware and software.	Lower risk. ASP assumes all hardware/ software costs and must meet minimum performance parameters or customer walks away.
Control	Greater control over administration, security, and change management.	ASP manages upgrades, maintenance, security checks, and other system changes.
Maintenance	Internal IT staff must be involved in fixes, patches, and upgrades.	No internal staff allocated to maintaining the system; fixes and upgrades all handled by ASP resources.
Security	Data is stored at the company's facilities; highly secure.	Data is stored at a data center managed by the ASP; encrypted data transmission; security level depends on the ASP—SAS 70 certification a major positive.
Reliability	Highly reliable since internal IT staff are involved in installation, maintenance, deployment.	Reliability depends on the quality of the ASP's data centers and the vendor's internal processes—SAS 70 certification a major positive.
Scalability	Highly scalable; internal IT staff can do load balancing and other enterprise functions; add servers, storage and other equipment as necessary.	Scalability depends on the ASP's data center and capabilities.
Performance	Only limited by the Project Workforce Management's benchmarks.	Performance depends on ASP's data center and the company's Internet access speeds and bandwidth.

Table 24.2   On-Premise and On-Demand Comparison

an on-demand only software vendor such as salesforce.com or a vendor who sells software licenses only. *Hybrid software* vendors, which are more common today, provide the customer with the most flexible delivery methods including the option to purchase licenses, a subscription, or an on-demand arrangement.

Some on-demand and hybrid vendors have also started to offer companies the option to purchase the software licenses as well as any other related third-

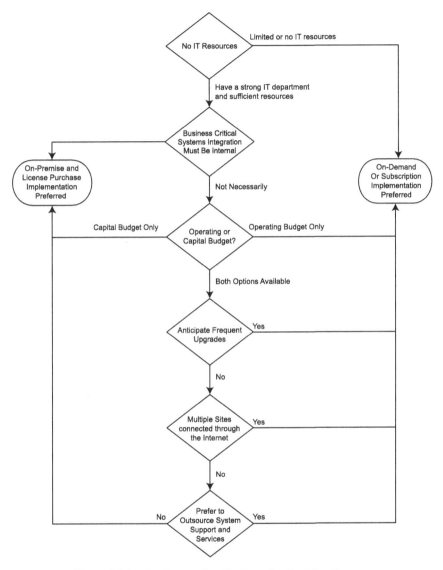

Figure 24.1   On-Demand or On-Premise Decision Process

party software and hardware, and manage the server(s) at the vendor's facility. This is similar to the co-location option offered by Web hosting service providers. The benefits of this option are that the customer reduces its long-term costs (by purchasing all of the licenses and equipment that are required one time). In addition, the customer outsources the support and services to the vendor who has the most capable resources for managing the application and servers. However, this may make the purchasing decision and process too complicated. The more common license purchase, subscription, and on-demand options are easiest to understand, to build a business case around, to secure approval, and allocate a budget for.

NOTE

1. For a quick description, see http://en.wikipedia.org/wiki/SAS_70. For a more in-depth understanding of SAS 70 compliance refer to *Service Organizations: Applying SAS No. 70, as Amended—AICPA Audit Guide,* published by AICPA, available at http://www.cpa2biz.com. The audit guide is listed as publication number 012775.

25

Building the Business Case

The end may justify the means as long as there is something that
justifies the end.

—Leon Trotsky

To the enlightened executive, the obvious benefits of faster and higher quality decision making are necessary prerequisites for survival in the flat world. However, many organizations and corporate boards demand financial justification before proceeding. Without knowing costs, decision makers refuse to allocate funds or personnel to carry out the needed infrastructure improvements. Top decision makers require a rigorous Business Case evaluation that explores alternative technologies, evaluates potential risks, and estimates costs and benefits. By documenting the expected costs, benefits, and risks of pursuing a Project Workforce Management approach, the Business Case determines a course of action for management.

This chapter works through the steps of building the Business Case for Project Workforce Management that are as follows:

1. Identify stakeholders.
2. Define desired outcomes.
3. Build a role-based value matrix.
4. Develop the key pain indicators.
5. Build the questions and return-on-investment calculations.
6. Build the return-on-investment financial dashboard.

The analysis process and the Project Workforce Management Business Case fundamentals proposed here have been developed in collaboration with VMC.[1] VMC focuses on delivering objective value estimation tools for software companies. The tool and process can be used to build the case for any type of enterprise software investment. A simplified and summarized version of the process applied to Project Workforce Management is explained here.

The tool is based on a model that includes a standardized needs analysis questionnaire. The end result of applying the tool is an executive financial dashboard that shows the project's business value, costs, and return on investment (ROI). This exercise is extremely valuable because it also details the status quo costs (cost of doing nothing) based on the challenges being experienced that would be addressed by a Project Workforce Management solution.

The pains, issues, goals, and solution proposals for internal and professional services projects are presented in separate tables, charts, and dashboards. If Project Workforce Management is being implemented enterprise wide and the company has a services division as well as an internal information technology (IT) department, then both types of tables and charts should be factored into building your Business Case and project justification.

Project Workforce Management solution vendors often have Business Case templates they will freely share with you. These Business Case templates are a set of documents or spreadsheets that you can complete with the vendor's help to measure your ROI and other benefits. If your executive team is not convinced that the investment is necessary, then the combination of the concepts presented here and the investment justification you build with the software vendor should provide you with an excellent foundation for putting together your own Business Case, executive reports, and presentations.

The Business Case also defines a baseline that can be used to review the project's performance in 3-, 6- and 12-month intervals, as well as serve as a set of project milestones to ensure the project meets or exceeds its original financial objectives.

The following encapsulates the information needed to build a Business Case before embarking on a Project Workforce Management initiative.

Typical roadblocks to projects of this type are:

- The executive committee is constantly postponing or delaying its decision.
- People have trouble making a good Business Case for Project Workforce Management.
- There are too many other high-priority projects to choose from.
- Internal confusion occurs from rushing into vendor demonstrations and seeking proposals without clearly communicating solution value.
- Shifting objectives and conflicting priorities harm the vendor selection process, possibly leading to misunderstandings and bad decisions.

A well-prepared Business Case is a credible, simple, accurate, and presentable document that provides a solid framework for all discussions involving the project's strategic fit, important milestones when implementation begins, and the metrics that measure whether success is achieved.

A well-planned Business Case results in:

- Improved communication with the executive committee earlier in the project cycle
- A value justification matrix (why buy, business issues per stakeholder, and desired outcome)
- A solid pitch that resonates with the finance executives (talking their language)
- An internal discussion shift from cost to value justification, supported by a well-documented Business Case
- A document that speaks directly to the main opponent, specifically highlighting the cost of doing nothing (the cost of status quo)

Identify Stakeholders

Once you have identified the overall issues you can then translate them into the daily challenges faced by various executives within your organization. Table 25.1 illustrates this for a professional services department.

Define Desired Outcomes

Once the stakeholders that are impacted by the project have been identified, it is time to agree on the desired outcome of the initiative. Will you be able to measure success? What are some quantifiable metrics that will establish a baseline and show progress that you can agree on with your sponsors?

Ideally, key players from finance, project and resource management teams, as well as the CIO (if this is an on-premise implementation or you are planning to integrate with an on-premise solution), and CFO would work together on this exercise to determine the processes directly impacted by the Project Workforce Management solution. Some examples are shown in Table 25.2.

Build a Role-Based Value Matrix

Building a role-based value matrix presents the Business Case in a summary table and helps create the buy-in needed from the internal decision-making circle, also referred to as the virtual buying committee (see Table 25.3).[2]

The idea is to first clearly define the business drivers on the "Why Buy" and then outline the "Business Issue" which gets directly impacted and the "Desired

STAKEHOLDER	PRIMARY RESPONSIBILITIES OF THE STAKEHOLDER
Vice President Professional Services	Increase billable revenue, maximize resource utilization rates, ensure customer satisfaction, streamline billing and collections.
Line of Business (LOB) Manager	Execute projects and deliver services effectively and profitably.
For an Internal IT Organization	
Vice President PMO	Implement enterprise wide project management best practices; launch process improvement initiatives.
CIO	Provide IT services to the rest of the company; manage IT assets and resources.
For a Generic Organization	
COO	Ensure efficient day-to-day operations, cost control, and investment in long-term strategic projects that improve operational execution.
CFO	Financial reporting, establish corporate governance and effective internal controls, and ensure compliance with accounting regulations, streamlined billing and collections for a professional services firm.
CEO	Define the company's strategy, build long-term value usually by profitable revenue growth, and drive initiatives that result in a competitive advantage.
Vice President Human Resources	Ensure compliance with labor laws and an efficient payroll and leave management system, plan hiring and training based on resource pool's current skill set, work load, and future demand.

Table 25.1   Identify Stakeholders

STAKEHOLDERS	DESIRED OUTCOMES
CIO, Director of Project Management Office	I want to reduce the number and cost of failed projects.
CIO, CEO	I want to reduce the number of non-strategic projects.
COO	I want to reduce the amount of time spent on overhead tasks. I want to control and reduce costs.
CFO	I want to reduce my days sales outstanding. I want improved forecasting.
Vice President Professional Services	I want to reduce unbillable work and late projects. I want to have good margins on fixed bid projects. I want to reduce or eliminate revenue leakage. I want to improve resource utilization.
Vice President Human Resources, Resource Manager	I want to reduce resource overload. I want to increase productivity. I want to reduce employee attrition.

Table 25.2   Define Desired Outcomes

Why buy	Articulate a specific reason to your company as to why it needs to buy a solution.
Business issue	Explain the specific needs to address, the problems to solve.
Desired outcome	Describe the expected outcome of buying a solution.
Stakeholder pain chain	Identify the stakeholders who have this business issue and will benefit from the expected outcome.
Solution	Introduce the specific features or modules of Project Workforce Management that will produce the desired outcome.
Category	Assign a category to this business issue. There are three categories to choose from: cost reduction, cost avoidance, revenue increase.
Value metric	Summarize all of the above information into a single value statement.

Table 25.3   Building a Role-Based Value Matrix

307

Outcome" once the issue is addressed; this all ties into specific "Stakeholder(s)" who would benefit from the problem being dealt with. The organization is then able to categorize the results in terms of cost reduction, cost avoidance, or revenue increase, thus identifying a "Value Metric."

Value Matrix for Service Organizations

Tables 25.4 through 25.8 show the value matrices for a professional services organization. They provide a good overview of the types of business issues each of your stakeholders are likely to be experiencing and how Project Workforce Management addresses those business issues.

Value Matrix for Internal Project Teams or IT Departments

Tables 25.9 through 25.13 show the value matrices for internal project teams or IT departments. They provide a good overview of the types of business issues each of your stakeholders are likely to be experiencing and how Project Workforce Management addresses those business issues.

Develop the Key Pain Indicators

The value matrix contains a wealth of information about a business executive's issues, pain, and goals as well as the stakeholders who care about those issues and how Project Workforce Management's features solve those business concerns. The value matrix is categorized, sorted, and analyzed to produce a set of unique key pain indicators (KPI). Any duplicate or noncritical pains are eliminated in this process, helping produce anywhere from 3 to 10 primary KPIs. Each KPI is a statement in the form of a question that describes a primary issue, pain, or goal. After completing this exercise, the following sets of KPIs were identified for a company with Project Workforce Management challenges.

For a Service Organization
- Are you able to maximize your resource utilization?
- Are you losing money on revenue generating projects?
- Do you spend too much on managing timesheets and expense reports?
- Are you losing revenue from an inability to track and bill (also referred to as revenue leakage)?
- Are you losing revenue due to customer attrition?
- Do you enter and reenter data into multiple systems?
- Are you spending too much on managing regulatory requirements?

WHY BUY	BUSINESS ISSUES	DESIRED OUTCOME	STAKEHOLDER PAIN CHAIN	SOLUTION	CATEGORY	VALUE METRIC
I need to know which opportunities/projects to take on.	Taking on the wrong projects is costly and time consuming.	I want to reduce the cost of failed projects.	COO, CFO, Vice President Professional Services	Dashboards, project demand management	Reduce cost	Percentage loss of failed projects
I can't approve the time for my employees.	It is too time consuming to collect timesheets.	I want to reduce the amount of time administering timesheets.	COO, CFO, Vice President Professional Services	Workflow based approval, automatic time entry, and management by exception	Reduce cost	Human Capital
I want to have visibility in all the work being done in professional services.	It is too costly for billable resources to focus on less profitable projects.	I want to increase profitability per project.	COO, CFO, Vice President Professional Services	Project reports, Dashboards	Increase revenue	Margin per project
I need to forecast resource utilization.	I want to do better planning to maximize billable output.	I want to increase billable output and reduce bench time.	COO, CFO, Vice President Professional Services	Workforce planning, timesheet	Increase revenue	Margin per project and revenue per employee
I want to see my project's health.	It is too time consuming to find the right information.	I want to reduce administrative overhead.	COO, CFO, Vice President Professional Services	Project reports, dashboards, project management workflows	Reduce cost	Human capital
I need to govern my projects.	Poor governance results in overspending, misallocation of resources, fraud, and penalties.	I want to reduce the cost of compliance and audits and reduce the time it takes to comply.	C-Level	Audit trails, project reports, dashboards, project management workflows	Reduce cost, avoid cost	Human capital, penalties, fines

Table 25.4 Value Matrix for Service Organizations

WHY BUY	BUSINESS ISSUES	DESIRED OUTCOME	STAKEHOLDER PAIN CHAIN	SOLUTION	CATEGORY	VALUE METRIC
I want to have best practices for project delivery.	It costs too much not to standardize project delivery.	I want to reduce my cost per project and improve my productivity.	COO, CFO, Vice President Professional Services	Workflow system, project templates	Reduce cost, increase revenue	Cost per project, revenue per employee
I need more accurate billing.	We are losing money on work we should be billing.	I want to reduce or eliminate revenue leakage.	COO, CFO, Vice President Professional Services	Time and billing solution with support for billing and rate dependencies	Increase revenue	Maximize revenue per consultant per client
I need to improve my time on billing projects.	We want to recognize our revenue sooner.	I want to reduce my days sales outstanding.	Controller, CFO	Multiclient invoicing, workflow invoice approval, online review	Reduce cost	Borrowing cost
I need to get timely reports on my projects.	It can cause delays in projects, and cost us more money on bad projects.	I want to reduce unbillable work and late projects.	COO, CFO, Vice President Professional Services	Real-time cost and billing rate engine, reporting	Avoid cost	Budget overruns, losing customers
I need to report on my employees project work.	I want them to be working on billable projects.	I want to increase billable (productive) projects.	CFO, Vice President Services	Utilization reports	Increase revenue	Margin per project, revenue per employee
I want to know my skill inventory.	It is costly not to have the right people on the right projects.	I want to reduce resource gap (skills), overload, and underutilization.	COO, Vice President Professional Services	Workforce planning, reporting	Increase revenue, reduce cost	Revenue per employee, human capital
I want to measure project performance.	I want to know the profitability of each project.	I want to eliminate nonperforming projects.	COO, Vice President Professional Services	Project reports, dashboards	Increase revenue, reduce cost	Margins, human capital

Table 25.5   Value Matrix for Service Organizations

WHY BUY	BUSINESS ISSUES	DESIRED OUTCOME	STAKEHOLDER PAIN CHAIN	SOLUTION	CATEGORY	VALUE METRIC
I need to manage project scope change.	I have trouble managing scope manually.	I want to avoid unbillable work, capture and invoice scope changes.	COO, Vice President Professional Services	Workflow system, project management workflows	Increase revenue	Unbilled revenue
I want a clear status of how we are doing against our deliverables.	It is too time consuming to collect data for billing.	I want to reduce the amount of time it takes to collect data and invoice.	COO, Vice President Professional Services, CFO	Real-time billing engine, reporting, invoicing, time and expense tracking	Reduce cost	Human capital
I want people to collaborate on project changes and issues.	It is too time consuming to hide timely project information.	I want to reduce the time it takes to report on projects.	COO, Vice President Professional Services, CFO	Workflow system, project management workflows, reporting	Reduce cost	Human capital
I need to manage fixed-bid project risk.	Unmanaged risks can result in project overruns and delays and could have financial impacts.	I want to reduce project delays and budget overruns.	COO, Vice President Professional Services, CFO	Real-time cost engine, budgeting, workflow system, project management workflows, reporting	Reduce cost, avoid cost	Cost per project, budget overruns
I want to easily access the project artifacts.	It is time consuming to locate information (if everything is decentralized and manual).	I want to reduce the time spent locating artifacts.	COO, Vice President Professional Services	Integration with document management	Reduce cost	Human capital
I want to automate my entire project and/or service delivery life cycle.	It is too costly to do it inconsistently and with disparate systems.	I want to reduce errors and cost overruns.	COO, Vice President Professional Services	Project Workforce Management solution	Reduce cost	Human capital

Table 25.6   Value Matrix for Service Organizations

WHY BUY	BUSINESS ISSUES	DESIRED OUTCOME	STAKEHOLDER PAIN CHAIN	SOLUTION	CATEGORY	VALUE METRIC
I need to track projects.	It is too time consuming to get project status face to face.	I want to reduce the amount of time on administrative tasks.	COO, Vice President Professional Services	Project reports, dashboards	Reduce cost	Human capital
I need accountability for fixed bid projects.	We are always over budget and over schedule.	I want to reduce the overbudget and over-scheduled projects.	COO, Vice President Professional Services, CFO	Audit trail, project reports, dashboards	Avoid cost	Budget overruns, losing customers
I need to comply with regulations.	It is too costly to do it manually.	I want to reduce the cost of compliance.	C-Level	Workflow system, audit trail, invoicing and revenue recognition policies, point of entry validation	Avoid cost	Overhead costs
I need a single point of entry.	Having duplicate data entry is time consuming (reduce duplicate entry).	I want to reduce duplicate entry.	COO, Vice President Professional Services, CFO	Integration with accounting systems, payroll, project planning, CRM	Reduce cost, avoid cost	Human capital
I am tired of using spreadsheets to track this stuff.	It is too time consuming to consolidate the data and it is error prone.	I want to reduce errors and duplicate entry.	COO, Vice President Professional Services, CFO	Web-based time and expense tracking	Reduce cost	Human capital
I want to make data collection more efficient.	It is time consuming to collect the right information.	I want to reduce the amount of time it takes to collect data.	COO, Vice President Professional Services, CFO	Validation at point of entry, management by exception	Reduce cost	Human capital
I need access to historical data (similar projects).	I can lose money on current projects.	I want to forecast more accurately on similar projects.	COO, Vice President Professional Services, CFO	Audit trail, reporting	Avoid cost	Budget overruns, human capital

Table 25.7 Value Matrix for Service Organizations

WHY BUY	BUSINESS ISSUES	DESIRED OUTCOME	STAKEHOLDER PAIN CHAIN	SOLUTION	CATEGORY	VALUE METRIC
I need to track overhead.	It is costly.	I want to reduce administrative overhead.	COO, Vice President Professional Services, CFO	Project Workforce Management solution	Reduce cost	Administrative overhead
We need better communication between managers and end users.	It is too costly for managers and end users to collaborate.	I want to reduce the amount of time providing updates on project status.	COO, Vice President Professional Services	Timesheet manager, project reporting, estimated time to complete	Reduce cost	Human capital, time
I need a Web-based data entry system for remote users.	It takes too long to collect data otherwise.	I want to reduce the amount of time spent on data entry.	COO, Vice President Professional Services	Web application, Off-line system	Reduce cost	Human capital
I want to be able to automatically send time and expense information to my payroll (and projects and billing) system.	It takes too long to do it manually and it is error prone.	I want to reduce duplicate entry and reduce errors.	COO, Vice President Professional Services, CFO	Integration with accounting systems, payroll, project planning, CRM	Reduce cost	Human capital
I want to eliminate duplicate entry into other systems.	It takes too long to do it manually and it is error prone.	I want to reduce duplicate entry and reduce errors.	COO, Vice President Professional Services	Integration with accounting systems, payroll, project planning, CRM	Reduce cost	Human capital
I want more streamlined reporting between executives and managers.	Constant and direct updates are too costly.	I want to reduce the amount of time executives and PM's are required to collaborate on projects.	COO, Vice President Professional Services	Reporting, workflow system, project management workflows	Reduce cost	Human capital

Table 25.8   Value Matrix for Service Organizations

313

WHY BUY	BUSINESS ISSUES	DESIRED OUTCOME	STAKEHOLDER PAIN CHAIN	SOLUTION	CATEGORY	VALUE METRIC
I need to know which projects to take on.	Taking on the wrong projects is costly and time consuming.	I want to reduce the cost of failed projects.	COO, Vice President PMO, CIO	Project reports, dashboards, project initiation	Reduce cost	Percentage loss of failed projects
I want to have visibility in all the work being done in the IT department.	It is too costly for IT to focus on poorly aligned projects.	I want to reduce the number of non-strategic projects.	CIO, CEO	Project reports, dashboards	Reduce cost	Cost per project
I need to forecast resource capacity.	I want to do better planning to maximize productivity (reduce resource overload).	I want to reduce the amount of resource overload and increase productivity, and reduce my employee attrition.	COO, CIO	Workforce planning, timesheet	Reduce cost, avoid cost	Human capital, overtime
I need to govern my projects.	Bad projects cost too much money.	I want to reduce the cost of failed projects.	CIO, CFO	Project reports, dashboards, project management workflows	Reduce cost	Cost per project
I want to see my project's health.	It is too time consuming to find the right information.	I want to reduce administrative overhead.	CIO, CFO, CEO	Project reports, dashboards, project management workflows	Reduce cost	Human Capital

Table 25.9   Value Matrix for Internal Project Teams or IT Departments

WHY BUY	BUSINESS ISSUES	DESIRED OUTCOME	STAKEHOLDER PAIN CHAIN	SOLUTION	CATEGORY	VALUE METRIC
I need to govern my projects.	Poor governance can result in overspending, misallocation of resources, fraud and penalties (& internal customer dissatisfaction).	I want to reduce the cost of compliance and audits, and reduce the time it takes to comply.	CIO, CFO, CCO, CEO, COO	Audit trails, project reports, dashboards, project management workflows	Reduce cost, avoid cost	Human capital, penalties, fines
I want to have best practices for project delivery.	It costs too much not to standardize project delivery.	I want to reduce my cost per project and improve productivity.	Vice President PMO, CIO	Workflow system, project templates	Reduce cost	Cost per project
I want to run my IT as a business.	I need to invest in the right IT projects.	I want to increase my project success with the current staff levels (resources).	CIO, COO, Vice President PMO	Workforce planning, project reports, dashboards, project management workflows	Reduce cost	Human capital
I can't understand the actual cost of a portfolio.	We don't have proper visibility.	I want to reduce the number of underperforming portfolios.	C-Level	Real-time cost engine, budgeting	Avoid cost	Project expense
I want to know my skill inventory.	It is costly not to have the right people on the right projects.	I want to reduce resource gap (skills), overload, and underutilization.	CIO, COO, Vice President PMO	Workforce planning, reporting	Reduce cost	Human capital
I want to allocate costs to my business units (chargeback).	I don't want to absorb the expense internally.	I want the ability to properly allocate expense to the correct business unit.	CIO, CFO	Real-time cost engine, budgeting, reporting, chargeback, time and expense tracking	Avoid cost	Human capital

Table 25.10   Value Matrix for Internal Project Teams or IT Departments

WHY BUY	BUSINESS ISSUES	DESIRED OUTCOME	STAKEHOLDER PAIN CHAIN	SOLUTION	CATEGORY	VALUE METRIC
I want to have visibility into IT for the business users.	I need to justify IT spending.	I want to reduce the time it takes to report on IT spending.	CIO, Vice President IT	Real-time cost engine, budgeting, reporting, chargeback, time and expense tracking	Reduce cost	Human capital
We need to manage project scope change.	Changes in projects are expensive.	I want to reduce scope changes.	CIO, Vice President PMO	Workflow system, project management workflows	Avoid cost	Additional (unnecessary) project cost
I want a clear status of how we are doing against our objectives (goals).	It is too costly to take action on the wrong (insufficient/incomplete) information.	I want to reduce the amount of time it takes to get reports (real-time), reduce the cost of errors.	COO, CIO, Vice President PMO	Real-time cost engine, budgeting, reporting, chargeback, time and expense tracking	Reduce cost	Human capital
I need to manage my outsourced projects.	Poorly managed outsourced projects can be very costly.	I want to reduce our cost per project.	LOB Manager, COO	Real-time cost engine, budgeting, reporting, chargeback, time and expense tracking	Reduce cost	Cost per project
I want people to collaborate on project changes and issues.	It is too time consuming to not share timely project information.	I want to reduce the time it takes to report on projects.	CIO, Vice President PMO, COO	Workflow system, project management workflows, reporting	Reduce cost	Human capital
I need to manage (define) project risks and impacts.	Unmanaged risks can result in project overruns and delays and could have financial impacts.	I want to reduce project delays and budget overruns.	CIO, Vice President PMO	Real-time cost engine, budgeting, workflow system, project management workflows, reporting	Reduce cost, avoid cost	Cost per project, budget overruns

Table 25.11 Value Matrix for Internal Project Teams or IT Departments

316

WHY BUY	BUSINESS ISSUES	DESIRED OUTCOME	STAKEHOLDER PAIN CHAIN	SOLUTION	CATEGORY	VALUE METRIC
I want to easily access the project artifacts.	It is time consuming to locate information (if everything is decentralized and manual).	I want to reduce the time spent locating artifacts.	Vice President PMO, CIO	Integration with document management	Reduce cost	Human capital
I want to automate my entire project life cycle.	It is too costly to do it inconsistently and with disparate systems.	I want to reduce errors and cost overruns.	Vice President PMO	Project Workforce Management solution	Reduce cost	Human capital
I need to track projects.	It's too time consuming to get project status face to face.	I want to reduce the amount of time on administrative tasks.	COO, CIO, Vice President IT	Project reports, dashboards	Reduce cost	Human capital
I need accountability.	We are always over budget and over schedule.	I want to reduce the over budget and over scheduled projects.	CIO, CEO, CFO	Audit trail, project reports, dashboards	Avoid cost	Budget overruns, losing customers
I need to comply with regulations.	It is too costly to do it manually.	I want to reduce the cost of compliance.	C-Level	Workflow system, audit trail, PR policies, data validation at point of entry	Avoid cost	Overhead costs
I need to see who is working on what.	Over- or underallocating resources can be very costly.	I want to improve productivity (increase resource utilization).	CIO, COO, Vice President PMO	Reporting	Reduce cost	Human capital
I need a single point of entry.	Having duplicate data entry is time consuming (reduce duplicate entry).	I want to reduce duplicate entry.	COO, CFO, Vice President PMO, CIO	Integration with accounting systems, payroll, project planning, CRM	Reduce cost, avoid cost	Human capital
I am tired of using spreadsheets to track this stuff.	It is too time consuming to consolidate the data and it is error prone.	I want to reduce errors and duplicate entry.	Vice President IT, CFO, Vice President PMO, COO, CIO	Web-based time and billing application	Reduce cost	Human capital

Table 25.12 Value Matrix for Internal Project Teams or IT Departments

317

WHY BUY	BUSINESS ISSUES	DESIRED OUTCOME	STAKEHOLDER PAIN CHAIN	SOLUTION	CATEGORY	VALUE METRIC
I want to make data collection more efficient.	It is time consuming to collect the right information.	I want to reduce the amount of time it takes to collect data.	COO, CIO, Vice President PMO	Validation at point of entry, management by exception	Reduce cost	Human capital
I need access to historical data (similar projects).	I can lose money on current projects.	I want to forecast more accurately on similar projects.	Vice President IT, Vice President PMO	Audit trail, reporting	Avoid cost	Budget overruns, human capital
I need to track overhead.	It is costly.	I want to reduce administrative overhead.	CFO, CIO, COO	Project Workforce Management solution	Reduce cost	Administrative overhead
I don't know how I am doing against my budget.	It takes too long to collect the data manually.	I want to reduce the amount of time it takes to collect data.	COO, CIO, Vice President PMO	Budget tracking system	Reduce cost	Human capital, budget overruns
We need better communication between managers and end users.	It is too costly for managers and end users to collaborate.	I want to reduce the amount of time providing updates on project status.	Vice President PMO	Timesheet manager, project reports, estimated time to complete	Reduce cost	Human capital, time
I need a data entry system for remote users.	It takes too long to collect data otherwise.	I want to reduce the amount of time spent on data entry.	COO, Vice President IT	100% web-based solution, Off-line system	Reduce cost	Human capital
I want to automatically send time information to Payroll (and PM and billing).	It takes too long to do it manually and it is error prone.	I want to reduce duplicate entry and reduce errors.	Vice President IT, Vice President HR, CFO	Integration with accounting systems, payroll, project planning	Reduce cost	Human capital
I want more streamlined reporting between executives and PMs.	Constant and direct updates are too costly.	I want to reduce the amount of time executives and PMs are required to collaborate on projects.	COO, CIO, Vice President PMO	Reporting, workflow system, project management workflows	Reduce cost	Human capital

Table 25.13   Value Matrix for Internal Project Teams or IT Departments

- Do you experience scope changes on your fixed-bid projects?
- Are your fixed-bid projects taking too long to complete?

For an Internal Project Team or IT Organization
- Are you allocating too many resources to low priority projects?
- Are you able to maximize your skill inventory?
- Are you spending too much on managing regulatory requirements?
- Are you able to easily determine nonperforming and underperforming projects?
- Do you enter and reenter data into multiple systems?
- Do collaboration and meetings take too long and slow productivity?
- Do you experience scope changes on your projects?
- Are you able to automatically allocate costs to a business unit?
- Are you able to effectively manage your outsourced projects?

Build the Questions and Return-on-Investment Calculations

The next step in building an ROI model involves breaking down each KPI into a set of needs analysis questions that describe the current situation, the measurable improvement that will be achieved by investing in a Project Workforce Management solution and the cost of continuing with the status quo. The calculations are based on the needs analysis questions for each KPI.

Figure 25.1 is a sample needs analysis questionnaire and ROI calculation for one of the KPIs of a service organization. Figure 25.2 is a sample needs analysis questionnaire and ROI calculation for one of the KPIs of an internal project team or IT organization.

Build the Return-on-Investment Financial Dashboard

After completing the needs analysis questions and building ROI calculations for each KPI, the ROI financial dashboards are built. Project Workforce Management dashboards are best understood by providing two examples: one for a professional services organization and one for an IT or internal project team.

In these two examples (see Figures 25.3–25.8), the assumption is that each organization will need approximately three months to deploy the entire solution. The estimation model allows the user to input a discount factor as well as to apply a risk-reduction factor to further manage the model results, helping to provide a more realistic value estimate. The investment delay is shown as the opportunity cost of postponing action.

Key Pain Indicator: 1- Are you able to maximize your resource utilization?

Increase your resource utilization

This section is designed to capture your current cost of resources.

Billable resources

Enter the number of billable resources:

Breakdown utilization: (Must equal 100% of time)

Time spent on billable projects:
Time spent on non-billable projects:
Time spent idle: (non-billable paper work, expense reports, etc.)

0%

Enter the average rate per hour for a billable resource:

	Per consultant	Total all consultants
Calculated amount of annual billings for billable resources:	$0	$0

Enter actual current annual billings:

Calculated annual loss of revenue: *(If less than zero, defaults to zero)* $0

Non-billable resources

Total number of non-billable resources:

Enter the annual average cost for non-billable resources:

Annual cost for above resources: $0

Enter the estimated utilization percentage for the above resources included in your pool:

Calculated annual cost for under utilization: $0

Figure 25.1   Key Pain Indicator Questions Sample 1

Key Pain Indicator: 1- Are you allocating too many resources to low priority projects?

Reduce your cost on low priority projects
with more visibility and project prioritization tools

This section is designed to capture your current cost of low priority projects.

Total number of projects: (From General Information)   0

Distribute your projects into the following categories:

	%	No. of projects
High Priority:		0
Medium Priority:		0
Low Priority:		0

0%   <Must equal 100%>

Average annual cost per project: (From General Information) $0

Calculated annual cost for low priority projects: $0

Figure 25.2   Key Pain Indicator Questions Sample 2

320

Value Estimation - Dashboard Summary

Customer: **Date:**   April 21, 2006

Investment vs. Return

Payback period

Financial Dashboard Summary

Total investment:		TBD
Annualized investment:	TBD	
Savings from Cost Reductions:		$686,374
Savings from revenue increases / recaptured:		$172,212
KPI summary:		$858,587
Estimated risk reduction factor:		25%
KPI Value Estimation delivery:		$643,940
External value delivered:		
KPI Total Value Estimation delivery:		$643,940
Amortized value delivered:		$3,219,699

Financial Dashboard Summary Metrics

Return on Investment Percentage:		194%
Enter the startup period: (Months)		3
Payback period: (Months)		8.0
Amortization period: (Years)	5	
Discount rate / Factor:	15%	
Net Present Value: (NPV)		TBD
Internal Rate of Return: (IRR)		TBD
Current annual cost affected by this solution:		$10,931,708
Daily savings post implementation:		$3,543
Investment delay: (days)	90	
Missed savings due to investment delay:		$318,838

Figure 25.3   A Sample Return-on-Investment Dashboard for a Service Organization

321

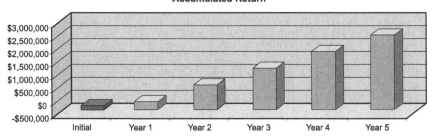

Accumulated Return

Figure 25.4   Accumulated Return for a Sample Service Organization

Value Estimation - KPI Summary			

Customer:			Date: April 21, 2006	
Key Pain Indicator descriptions		**Current cost**	**Revised cost**	**Value estimated**
Annual revenue recaptured:		$7,040,000	$6,758,400	$281,600
Annual reduction in resource costs:		$750,000	$720,000	$30,000
Annual revenue increase:		$500,000	$450,000	$50,000
Annual reduction in time tracking and processing timesheets:		$30,000	$9,000	$21,000
Annual reduction in time tracking and processing Expense Reports:		$30,000	$9,000	$21,000
Annual revenue recaptured from a reduction in revenue leakage:		$202,020	$80,808	$121,212
Annual revenue recaptured from a reduction in customer attrition:		$300,000	$240,000	$60,000
Annual cost reduction in cost of duplicate data entry:		$44,928	$8,986	$35,942
Annual cost reduction in cost to correct errors:		$149,760	$44,928	$104,832
Annual reduction in cost to comply with government regulations:		$10,000	$2,000	$8,000
Annual reduction in unnecessary scope change costs:		$1,250,000	$1,125,000	$125,000
Annual reduction in project cost lifecycle:		$625,000	$562,500	$62,500
Summary totals >>>>		$10,931,708	$10,010,622	$921,087

Figure 25.5   Summary for a Sample Services Organization

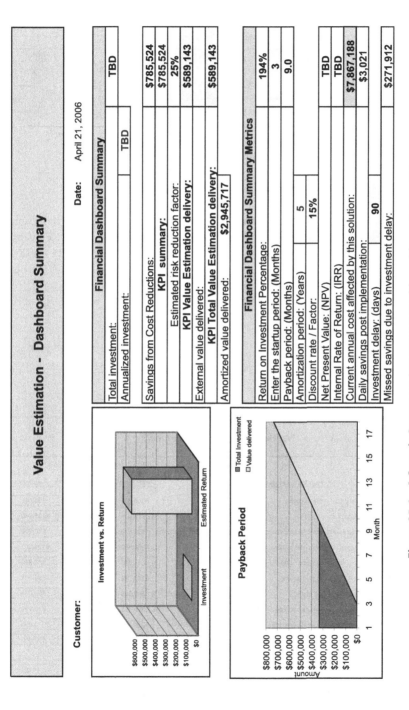

Value Estimation - Dashboard Summary

Customer: Date: April 21, 2006

Investment vs. Return

| $600,000 |
| $500,000 |
| $400,000 |
| $300,000 |
| $200,000 |
| $100,000 |
| $0 |

Investment   Estimated Return

Payback Period

Amount

| $800,000 |
| $700,000 |
| $600,000 |
| $500,000 |
| $400,000 |
| $300,000 |
| $200,000 |
| $100,000 |
| $0 |

1 3 5 7 9 11 13 15 17
Month

■ Total Investment
□ Value delivered

Financial Dashboard Summary

Total investment:	TBD
Annualized investment:	TBD
Savings from Cost Reductions:	$785,524
KPI summary:	**$785,524**
Estimated risk reduction factor:	25%
KPI Value Estimation delivery:	**$589,143**
External value delivered:	
KPI Total Value Estimation delivery:	**$589,143**
Amortized value delivered:	$2,945,717

Financial Dashboard Summary Metrics

Return on Investment Percentage:		194%
Enter the startup period: (Months)		3
Payback period: (Months)		9.0
Amortization period: (Years)	5	
Discount rate / Factor:	15%	
Net Present Value: (NPV)		TBD
Internal Rate of Return: (IRR)		TBD
Current annual cost affected by this solution:		$7,867,188
Daily savings post implementation:		$3,021
Investment delay: (days)	90	
Missed savings due to investment delay:		$271,912

Figure 25.6   A Sample Return-on-Investment Dashboard for an Internal Team

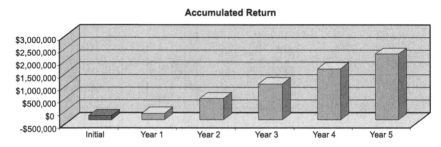

Figure 25.7 Accumulated Return for an Internal Team

When building a Business Case, one of the key considerations is to closely examine the KPIs which result in very large or small revised costs, to ensure data validity and then exclude any amounts that result in very little to no savings; making sure the analysis is focused on the top-value generators. A one- to three-year amortization term is typical for most organizations.

Table 25.14 describes the terms that typically appear in an ROI financial dashboard.

Value Estimation - KPI Summary

Customer: **Date:** April 21, 2006

Key Pain Indicator descriptions	Current cost	Revised cost	Value estimated
Annual reduction in low priority project costs:	$500,000	$450,000	$50,000
Annual reduction in labor costs:	$2,625,000	$2,493,750	$131,250
Annual reduction in cost to prepare for audits and comply with government regulations:	$22,500	$9,000	$13,500
Annual reduction in losses due to non-performing projects	$1,250,000	$1,125,000	$125,000
Annual cost reduction in cost of duplicate data entry:	$44,928	$8,986	$35,942
Annual cost reduction in cost to correct errors:	$149,760	$44,928	$104,832
Annual reduction in communication costs:	$1,800,000	$1,710,000	$90,000
Annual reduction in unnecessary or unapproved scope change costs:	$1,000,000	$950,000	$50,000
Annual labor cost avoided that is mis-allocated to IT:	$225,000	$90,000	$135,000
Annual cost reduction in outsourced project costs	$250,000	$200,000	$50,000
Summary totals >>>>	$7,867,188	$7,081,664	$785,524

Figure 25.8 KPI Summary for an Internal Team

ELEMENT	SOURCE
Key pain indicators (KPI) summary	Summarized KPI descriptions and projected ROI from Needs Analysis Questionnaire.
Category charts, investment versus cost charts	Graphical displays of information collected and calculated on the dashboard.
Investment input	Prospect's cost, either entered into dashboard or interfaced from a pricing spreadsheet or application.
Net present value (NPV)	Calculation using standard spreadsheet NPV formula and based on projected ROI and entered NPV factor.
Internal rate of return (IRR)	Calculation using standard spreadsheet IRR formula.
Return on investment (ROI) percentage calculation	Calculation based on total projected ROI, investment, and payback period.
Payback period	Amount of time required for the company to recoup its investment, generally including a start-up factor for product implementation.
Discount rate/factor	Data entry field on dashboard supplying a variable used in NPV calculation.
ROI category summary (reduce cost, avoid cost, increase revenue)	Summarization of ROI by category based on data from Needs Analysis Questionnaire.
Start-up factor (time it takes to implement solutions)	Data entry field on dashboard used in calculation of payback period.
Cost of waiting (ongoing cost of not purchasing a system)	Calculation on dashboard showing cost per time period (day, week, month, year, etc.) of not purchasing a Project Workforce Management system.

Source: Michael J. Nick and Kurt M. Koenig, *ROI Selling Book.*

Table 25.14   Financial Dashboard Glossary of Terms

Are You Ready for Project Workforce Management?

The quick test presented in this section will help you assess your company's readiness for a Project Workforce Management System. The test is divided into four sections: Preparing for implementation and deployment, integration, reporting, and establishing the right culture.

This test has the following objectives:

- To provide your organization with a quick assessment of its Project Workforce Management maturity level
- To highlight some of the key areas you should be aware of, before you jump into a potentially disruptive and expensive enterprise software initiative
- To arm you with the basic information you need to create awareness and "buy-in" about this initiative in your organization
- To serve as a simple checklist as you prepare to embark on a successful project and workforce management initiative

It is recommended that you ask several individuals in your company (including all of the key project stakeholders), to complete this test independently so you can then meet and discuss the results to compare your score and responses. If there are areas of conflict, the lowest score should be assumed.

Note: Anything less than a very high mark on this test indicates that more preparation, education, and planning is necessary in the analysis, selection, and pre-implementation phase of this project.

Test 1: Time and Expense Tracking and Cost and Revenue Accounting Modules

Scoring: Every Yes answer scores 3, Somewhat scores 1 and No scores 0. If a question is not applicable in your phased implementation (such as an integration you do not intend to start with), score it at 3 so that it does not impact your score.

Preparing for Implementation/Deployment

1. You have executive sponsorship for the project.
   The company's senior executives must be aware of and fully engaged in the company-wide rollout of such a solution. If this is a departmental or business unit initiative, then the same comments apply to the line-of-business manager. Without executive sponsorship, the project is likely to face internal resistance, budget threats, and other obstacles.

2. You have clearly identified a budget range and agreed to the target ROI with the desired tangible and intangible goals for rolling out the system,

   Clearly establish written quantitative and qualitative objectives and share them with the vendor; agree to milestones and timelines for achieving such objectives.

3. You have designated a single person as the project owner for this initiative.

   A single solution champion who is held accountable for the success or failure of the project is absolutely essential. The solution champion must allocate ample time to this project, especially for the first few initial phases.

4. You have designed an organization breakdown structure (OBS).

   The OBS consists of the hierarchy of the company's business units, groups, subgroups, and users. Reporting is one of the most critical aspects of a Project Workforce Management system. If the OBS is too deep, then it takes longer to maintain but substantially improves analysis and reporting. A shallowr OBS is much easier to maintain but reduces the amount of detail available in reports and analytics. You have to strike the right balance of OBS depth and simplicity based on your organization's reporting needs.

5. You have designed a work breakdown structure (WBS).

   The WBS consists of the hierarchy of the company's customers, projects, subprojects, and tasks. Reporting is one of the most critical aspects of a Project Workforce Management system. If the WBS is too deep, it takes longer to maintain and gets more cumbersome for people to choose the right activities to work against. A deep WBS substantially improves analysis and reporting. A shallow WBS is much easier to maintain but reduces the amount of detail available in reports and analytics. You have to strike the right balance of WBS depth and simplicity based on your organization's reporting needs.

6. You have a written company-wide time and expense reporting policy.

   A documented and written time and expense reporting policy that everyone has agreed to (and possibly signed off on) is essential. Project Workforce Management software will substantially facilitate the enforcement of your time and expense reporting policies.

7. You have a written company-wide leave time and Paid Time-Off (PTO) policy.

   A documented and written leave time policy for sick leave, personal day, vacation, and other types of paid and unpaid time-off. Project Workforce Management will substantially facilitate the enforcement of your leave time policies.

8. You have identified the government regulations that you must comply with. You have communicated to your executives how the system

helps your company comply with the regulations that relate to your organization.

Regulations that are impacted by the Project Workforce Management system include Sarbanes-Oxley (sections having to do with effective internal controls), DCAA (cost accounting and reporting for government contractors), SOP 98 (capitalized software costs), FMLA (family leave act), and FLSA (fair labor law pertaining to work time, leave time, and overtime rules) that you must comply with.

9. Your internal teams have mutually agreed on the format and content of end-user forms for all work processes that are to be automated for various business units and resource types.

Every company (and sometimes every department) has its own preferences and needs for time and expense reporting. For example, one team may prefer to enter percent of effort spent against a project on a weekly basis (such as an engineering department), whereas other companies may ask their employees (or consultants) to enter the actual numbers of hours against a specific task down to 5 minute increments. Other details include identifying billable work, overtime, leave time, on call time, requiring notes for certain types of time entries, and other exceptions. Your Project Workforce Management initiative must ensure that all user requirements and team specific needs have been documented prior to implementation planning.

10. Your internal teams and management have agreed on the approval processes.

Every department may have its own timesheet, expense reporting, and billing approval processes that may or may not include administrative staff, group managers, project managers, and billing or payroll managers. These approval processes have to be documented and agreed on prior to implementation planning.

11. You have clearly documented cost and billing rules, and an explanation of any special cost and billing scenarios.

Every company has a few types of cost and billing rules, such as hourly paid employees (or hourly billed consultants), fixed cost employees, milestone-based projects, cost plus projects, and others. These rules need to be clearly documented, along with any exceptions and scenarios. The Project Workforce Management system has to be able to support these scenarios with little to no customization, and it should be configured accordingly at implementation time.

Reporting

12. You have the list of reports and the specifications for each report that are needed by managers, executives, and administrators.

Define the reports required, their overall format, and details to ensure the system's OBS, WBS, roles, cost and billing rules, design, and other configurations are set up accordingly.

13. You have identified and defined key performance indicators and executive dashboards that are necessary for your top executives.

    Define the KPIs and executive dashboards required; identifying data sources to be aggregated into the dashboards (may include information from other enterprise systems). The overall format and details of the dashboards you need are necessary in order to ensure that the system's OBS, WBS, roles design, and other configurations are set up accordingly.

Integration

14. Your project and resource group structures are mapped to general ledger accounts in the accounting system.

    The operational part of the company (such as COO, project managers) should work with the finance team to establish a mapping between project work and the company's accounting system. Most companies prefer to keep project details outside of their financial system and map multiple projects into one general ledger account (such as a cost center) for financial reporting purposes.

15. If payroll integration is planned there is a clear agreed on strategy to link time tracking data to the payroll system.

    The operational part of the company (such as COO, project managers) should work with the finance team to establish a mapping between project work and the company's payroll system. Pay codes can be associated with groups, users, or specific tasks. The Project Workforce Management system will use the pay-code mapping to determine which data is exported to the payroll system.

User Adoption

16. Management is using the Project Workforce Management software.

    The company's executives have committed to using the reports, dashboards, and other information from the system in their decision-making process. Regular executive involvement and system use is highly likely to reinforce and encourage user adoption.

17. You have a plan with full executive sponsorship to ensure minimal resistance to work tracking and approval.

    The solution champion has a plan to educate users about the benefits of the system; and the company's executives have expressed their full support in case resistance or internal politics emerge during the rollout process.

Readiness Test Scorecard

				SCORE
Q1	☐ Yes	☐ Somewhat	☐ No	
Q2	☐ Yes	☐ Somewhat	☐ No	
Q3	☐ Yes	☐ Somewhat	☐ No	
Q4	☐ Yes	☐ Somewhat	☐ No	
Q5	☐ Yes	☐ Somewhat	☐ No	
Q6	☐ Yes	☐ Somewhat	☐ No	
Q7	☐ Yes	☐ Somewhat	☐ No	
Q8	☐ Yes	☐ Somewhat	☐ No	
Q9	☐ Yes	☐ Somewhat	☐ No	
Q10	☐ Yes	☐ Somewhat	☐ No	
Q11	☐ Yes	☐ Somewhat	☐ No	
Q12	☐ Yes	☐ Somewhat	☐ No	
Q13	☐ Yes	☐ Somewhat	☐ No	
Q14	☐ Yes	☐ Somewhat	☐ No	
Q15	☐ Yes	☐ Somewhat	☐ No	
Q16	☐ Yes	☐ Somewhat	☐ No	
Q17	☐ Yes	☐ Somewhat	☐ No	
Your Score				

Score Interpretation

1 to 10: You need to prepare much better for this project. Ensure that the executive sponsorship is present and strong and that sufficient time is invested in the analysis and pre-deployment phase of this project to ensure success.

11 to 39: You need to plan and prepare more. Review the areas where you have weaknesses and work with your project stakeholders to address those weaknesses.

40+: You have a mature and consistent approach to Project Workforce Management; you are very likely to execute a successful project with a substantial ROI.

Test 2: Workforce Planning

Note: Test 1 must be completed prior to Test 2.

For this test, the score needs to be 100 percent before you can move forward. If the answer to any of these questions is no, you need to plan and prepare more before embarking on a workforce planning initiative.

Preparing for Implementation/Deployment

1. You have defined a set of skills and competencies.

    You have documented and catalogued your industry's certifications and company's skills. There is a well-documented process to acquire a new skill or to get more experience in a given skill.

2. You have defined a workforce planning process and policy.

    How does a project manager ask for resources? Is there a designated resource manager? How are booking conflicts for critical resources handled? What are the recommended resource allocation parameters? Is less cost more important than better skill matching? Should the employee's interests be given any weighting? If yes, how much? Can you overload resources? All of this has to be documented and explained to participants.

3. You have a well-defined and agreed on strategy for maintaining up-to-date skill information.

    One of the biggest challenges of any workforce planning initiative is to keep an updated skill database. Asking administrative resources to associate skills to resources on an ongoing basis creates too much overhead and data entry work nobody wants to do. Employees have to be given the tools and the rewards to maintain their skills themselves. For example, employees can use a Skill Update Request workflow to report new skills and get them approved. The company has to define its skill update policy and make sure employees have an incentive to manage this information on their own.

Reporting

4. You have a list of workforce planning and forecast reports, and the specifications for each report that are needed by managers, executives, and administrators.

    Define the resource planning, forecasting, and utilization reports, as well as dashboards required, and their overall format and details.

Integration

5. The integration and interaction between workforce planning, project planning, and effort tracking has been clearly defined and agreed on.

   Assuming that you implement and roll out a Workforce Planning system, how does this module interact with your project planning and timesheet systems? What are the integration points? How much control do users have in assigning work to themselves? How is planned and unplanned work managed? The processes, connections, and "work" hand-offs between these systems need to be discussed, documented, and agreed to.

User Adoption

6. Project managers, resource managers, and project contributors will use Workforce Planning to plan all the work.

   The company's project and resource managers have committed to using the system for all project bookings. No one can use "unofficial" or "buddy" channels to book resources to work on their projects or initiatives. Furthermore, project contributors understand that they have to work on the projects they are assigned to through the system; they cannot simply choose other priorities. Establishing the right culture and enforcing workforce planning processes will be a major challenge in making this project successful.

Test 3: Project Process Management

Note: Test 1 must be completed prior to Test 3. Test 2 is optional.

For this test, the score needs to be 100 percent before you can move forward. If the answer to any of these questions is no, you need to plan and prepare more before embarking on a workflow planning initiative.

Preparing for Implementation/Deployment

1. You have established an enterprise-wide risk assessment policy, designated a risk management team, defined a list of risk types, and agreed on how and when to report risks to stakeholders.

   You have documented, catalogued, and classified the types of risks your projects face. Management has agreed to adopt a formal risk management and reporting system. The process (the workflow, the roles, and responsibilities) has been agreed to.

2. You have defined a scope management process and policy.

   Scope change is generally not handled consistently throughout an enterprise. Some departments may have highly mature scope change policies (professional services teams generally do), while other departments do not have any official scope change policy (such as IT and software development teams). The company has to document scope change policy per department and all line-of-business managers have to commit to institutionalizing scope management.

3. You will establish an enterprise-wide project initiation policy.

Without a workflow system, some projects are approved using the "buddy" system where an executive or project manager who is highly regarded or well-liked by senior management gets his or her projects approved with little scrutiny or due process. The company's management team has to agree to a very well-documented, strictly followed, transparent, and audited project proposal, review, and approval processes.

4. You are committed to treating project issue tracking as an enterprise initiative, not a departmental spreadsheet, custom-built program, or a siloed "bug" tracking application.

In almost any company, you will find one or more homegrown or departmental issue tracking systems that have no integration with the company's project management, effort tracking, or financial management systems. Issue tracking is treated as a "my department's system" and solved using point solutions or custom applications. To have enterprise-wide real-time visibility into all project work, risks, and issues, the company has to move toward establishing a global strategy for issue tracking. If multiple issue tracking systems are used, points of integration between such systems have to be defined so that data can be summarized into Project Workforce Management executive dashboards for global visibility.

Reporting

5. You have a list of project pipeline analysis, scope change, and risk reports, as well as the specification for each report that are needed by managers, executives, and administrators.

Define the project pipeline, scope tracking, risk reports, and dashboard required, in addition to their overall format and details.

Integration

6. The integration and interaction between project process management and project management has been clearly defined and agreed to.

Work process management has traditionally been treated as a set of processes that are independent of project management. With project process management in place:

- Projects can only be created, planned, and executed when the project proposal is approved using the project initiation workflow.
- Scope cannot change until the scope change request workflow is approved; if the scope change requires a new budget then the budget request must be approved before the project plan and baseline are updated and resources assigned.
- Project managers, stakeholders, and contributors collaborate on the project risks, scope changes, and issues using dashboards, work process queues, and reports as they do with project plans, Gantt charts, and timesheets. They will not resort to meetings, verbal conversations, e-mails, and spreadsheets to get agreement on project processes and seek approvals for any changes or new projects.

If project planning and execution is not intimately linked to and dependent on project process management (and vice versa), then much of the benefits gained from instituting project process management will not be realized.

User Adoption

7. Processes cannot be skipped.

There will be a tendency for users not to take action following a meeting where people unofficially agree on certain courses of action. Also project contributors and customers will try to skip the red tape and bypass certain processes with the argument that this is too much overhead, repetitive, and so on. If project processes are designed correctly, kept simple, and everyone is trained on how to use them, there should be absolutely no excuses. The benefits of tracking these processes far outweigh the few extra minutes of work people have to do to document and get audited approval for what has already been unofficially agreed to.

Summary

As the tests demonstrate, a considerable amount of planning and analysis goes into a well-thought-out Project Workforce Management initiative. This type of solution has tremendous benefits, such as improved efficiencies, faster decision making, more effective internal controls, and streamlined compliance with labor and governance regulations.

NOTES

1. ROI4Sales, Inc., visit http://www.roi4sales.com.
2. Also referred to as the virtual buying committee.

26

Conclusion

The world is being flattened. I didn't start it and you can't stop it, except at great cost to human development and your own future. But we can manage it, for better or worse.

—Thomas L. Friedman[1]

At the turn of the last century, buggy whip manufacturers were becoming obsolete—they didn't know it yet, but no matter how good a product they made, no matter how satisfied their customers, they would soon be out of business. Need for their products evaporated very quickly as the automotive revolution swept the globe. Similarly, at the dawn of this new century, no matter how efficiently a business operates, if it is not adapting to faster, cheaper, flat world realities, it too will perish.

Thomas Friedman predicts, "Wealth and power will increasingly accrue to those companies who get three basic things right: the infrastructure to connect with this flat world platform, the education to get more of their people tapping into this platform, and finally, the governance to get the best out of this platform . . ." The rest will go the way of the buggy whip manufacturers.

Define Project Workforce

Managing a Project Workforce in this new, flat world requires that decentralized project teams are provided the infrastructure to connect to this new platform. Project managers need real-time visibility into project status to anticipate and mitigate issues before they become crises. Project teams should be educated on how to communicate and collaborate more effectively with all project contributors and stakeholders regardless of their time zone. And projects must comply with government regulations, corporate policies, established best practices, and processes to produce optimal results.

The performance of a strong, value-creating company has two characteristics. First, the company's returns exceed its cost of capital—meaning it runs cost-efficient, streamlined operations. Second, the company captures its full market potential, leaving little, if any, money on the table. To perform at this level, project managers and executives must develop an understanding of their businesses that goes beyond that reflected in "How well are we doing and why?" information systems. They need more than densely descriptive explanations of past and present performance. More importantly, they must also answer the question: "How well should we be able to perform?" And, they must incorporate the answer to this question into all of their fundamental performance management processes.

By focusing on decision making and problem anticipation rather than on administration and problem description, project managers who look forward rather than backward will leverage this flat world infrastructure to effectively focus organizational attention and resources on the best opportunities for creating value. Companies that successfully govern project processes globally, in real time, will optimize the utilization rates of their project workforce and enjoy a sustainable competitive advantage. The speed of their decision making from a new-found agility and uniform global visibility will permit them to seize opportunities that would have otherwise passed them by. Profits from just one of these new opportunities will more than justify the investment made in the new infrastructure, education, and governance.

In the chapters of this book, you learned about the relationship between project management, workforce management, and financial reporting. We then covered the fundamental building blocks of Project Workforce Management: the organization and work breakdown structures as well as the workflow system. Next, we delved into project processes such as project selection, prioritization, initiation, and planning; human capital management processes such as workforce planning, timesheet and leave management; and financial processes such as budgeting, cost accounting, billing, and purchasing. Subsequently, we reviewed project processes that control scope, manage risk, and enable enterprise-wide collaboration on issues. With reliable, accurate, and audited cost and revenue information captured and stored using workflows in a centralized repository, we then discussed the challenges and benefits of real-time reporting and analytics. Finally, a detailed process was presented to build a Business Case for a Project Workforce Management investment.

The world in which we must compete is not *transforming* into a flat world— it is already there. Aided by a global network of fiber optic connectivity, new ideas are propelled across geographic and bureaucratic boundaries—literally at the speed of light. Executives who remain oblivious to the realities of competing in this fragmented, high-speed, global economy will fall behind. Their companies will be obliterated with a ferocity and pace never before witnessed in the history of global business.

Speed exhilarates and energizes. Ask anyone addicted to fast cars, extreme skiing, or flying jets. Speed injects fun and excitement into an otherwise routine activity. Organizations equipped to compete in today's flat world are built for speed, however, speed limits on the road to success are optional.

NOTE

1. *The World Is Flat* (New York: Farrar, Straus and Giroux, 2006), p. 469.

Index

Account executives, 20–21
Accounting:
  budgeting, 165–172
  for differentiated time, 114
  generally accepted accounting principles
    (GAAP), 27, 33, 61–63, 189
  integration, 154, 163–164, 259–262, 329
  phased deployment and implementation,
    271–272, 279
  project planning and, 124
  Project Workforce Management system
    component, 13
  readiness test, 326–330
  regulations, 17, 57–59, 61–63, 70
  revenue recognition, 33, 190–193
  software investments (GAAP SOP 98-1),
    61–63, 328
  threats (symptoms/causes/solutions), 28–34
Accounts payable/receivable, 23–24, 260, 262
Accretion approach, revenue recognition,
    192–193
Activity-based costing, 141–142
Activity monitoring, 95
Actual cost of work performed (ACWP), 130,
    132–133
Administration costs, as adoption challenge, 291
Administration/operations, 276–278
Administrative staff, 22, 150
Administrator, system. See System
    administrator
Adoption challenges. See User adoption
Analysis/analytics:
  benefits of, 242
  phase deployment and implementation, 274,
    282
  Project Workforce Management function, 13
  real-time, 13, 237–238

timesheet, 146
workflow system component, 95
workforce planning, 121
Application service provider (ASP), 295
Approval:
  budget, 108, 273
  chargeback, 272
  document (workflow sample), 93
  invoice, 186–187, 272
  line item, 152, 160–161, 217
  processes for, 328
  scope change request workflow, 334
  threats (symptoms/causes/solutions), 36–37
  timesheet, 92, 151, 152
  unapproved changes, 201
  workflow, 216–217
Arthur Andersen, 55
Assigning resources. See Resource(s),
    allocation/assignment of
Assignment rules, 96–97
Assumptions, changing, 201
Auditing, 27, 109, 281, 296–298

Background processing, 282–283
Barriers/roadblocks, 290, 304
Basel II versus Sarbanes-Oxley, 45
Baselines:
  budgets, 168–169
  business case, 304
  existing project portfolio, 233
Benioff, Marc, 295
Bennett, Dan, 165
Best practices:
  identifying/implementing, 99
  scoping, 205
  threats (symptoms/causes/solutions), 34–35
Billable time tracking software, 9

339

Printed in the United States
By Bookmasters